TRAGEDY PLUS TIME

TRAGEDY PLUS TIME

National Trauma and Television Comedy

PHILIP SCEPANSKI

UNIVERSITY OF TEXAS PRESS
Austin

Copyright © 2021 by the University of Texas Press
All rights reserved
Printed in the United States of America
First edition, 2021

Requests for permission to reproduce material from this work should be sent to:
Permissions
University of Texas Press
P.O. Box 7819
Austin, TX 78713-7819
utpress.utexas.edu/rp-form

♾ The paper used in this book meets the minimum requirements of ANSI/NISO Z39.48-1992 (R1997) (Permanence of Paper).

Library of Congress Cataloging-in-Publication Data

Names: Scepanski, Philip, author.
Title: Tragedy plus time : national trauma and television comedy / Philip Scepanski.
Other titles: Tragedy + time : national trauma and television comedy
Description: First edition. | Austin : University of Texas Press, 2021. | Includes bibliographical references and index.
Identifiers: LCCN 2020032962
ISBN 978-1-4773-2254-3 (hardback)
ISBN 978-1-4773-2255-0 (library ebook)
ISBN 978-1-4773-2256-7 (non-library ebook)
Subjects: LCSH: Television comedies—Social aspects—United States. | Psychic trauma—Humor—Social aspects—United States. | Disasters—Humor—Social aspects—United States. | American wit and humor—Social aspects. | Americans—Psychology.
Classification: LCC PN1992.8.C66 S3 2021 | DDC 791.45/6170973—dc23
LC record available at https://lccn.loc.gov/2020032962

doi:10.7560/322543

To Mom and Dad

CONTENTS

ACKNOWLEDGMENTS

This book is the result of many years, relationships, influences, and favors. Since it grew out of my dissertation, I must thank Jeffrey Sconce, my advisor, as well as committee members Lynn Spigel and Robert Hariman, without whom this project could never have begun nor developed into anything resembling what it is today. I must also thank the professors from my undergraduate and graduate studies who taught me so much, all of whom are represented in this work. At Northwestern, Scott Curtis, Penelope Deutscher, Hamid Naficy, Jacqueline Stewart, Domietta Torlasco, Amy Villarejo, and Mimi White were especially influential, while at UCLA, John Caldwell, Jennifer Holt, and Stephen Mamber proved particularly important to my development as a scholar.

In my time since graduate school, colleagues and administrators at Marist and Vassar Colleges have earned my thanks for support and friendship. At Marist, colleagues Daniel Amernick, Jeff Bass, Sally Dwyer-McNulty, Jenn Eden, Sue Lawrence, Kevin Lerner, Robyn Rosen, and Adam Zaretsky provided enormous, if varied types of, support, as did administrators Lyn Lepre and Thomas Wermuth. Marist library staff members Becky Albitz, Greg Carr, and Zachary Grisham, and especially Elizabeth Clarke, were also incredibly helpful. At Vassar, I am particularly grateful for the support of Dara Greenwood, Sophia Harvey, Sarah Kozloff, Mia Mask, and Christopher White.

I owe enormous thanks to my peer reviewers on this project, Matt Sienkiewicz and Rebecca Krefting, whose advice and support improved the book's quality immensely and ushered me past imposter syndrome. I need to also thank the entire University of Texas Press, its faculty board, editors, and additional team members for seeing this project through. In particular, thanks goes to Lynne Ferguson, Sarah McGavick, and Sarah Hudgens. Special thanks also go to my editor Jim Burr, who has been a supporter of this project since long before I even sent in the proposal.

I have been lucky enough to be friends and colleagues with many others through graduate school and my early career. Some deserve particular thanks for reading through portions of this and offering notes, including Peter Kunze, Nick Marx, Luke Stadel, and Beth Corzo-Duchardt. Other scholars who have influenced this project through their advice and expertise include Ashley Nicole Black, Nina Bradley, Jared Champion, Jonathan Cohn, Alla Gadassik, Amelie Hastie, Alex Kupfer, Jenn Porst, David Sagehorn, Ethan Thompson, and Laura Weinstein. Others who might not have overlapping expertise but who have been good friends through my academic pursuits include Susan Ericsson, Tara Flanagan, Dawn Fratini, Harrison Gish, and Jason Roberts. A special thanks also goes to Adam VanWagner for his legal expertise.

Finally, I need to thank all of my family members—each of you has made this possible and provided support for my education and eventual career. William, Linda, and Rachel Scepanski got me to the point where I could begin this project and continue to provide me with all manner of support. Most importantly, I need to acknowledge the love, support, and sacrifice of Martha Warner-Scepanski and Henry Scepanski, the two most important people in my life.

TRAGEDY PLUS TIME

On September 29, 2001, the same month as the 9/11 terror attacks, cable television channel Comedy Central and the New York Friars Club hosted a roast of Hugh Hefner. Introducing the event, Freddy Roman justified its questionable frivolity by invoking the orders of newly sanctified leaders. "It's time we get back to normal, like Mayor Giuliani and President Bush have asked. . . . And for the Friars, this is normal. Telling dirty jokes, making fun of people. That's what we do, and we're proud to do it for you. . . . So you can get some laughter back in your life and into your hearts."[1] Roman's earnestness also conveyed the sense that within this context, not everything spoken at the comedy show would be funny. Interviews with attendees and its edited broadcast suggest that despite the roast's reputation for offensive humor, most of the comics avoided certain kinds of offense even when cracking jokes.[2] After all, numerous critics had already declared that the end of the age of irony was at hand.[3] Jeff Ross proved an early exception to this rule, however, as he mocked Rob Schneider's flagging set: "Rob, hasn't there been enough bombing in this city?" Other comics followed Freddie Roman's lead, offering more earnest reactions to the terror attacks. For instance, Dick Gregory used the occasion to first praise Hefner for his early integration of the Playboy Club before appealing to a sense of national community, delivering an inspirational speech:

> I hear people talking about what a great nation this is today like something just happened a couple of weeks ago and we just got great. Fear and God do not occupy the same space, understand that. . . . If you stop to think about what makes America great . . . it's the firemen that left home this morning and intended to come back tonight and ran into a building when everybody else was running out.

At the same time, one could hardly call Drew Carey's verbal assaults on Osama bin Laden insincere, even if he meant them to be funny. After repeatedly calling bin Laden a "cock" (a word bleeped in Comedy Central's airing), Carey smiled and added, "I'm calling him a cock because Comedy Central didn't want me to say 'towelhead.'" Toward the end of the evening, Gilbert Gottfried flouted the rule proscribing irreverent 9/11 jokes: "I have to leave early tonight, I have to fly out to L.A. I couldn't get a direct flight," he joked in his trademark scream. "I have to make a stop at the Empire State Building."[4] The crowd responded with gasps, boos, and shouts of "too soon." Eventually, and famously, Gottfried won the crowd back with his telling of "The Aristocrats," a famously dirty shaggy dog joke. However, the 9/11 joke and everything that followed in Gottfried's appearance were cut from Comedy Central's airing of the roast.

September 11 was certainly the largest mediated American national trauma at least since the 1963 Kennedy assassination. Nevertheless, it proves instructive not only for its familiarity as opposed to other, less totalizing traumas, but also for the continuities it has with other catastrophes before and since. The events of that night's roast serve as a microcosm of the role of humor in society and on television and highlight key tensions. Does comedy function to unite groups, as Roman and Gregory indicated? Does that unity necessarily rely on othering those perceived as enemies, as Carey's set suggested? In that case, is comedy more unifying or divisive in the balance? African American Dick Gregory's speech draws attention to the way that members of disenfranchised groups negotiate their relationship to the nation. In yet another way, his performance calls attention to the way comedy can reengage historical memories of events like the black civil rights movement of the 1950s and '60s. Gottfried's joking also emphasizes the way humor serves as cover for breaking taboos and testing the limits of expression around sensitive issues. The censorship of his and Carey's routine for television underscores how, even in the relatively freely expressive genre of comedy, speech is limited. More generally, these examples point to the function of comedy in television's larger role of transmitting and remembering incredibly serious and powerful moments in American culture.

Since the rise of television as America's most ubiquitous and significant mass medium, national traumas have proven to be the most important moments in which the medium creates and reinforces the sense of the United States as a nation. Moreover, they act as critical moments for defining and narrating national history. As defined in journalistic coverage, national traumas are sober and unfunny. Nevertheless, American television has, at least since the 1980s, considered events like assassinations, civil unrest, terror attacks, and natural disasters to be fodder for comedy. Unlike journalism and drama, which are forced by genre expectations to more closely follow the discursive rules surrounding such events, comedy's expressive freedom allows it more leeway. Comedy can forgo this privilege and reinforce the seriousness that frames such moments, but it can also use its ability to bend and break taboos to negotiate or outright reject popular understandings of national traumas and the issues that surround them. Because the genre follows a different set of rules than others, television comedy acts as a key component to the way mass media makes sense of American nationhood in relation to national traumas. It does so by acting as a forum for testing and defining the limits of expressible ideas, negotiating popular memory and history, and policing the boundaries of group identity.

Television comedy frequently tests and defines the limits of the sayable. Sick humor especially occupies a liminal position as acceptable in some venues but not others. As television comedy evolved from the relatively staid forms of the network era to the more risky fare that sometimes appears in post-network television in the 1980s and after, comedy began to help shift the discourse surrounding historical and recent traumas by joking about things that serious genres and safer comedy could not. For example, as "edgy" humor became a possibility on television, comedy grew able to dissipate the air of solemnity that surrounded the John F. Kennedy assassination, which impacts the president's legacy. At the same time, jokes that had been acceptable for years suddenly became "sick" on 9/11, precipitating a change to the way reruns and other forms of programming distribution narrate the medium's history. Because national traumas are so important to America's politics and larger sense of identity, comedy's role as both an active agent of boundary-stretching and a passive test of changing discursive rules makes it a critical site in defining the way we speak of significant historical events.

Comedy also negotiates viewers' relationships to the nation in the way it plays around with history. As a genre defined by its appeals to laughter and its associated emotions, to joke about collective traumas presents a conflict. For viewers attuned to jokes that comfort, deflate the senses of fear and mourning, or otherwise respond to the emotions surrounding national trauma, comedy acts as a significant method through which we feel our way through history. In a political sphere where rhetoric frequently relies on emotional understandings of events, confronting, working through, and rejecting such feelings become especially significant. In other ways, comedy acts as a battleground over truth. Conspiracy theories commonly pop up in the wake of national traumas, and the playful relationship that comedy has with reality often mirrors or recreates this mode of thinking.

In practice, this has allowed some comedians to slip back and forth between political comedy and more earnest conspiracy theorizing. At the same time, humor can be used to criticize unorthodox thinking in an assertion of more orthodox understandings of history.

Comedy also polices the boundaries of national and subnational identity. American culture is neither singular nor homogenous, but is instead a complex mixture of overlapping "subnational" communities joined in affiliation under a single banner of American identity. Any group of Americans that does not encompass the entirety of the population, including African Americans, Muslim Americans, working-class Americans, and so forth, form a subnational identity. This of course makes them American, but it can also put such groups or identity categories in tension with others as well as with the very idea of a singular American identity. When a subnational culture experiences a trauma that results from friction between the part and the whole, as when African American communities respond to police brutality with civil unrest, comedy's ability to mediate between exclusionary and inclusionary impulses is critical to multiple senses of national identity. At other times, as was the case with Muslim Americans and those of Middle Eastern descent after 9/11, comedy polices the boundaries of national identity in relation to those defined more by otherness. Finally, television comedy is so powerful in its ability to define group identity that it is increasingly significant in defining national trauma for a subset of Americans, as examples of comedy in the Trump era demonstrate.

TELEVISION AND THE NATION

Since its development as a popular medium, television has been the most significant medium in defining the experience of American nationalism. As a new technology, it inflected this experience in unique ways. However, it also continued a tradition of national appeals with a much longer history in the modern era. If you ask theorists working in the modernist tradition of nationalism studies, they say that nations are particular to the last few hundred years.[5] Of the most significant theorists in this area, Benedict Anderson ties the nation most specifically to communication technology. He posits that nation-states arose largely due to the spread of the printing press and print capitalism. Since nationalism in these models is neither a given nor a constant, it is in continual need of reinforcement and renewal. To Anderson, newspapers were a particularly important site to create feelings of nationalism during the formative years of modern nations. In reading the newspaper, each "communicant is well aware that the ceremony he performs is being replicated simultaneously by thousands (or millions) of others of whose existence he is confident, yet of whose identity he has not the slightest notion."[6] By its very form, mass culture helped foment modern notions and experiences of the nation.[7]

In Anderson's schema, the ritual engagement with the idea of the collective forms the psychological and cultural foundations for nationalism. In his study of early modern bourgeois spaces such as coffeehouses and salons, Jürgen Habermas's notion of the "public sphere" places more emphasis on debate as productive discourse, focusing on not only physical spaces like early modern coffeehouses but also more virtual ones like nineteenth-century newspapers.[8] Broadcasting has obvious parallels to newspapers in both Anderson's and Habermas's conceptions. Franklin Roosevelt's fireside chats on radio made explicit the metaphor of broadcasting media as a virtual hearth for the national family, much like the newspaper served the construct of an imagined community. At the same time, newspapers publishing stories and opinions about national politics or other matters framed in nationalist terms spoke to the nation as well. So while the simultaneous virtual gathering represented by fireside chats gave Americans a feeling of communal existence, Roosevelt's role as president and his explicit discussion of the federal government further naturalized the sense that listeners were all part of a singular community.

Live broadcasting was significant to many of the founding works of television studies, helping to differentiate the medium from cinema, which could only show past events, and underscoring the sense of collective experience.[9] In these understandings, the simultaneity between on-screen events and viewers is important to the way people understand television, as is the sense that all audience members are witnessing the events at the same time. Although by the time this foundational work was written in the 1980s and '90s television was infrequently live, scholars such as Mary Ann Doane, Daniel Dayan, and Elihu Katz nevertheless emphasize the particular and continuing momentousness of the live event for bringing people together around shared witnessing.[10] Indeed, in the contemporary era of time-shifting and on-demand television, events including State of the Union addresses, Super Bowls, terror attacks, and school shootings are increasingly significant as rare moments of broad collective, simultaneous witness.

Although television began with a stronger regional sensibility, the technological and economic development of the medium toward the network era that ran from the mid-1950s through the 1970s consolidated control in the hands of NBC, CBS, and ABC. The concentration of economic control and talent in New York and Los Angeles meant that the cultures of those cities would largely stand in on television for the nation as a whole. There were of course countervailing factors that pushed back against this tendency. The Federal Communications Commission (FCC) has long used localism and diversity as measures of whether broadcasters are fulfilling their public service duties.[11] The desire to speak to "middle America" kept figures like Milton Berle and Carl Reiner off the airwaves, lest their Jewish New York sensibilities alienate viewers.[12] While television may have historically resisted a too-strong regional sensibility, aspirants in the entertainment and news industry come from all over, bringing their home culture to television.[13] Nevertheless, network broadcasting's industry and culture subsumed even these counterbalances to television's nationalizing tendencies, counterintuitively making them aspects of television's cultural homogenization.

In the decade between the mid-1970s and mid-1980s, the hegemonic power of the three networks eroded in the face of new competition from cable television, video recorders, video games, and the upstart network Fox (later to be joined by the UPN and WB networks). This shift to the so-called post-network era changed the inflection of American television's nationalism but did not eliminate it. Thinking back to Anderson's model, newspapers in Europe and the United States, especially during the formative years of the nation-state, were typically local, meaning that while readers from Boston to Atlanta were all engaging in the idea of the nation, they were typically reading different copy.[14] In contemporary television, while audiences might be split between local, network, and politically targeted cable news, they nevertheless engage with the concept of the nation when they watch the news.

Demographic targeting has existed since the beginning of television, growing more pronounced over time. However, there are particular moments of television that tend to bring majorities and sizable pluralities of viewers to witness the same events. Dayan and Katz highlight planned media events like the Olympics as bringing audiences together in large numbers and hailing them with explicit nationalism.[15] Katz, with coauthor Tamar Liebes, has in more recent years drawn distinctions between media events as "integrative" versus catastrophe coverage as "disintegrative," but this dichotomy deserves scrutiny.[16] Authorities may not plan school shootings and terror attacks, and they are marked more by violence than conciliation. However, these events also draw considerable national attention through television coverage and slip, seemingly naturally, into nationalist discourses, effectively recreating the nationalistic form and rhetoric of the media event discussed in Katz's earlier work. American television always has and continues to represent and smooth over the tensions and conflicts between local and national, in addition to other ways in which parts form a sense of the whole.

NATIONAL TRAUMA AS NATIONALISM

In the period immediately following 9/11, television narrated the national mood as mournful but also resilient and unified. When Rudolph Giuliani appeared on *The Late Show with David Letterman*, he stated that those events were "a beautiful and dramatic representation of how these cowardly terrorists tried to separate us . . . and what they achieved in doing was unifying Americans more than it's ever been before."[17] Similarly, but with more focus on the means that create that unity, Matt Roush of *TV Guide* wrote, "In the days and weeks since September 11, the country has come together—inspired, in part, by the moving images brought home by television."[18] The article that followed emotionally recounted post-9/11 highlights of nationalist pride and unity on television, such as when the New York Yankees "represent[ed] the Ground Zero of our wounded yet resolute national psyche" in the World Series.[19] Reflecting the spiritualist tenor of that period's patriotism, he claimed that "everything we do, everything we see takes on new, greater significance. And whether in the news we absorb or the entertainment we choose to enjoy, TV has played an essential role in our lives these last few historic months."[20]

National traumas perform nationalist ideology in both the Marxist sense of a determining worldview and the more conventional sense of everyday politics.[21] "[Benedict] Anderson's concern, of course, is not with trauma per se, but with the kinds of self-consciously ideological narratives of nationalist history," writes Jeffrey C. Alexander. "Yet these collective beliefs often assert the existence of some national trauma. In the course of defining national identity, national histories are constructed around injuries that cry out for revenge."[22] In dealing with moments such as these, the term *ideology* can have different meanings. On the one hand, the classically liberal definition uses the word to mean conscious and coherent sets of beliefs, the way one might commonly describe a Democratic or Christian ideology. Obviously, such use of the term is key to understanding the everyday politics of events like 9/11 and mass shootings when battles between progressives and conservatives, among others, become significant. More Marxist thinkers use the term in a different sense, where ideology functions as a largely unconscious but determining worldview. In this sense, the nation itself, as well as any construction of collective trauma, would function as an ideological expression of the deeper conditions of capitalism. That is, the nation exists as ideology in that it appears to be common sense and serves the interests of ruling classes.

While noting their differences is important, this book examines ideology in both the Marxist and everyday senses. Stuart Hall proves instructive here in the way he puts the two senses of the term *ideology* in dialogue and, while maintaining a distinction between them, finds value in both.[23] Understanding ideology as "false consciousness" should not confuse us into thinking that such ideas are somehow ineffectual. Indeed, the concept of nation has proven to have very real effects in modern history. Nor does he believe that we can ignore the real effects of the more mundane usage of the term *ideology*, as he notes the powerful effects of Thatcherite thinking in the United Kingdom. Like Hall, I aim for a middle ground where both understandings of ideology are legitimate and useful for understanding the machinery of culture. By this understanding, national trauma serves the idea of the nation as an ideological construct, but also matters for the way Americans understand and respond to such events through everyday politics.

A complete and simple refusal of shared experience as false consciousness would elide the fact that there are clear collective social operations at work here. Obviously, there are real people either directly cooperating to produce specific content or contributing to a larger discursive tendency by producing similar content without direct contact. And at the same time, viewers effectively choose among a finite number of readings of television content, meaning that large groups of viewers will experience similar reactions. Thus, while rejecting a romantic notion of an anthropomorphized society and examining how mass media constructs this idea, it is still safe to generalize to some extent about the ways in which these discourses construct and manage national traumas. The ideology of nationalism in the Marxist understanding has real and varied effects, including its continued support of capitalist economies, even if it appears too commonsensible for us to always notice its effects. At the same time, there are real impacts for people living and voting in societies where mundane concepts like Republican and Democratic ideologies face off in the public sphere. This book follows the cues of these and other thinkers in working to make clear and understand the effects that these discourses and ideologies have on our understandings of self and history through nationalism.

National traumas are *rituals* in that they inspire meaningful forms of media coverage that reinforce a sense of national community and identity.[24] While television's nationalism sometimes dabbles in overt propaganda, it is more typically subtle in its ideological appeals.[25] In this mode, television enacts what Michael Billig refers to as "banal nationalism," which describes the largely unrecognized ways in which we are asked to imagine ourselves as part of a nation.[26] At other times, national traumas being particular examples, the nationalistic rituals become more obvious. After 9/11, flag-waving patriotism became the rule of the day. But even more minor traumas like school shootings or even celebrity deaths prompt an explicitly nationalist response, such as the ubiquity of American flags in makeshift memorials and the focus by news on such images. Most significantly, and as many of the responses to 9/11 noted above indicate, the discourse surrounding national traumas reflects ideas of national unity. Emile Durkheim, one of the founders of anthropological ritual theory, believed that rituals not only denoted what was sacred to a culture but also gave it a sense of belonging.[27] Sara Ahmed further develops Durkheim's ideas, arguing that emotion is in fact constitutive to the nation, noting, for example, the immense significance of saying, "The nation mourns."[28] The nation is not simply about thinking of oneself as part of an abstract concept, but about imagining oneself as part of a collection of human beings held together by common identity. In the contemporary era, this sense of sacredness and collectivity is perhaps most acutely felt in relation to national traumas as highly emotive events.

NATIONALIZING TRAUMA

In the three *South Park* episodes collectively titled "Imaginationland," the main characters travel to a magical land full of fictional characters from leprechauns to Luke Skywalker.[29] Once there, however, terrorists bomb Imaginationland, comically literalizing the notion that terrorism's primary target is the public imagination. Similarly, Jean Baudrillard and Slavoj Zizek are among the most notable proponents of understanding the primary importance of 9/11 as a virtual event.[30] This is to argue neither that there was not real violence on that day nor that the conventionally accepted account of the events were inaccurate. In fact, the power of 9/11 as opposed to more purely ceremonial, less lethal events arises in part from the realness that physical death and destruction connote. "It is a kind of duel between [reality and fiction]," in Baudrillard's words, "a contest to see which can be the most unimaginable."[31] The events on 9/11 killed three thousand people, but they also attacked the nation as a symbolic, ideological construct. In many ways echoing Michel Foucault's ideas on discourse analysis, we can understand the nation and particular events like 9/11 through the ways people communicated about them.[32] Of course, this requires accounting for not only the serious discourses but also the ways informal, contentious, humorous, and other discourses construct and deconstruct these ideas.

Baudrillard and Zizek argue that, in the long run, this terrorism of the media imaginary was more tactically significant than the physical destruction and carnage. Moreover, this position argues that the vast ripple of 9/11—its impact on everything from financial markets to flag-themed apparel—was primarily accomplished symbolically through mass media. In other words, despite the massive physical destruction, psychological distress to individuals caused by mass-mediated images created the more consequential impacts in the political and social sphere of the nation. September 11 was a twisted play on what Daniel J. Boorstin classifies as a pseudo-event. While his work tended away from violent destruction of this nature, these terrorist attacks fit his definition of a pseudo-event, especially since it was planned and intended "for the immediate purpose of being reported or reproduced."[33] The attacks accomplished their goals through news media that could not help but cooperate in reproducing their images. This symbolic destruction, along with the necessary and unavoidable cooperation of media producers, remains the paradigmatic example and most "successful" act of terrorism in American history. However, as the New York Friars Club roast demonstrated, genres besides strictly earnest news and documentary quickly joined the discussion, both reinforcing the sense of a nation that had been wounded and flagrantly breaking taboos as if to demonstrate that the wound was not terribly deep.

The "imagined" nation and "virtual" event are similar in construction and form, so it is no wonder they tend to collude ideologically. Trauma coverage amplifies television's nationalistic tendencies, making them privileged moments in the contemporary experience of nation. Their ability to capture large national audiences makes such events unique. Additionally, disasters often take on a national character. Some are explicitly linked to the national government when it involves a public servant, as was the case with the Kennedy assassination or the Gabby Giffords shooting. Other times, they represent the violent failure of an American project, the Space Shuttle Challenger explosion being an obvious example. Even when such events are less obviously national by virtue of their links to the federal government, they take on a national character in news coverage. On February 14, 2018, television news sent helicopters and interrupted regular programming to place viewers "at the scene" of the Marjory Stoneman Douglas High School shooting in Parkland, Florida. Less than an hour after the actual shooting, KTVU in Oakland, to take just one example, broke into its noon newscast to report on the events, virtually bridging the geographical distance between the coasts to allow Bay Area viewers witness.[34] Technological form made possible this particular nationalizing address, but news coverage added to the discourse. About ten minutes after the story first broke, Oakland's coverage began to nationalize its framing by noting, "This scene, not unfamiliar in 2018 or years prior. There's been more than a dozen school shootings *in our country* since the calendar year turned from 2017 to 2018" (emphasis added). Not long after, anchors reported that President Trump had tweeted his condolences, suggesting the importance of a federal response, whether symbolic or material, in understanding such events as national.[35] By the evening, network newscasts formalized their coverage. Lester Holt of *NBC Nightly News* narrated video highlights of the day: "*The nation* once again witnessed the awful images of students' hands raised fleeing from an *American* school along with the emotional reunions of children with their anguished parents" (emphasis added). Holt explicitly references the national character of this localized event twice in one sentence. At the same time, he drew attention to the affective weight of the coverage, heightening the emotional resonance of the event by tying it to the relationships between parents and children. Comedy shows may echo such sentiments, as did late night comedy talk show hosts like Jimmy Kimmel and Jimmy Fallon, who earnestly spoke against gun violence and in support of the students in the aftermath of the shooting.[36] At the same time, other shows like the purposefully raunchy *Family Guy* made light of school shootings, lessening the emotional weight granted such events by news coverage.

Both technology and discourse aid in the nationalizing of these events; so, too, were these tools put to use building the sense that this was a trauma. Stacy Takacs argues that 9/11 was understood in a "trauma frame" because news coverage used melodramatic performance in its coverage.[37] Indeed, Peter Brooks's listing of melodramatic techniques could easily describe television news's coverage of national traumas: "The indulgence of strong emotionalism; moral polarization and schematization; extreme states of being, situations, action; overt villainy; persecution of the good; inflated and extravagant expressions; dark plottings, suspense, breathtaking peripety."[38] Of course, not every violent event receives this same melodramatic coverage. While Lynne Joyrich highlights the melodramatic tendencies of news programming more generally, overtly emotional framing distinguishes trauma coverage from more pedestrian reportage of violent or otherwise troubling events.[39] This contrast was particularly stark to me as a Chicagoan during the summer of 2012, when gun violence led to an alarming weekly body count that was reported straight and with little

CNN's coverage of the 2012 Aurora, Colorado, shooting included a slow push-in on a still photograph of a makeshift memorial.

emotional reaction aside from interviews with family members. However, after twelve died and fifty-eight were shot at a movie theater in Aurora, Colorado, the same summer, television news was awash with the affective markings of a national trauma, including mournful interstitial music, still photograph montages of the wounded and grieving, and a strong focus on the psychological aspects of suffering and recovering from physical and psychological wounds. In this case, the weekend after the attack, a CNN anchor even remarked how the widespread violence in Chicago, whose casualty numbers dwarfed those in Colorado, had all but been ignored in the wake of the Aurora incident.[40]

The shooting at Marjory Stoneman Douglas was of course simply a more recent example of a phenomenon that existed in broadcasting for a much longer period. Television coverage of 9/11 brought together events in New York, Washington, DC, and Pennsylvania, delivering them to a national audience with branding as "Attack on America" and "America Under Attack."[41] Coverage focused heavily on the response by federal officials, especially George W. Bush, while declaring Rudy Giuliani to be not just the mayor of New York but "America's Mayor."[42] Interviews with witnesses focused on their emotional responses while formal television techniques like slow motion and music denoted anxiety or sadness. Forty years earlier, coverage of John F. Kennedy's assassination, while not quite as technically slick, offered a similar construct of national trauma.

A national trauma, then, is a media ritual that frames certain events as both unusually negative and national in scope and character using emotional appeals. A sizable portion of the population must also buy into the construction offered by media for it to function as a national trauma. While national traumas have elements in common with more clinical understandings of psychological trauma, this is not to argue that media coverage causes post-traumatic stress disorder (PTSD) on a mass scale. Although they are separate phenomena, the repetition compulsion of clinical trauma in the form of flashbacks, nightmares, and insistent thoughts is a useful metaphor to think through the tendency of culture to repeat images and narratives of national trauma.[43] Indeed, news coverage is repetitive, but the events it covers continue to echo through culture in dramatic and comedic art as well. As I argue most specifically in chapter 3, the repetition of national trauma as news and comedy is meaningful. Susannah Radstone offers a useful analogy between the experience of broken and incomplete memories that define PTSD and the experience of wanting to know, but never fully knowing, the past.[44] Trauma theory helps describe the tendency to repeatedly return to the event in news and documentary coverage in order to understand them better. Repetition is evidence that certain parties can never be satisfied with the level of knowing offered by such reengagements. Some, like 9/11 "truthers," grow so dissatisfied with this situation that they write their own history. I explore this topic in more detail in chapter 4.

As the examples used in this introduction already indicate, national traumas are relative. Some, like 9/11 and the JFK assassination, are more totalizing by virtue of their overwhelming media coverage and apparent impact on audiences. Others, like more localized natural disasters or even celebrity deaths, may take on the character of national traumas to a lesser degree. And while they speak meaningfully to nationalism itself, they also speak to related issues within the national frame. For instance, chapters 5 and 6 examine the ways that comedies engaged issues of ethnic and religious identity following the 1992 Los Angeles riots and 9/11. Although news has historically been the genre in which national trauma first registers (see chapter 7 for a discussion of exceptions), fictional and entertainment genres act as important sites to negotiate these constructs. Comedy's unique address and rhetoric are especially significant as places where the sacred tone surrounding national traumas can be questioned.

COMIC RITUALS

The ability to engage with and continue thinking through such issues is significant, but far from the only way in which comedy's response to national trauma matters. Comedy's appeals, modes of address, and ability to dabble in fantastic and experimental storytelling, among other characteristics, makes it a unique site for society to work through its most serious moments in unserious ways. To Jane Feuer, liveness is significant in part because the ability to show actual events in real time makes television feel more real and truthful. In focusing primarily on live television as a medium for news, this argument echoes the focus of theorists like Anderson and Habermas on news and other nonfictional genres of literature. While informational genres of television hold greater sway in presenting audiences with versions of reality and truth, fictional and entertainment genres can operate similarly, albeit to different effects. Entertainment programming has a similar ritual function to catastrophe coverage when, say, large numbers of people tune in for a series finale. However, in the era of narrowcasting and on-demand viewing through technologies including DVRs and Netflix, the expectation that anyone outside of your demographic sliver might be watching the same programming as you, much less at the same time, wanes. Nevertheless, even demographically targeted, time-shifted entertainment programming has nationalistic tendencies.

Anderson builds his model of imagined community primarily around engagement with factual genres, but he also includes fictional literature printed in vernacular language (a step that in many ways created the necessary conditions for contemporary popular culture) as a factor in the creation of the modern nation. As far as television goes, any engagement with a national medium, including more lighthearted programming, encourages nationalistic thinking. Of course, watching a sitcom as opposed to, say, a press conference emphasizes different aspects of imagined community. The ability of Netflix in its distribution of older shows to offer a lingua franca in my television studies classes is striking. The continuing relevance of the television shows *Friends* and the US version of *The Office* to in-class discussions and online meme-producers suggests, even keeping in mind that my students and online communities do not represent the entire nation, that popular television entertainment continues to serve as a cultural unifier. At the same time, television comedy is given to the siloing of culture, perhaps more so than other television genres. The broad array of subgenres—from formally staid fare like CBS's multi-cam sitcoms, to experimental Adult Swim shows and politically polarized content from Tim Allen's *Last Man Standing*, to late night talk shows' (mostly) left-leaning humor—allow a wide variety of viewing options to fit viewers' tastes and values. Although the Fox News–MSNBC viewership dichotomy remains telling, it nevertheless speaks to a one-dimensional understanding of political culture that understands viewers mostly as merely left or right in political orientation.[45] The examples above suggest that comedy divides people up not just politically but in terms of their tolerance for formal experimentation. This only begins to suggest the far wider variety of subcultural appeals across the range of television comedy. Nevertheless, comedy speaks to a collective sense of Americanness. Political comedy, especially when engaging with the most well-known moments in American culture, offers a way to engage in the national while maintaining the more narrow appeal required in the contemporary television industry. While specifically important to comedy in this project, this model speaks to the larger ways in which contemporary nationalism operates as a dialectic between national and subnational identity.

Though certainly significant for creating a sense of unity, the seriousness with which television and other mass media discourses treat national traumas indicates their ritual value in forming a sense of the sacred. Entertainment television often recreates the sense of seriousness surrounding such events, reinforcing their ritual value. In television studies, much of the focus on post-9/11 television was on dramas. While both Lynn Spigel and Stacy Takacs offer some engagement with programs like *Saturday Night Live*, *South Park*, and *The Daily Show*, both focus more on serious-minded fare like *The West Wing*, *24*, and *Battlestar Galactica*.[46] Both authors note that in the longer term, culture in general and television more specifically moved away from the short-lived political consensus that followed 9/11 by speaking to subgroups across political and taste spectrums. In this sense, television returned, after a brief hiatus, from a model of nationalism as simplistic unity and toward a more Habermasian one that understands political, and therefore national, culture as characterized by debate. Matt Sienkiewicz notes that while irony did not end with the 9/11 attacks, ironic comedy shifted from a largely uncritical form to one more political and barbed.[47] As both Sienkiewicz and Takacs argue more explicitly, comedy programs like *The Daily Show* served an important role in this shift back to a form of national culture typified more by debate.

For the most part, topical late night comedies treated 9/11 as a sacred event. Most notably, the New York–based shows—*The Late Show with David Letterman*, *The Daily Show with Jon Stewart*, and *Late Night with Conan O'Brien*—came back to air after a week off with a similar pattern. All three were solemn, with hosts practically apologizing for their role as comedians in that moment, responding to the larger sense that comedy and humor were inappropriate. But for slight self-deprecation ("I make a living acting like an ass," said O'Brien), there was little humor in these episodes. Even in those instances, self-deprecation served as a rhetorical tool to venerate by comparison first responders and politicians like Rudy

Giuliani and George W. Bush. Nevertheless, hosts justified the humor that would slowly return to these programs as a necessary comfort and as examples of New Yorkers getting back to work. Nevertheless, in the wake of 9/11 as well as other national traumas like devastating hurricanes and mass shootings, comedians turning serious has symbolic value to the sense of the national sacred.

Of course, as Gilbert Gottfried indicated in his performance at the Friars Club roast, comedy need not adopt this approach to national trauma. His sick joke about his plane hitting the Empire State Building did not exactly perform a high theory critique of 9/11 as a discursive object, but it flagrantly rejected the sacred tone of those events, which is an important element of their ritual power. In this way, he suggested the ability of humor to counter sacred rituals. Mary Douglas explains,

> Great rituals create unity in experience. They assert hierarchy and order. In doing so, they affirm the value of the symbolic patterning of the universe. Each level of patterning is validated and enriched by association with the rest. But jokes have the opposite effect. They connect widely differing fields, but the connection destroys the hierarchy and order. They do not affirm the dominant values, but denigrate and devalue. Essentially a joke is an anti-rite.[48]

Of course, this characterization is overly broad. Jokes can denigrate some values while reinforcing others, and humor may have little subversive quality at all. Nevertheless, humor's ability and tendency to operate outside and against sacred frames makes it unique among mass media discourses.

To the extent that jokes act as anti-rites, they would appear to disintegrate the sense of unity created by the rituals of Durkheim's formulation. Indeed, humor theorists like Sigmund Freud and Henri Bergson particularly note the tendency of jokes to be at the expense of some, separating humor's targets from the more unified community. At the same time, both theorists also note that separating out some people forms a social bond among those laughing at them.[49] Ted Cohen describes the ways that joking reinforces established bonds among comics and audiences by ritual engagements with linguistic codes.[50] Group laughter signals common knowledge and values, and thus reinforces group bonds and identity. And while admitting its potential for divisiveness, Lawrence E. Mintz believes that American humor developed the way it did as a way to smooth over divisions within the nation's "dynamic and heterogeneous" culture.[51] John Limon has a similar take, though instead of seeing comedy as an ever-present force unifying all Americans, he proposes that comedy of a type has spread to unite Americans. "America, between 1960 and the millennium," he writes, "in a process that began around the ascension of Johnny Carson or the Kennedy Assassination, comedified. Stand-up was once a field given over to certain subsections of a certain ethnicity. By now, roughly speaking, all America is the pool for national stand-up comedy."[52] Much of the scholarship around news parody considers nationalism explicitly or implicitly by examining the way that the genre comments upon nonfictional politics and news.[53] Still others focus on concepts like comedy's mediated intimacy or media industries as formative to a sense of nationalism.[54] Where *Tragedy Plus Time* differs is in its particular focus on the ways in which comedy negotiates experiences of the nation with and through what appear to be the most serious and sacred constructs in culture.

Mary Douglas's ideas about jokes as anti-rites relate closely to the work of Mikhail Bakhtin, who is, in comedy studies circles at least, best known as the theorist of the carnivalesque.[55] To Bakhtin, medieval carnival celebrations represented the rebellious spirit of the people against more official ceremonies of the church and state. While contemporary society does not have anything quite so regularly scheduled or totalizing as the church ceremonies of medieval Europe, national traumas operate in much the same way by offering moments of collective imagining marked by high seriousness. Comedies that joke about traumas often function similarly to Bakhtin's carnival by providing the anti-rite to the more sacred ritual of national trauma.[56]

Often, the sense of sacredness in national traumas narrows the range of expressible ideas surrounding them. This tendency applies to serious rituals more generally, as one is typically expected to limit their use of foul language, for instance, at a church service. After the deaths of significant figures like politicians and celebrities, criticism is muted in favor of more laudatory discussion. Marita Sturken discusses the ways that honest political introspection regarding the causes of anti-Americanism abroad was quieted in favor of discourses of national innocence following 9/11.[57] After every mass shooting in the United States, a number of conservative politicians can be expected to attempt to limit the extent to which gun-control advocates will discuss ways to limit firearm violence by arguing that it is vulgar to talk politics in that moment. The absence of certain kinds of speech is meaningful in that it signifies and helps create a sense of sacredness surrounding these events. But as all of these examples also suggest, it can have negative effects on political culture when it prevents significant discussion and debate from taking place. However, comedy is less beholden to the rules of what may or may not be said. In fact, in certain corners of the comedy industry, the willingness to "go there" is the draw.

Friars Club roasts are formal events presented on television, making clear their role as anti-rites in the sense that they are ritualistic in form but invert its meaning. Speakers follow a meaningful pattern whereby they insult attendees generally, then the guest of honor, before changing modes to more sincere admiration. At the same time, the ritual expects attendees to push boundaries. The Hefner roast presented a uniquely challenging moment in that there was a clear sacred construct about which there were many restrictions on speech. If Gottfried was fairly alone in violating taboos that evening, many on television followed his lead in the ensuing years. Shows like *Family Guy* were especially notable in the early 2000s for attacking social and expressive restrictions, and 9/11 proved especially useful as a way to prove their offensive bona fides, as did other traumas from the JFK assassination to the death of Trayvon Martin. As will be explored in various ways in the chapters that follow, taboo-breaking comedies serve to test and expand the boundaries of the sayable.

I am cautious about celebrating or condemning this kind of humor as a whole. Some sacred constructs deserve criticism, while others serve more legitimate purposes. Shows like *Family Guy*, along with Letterman, Jon Stewart, and others, helped reopen the door to criticism of the Bush administration after 9/11. When the Griffins, *Family Guy*'s titular family, visit the site of the attacks, the following discussion takes place between the idiot patriarch Peter and his wise anthropomorphic dog.

> BRIAN: Peter, this is the site of the 9/11 terrorist attacks.
> PETER: Oh, so Saddam Hussein did this?
> BRIAN: No.
> PETER: The Iraqi army?
> BRIAN: No.
> PETER: Some guys from Iraq?
> BRIAN: No.
> PETER: That one lady that visited Iraq that one time?
> BRIAN: No, Peter, Iraq had nothing to do with this. It was a bunch of Saudi Arabians, Lebanese, and Egyptians financed by a Saudi Arabian guy living in Afghanistan and sheltered by Pakistanis.
> PETER: So you're saying we need to invade Iran?[58]

This exchange is a clear critique of the neoconservative logic by which post-9/11 fears of terrorism justified the 2003 invasion of Iraq. Joking

Family Guy *makes light of mass shootings.*

about 9/11 at all helped to break the sacred frame around those events, but instances like these were especially notable for joking about 9/11 while also criticizing the ways in which the administration used the emotional fallout from those events to justify questionable policy.

At the same time, *Family Guy*'s willingness to play around with national traumas of other types is less clearly useful. In one example, Peter involves himself in a classic role-reversal sitcom narrative as he plans to attend high school while his children play the roles of adults.[59] Despite seemingly never suffering from the bullying that ostensibly triggered Columbine, Peter prepares to commit a massacre: his black trench coat directly alludes to those shooters' membership in the so-called Trenchcoat Mafia.[60] Lois corrects him, telling Peter to play the part of a normal high schooler, but it is too late. Peter phones his co-conspirator in order to call off his plan but is only met with the sounds of gunfire and terrified screams.

In yet another example, Peter shoots black teenage character Cleveland Jr. Although nonfatal, the episode is a clear allusion to the 2012 Trayvon Martin shooting.[61] In the cases of gun violence in general and deaths of young black men more specifically, positive political engagement requires that the public become and remain angry, frightened, and otherwise emotionally engaged. Reflecting Lauren Berlant and Sianne Ngai's concern that media culture maintains a constant sense of carnival, *Family Guy*'s and others' breaking of the sacred frame might speed viewers too quickly through the stages of grief, and acceptance does not typically lead to positive social change.[62]

This ability to emotionally reframe national traumas is indicative of parody's power to engage events more generally. National traumas clearly hold major positions as historical events and in historical narratives. They serve as turning points in tellings of popular history. By this logic, the 1960s didn't *really* begin until Kennedy was shot, and Columbine began the era of mass shootings in America. At the same time, their quality as flashbulb memories—the tendency to clearly remember the moment when one heard about JFK or 9/11—makes them significant moments for the way people consider themselves in relation to larger historical events and the nation. Parody, which is the technique of imitating texts to comic effect, is also a significant way in which comedy reengages these historical moments. As the chapter about dead Kennedy jokes on television makes clear, television's ability to joke in this manner has been mostly limited to the post-network era. But since then, this humor has been significant to emotional responses people attach to these histories and, in many cases, actually serves a role in debating the truth of orthodox historical narratives.

These comic rituals are neither fully subversive nor fully hegemonic in their relationship to the nation. In fact, as writers like Umberto Eco and Linda Hutcheon argue, irony and humor are especially slippery in ideological terms.[63] Eco in particular argues that the carnivalesque, by nature of being sanctioned rebellion, allows people to blow off steam rather than changing unjust aspects of society. Comedy, it seems, is especially well suited for holding contradictions in tension, resolving the discomfort with a laugh rather than logic or action. Comedy television, then, is an especially complex form of address. Television is nationalist but continually speaks to smaller demographic slices. Comedy in particular often provides a sense of community through laughter, but does so by othering, thereby separating some from the sense of unity. Television is responsible for many of the ways in which national traumas take on the characteristics of rituals, but comedy programs in the same medium provide us with anti-rites. To call these "comic rituals," as opposed to simply rituals, is to note the complexities and contradictions inherent to television comedy. This book sketches out the various ways that comic rituals respond to the most serious moments of secular culture and what that means for how culture relates those events to the sense of nation.

CHAPTER DESCRIPTIONS

The following two chapters examine the way that television comedy manages popular history, especially inasmuch as history is impacted by what can be expressed about it. According to Anderson, a sense of collective history is a critical factor in the way that culture creates and maintains a sense of the modern nation.[64] For various reasons, including parody's ability to play around with existing media texts and the low cultural status of comedy as compared to other genres, television comedy is an important site where the historical significance of national traumas can be narrated, negotiated, and even erased. At the same time, television comedy's negotiation of national trauma is important to popular history because national traumas are themselves so significant to the way Americans understand and narrate the nation's history.

Chapter 1 specifically concerns television history and the ways in which it has come to use sick humor to narrate traumatic history, demonstrating how the television industry has come to allow certain types of taboo humor to develop on-screen since the 1980s. As demographic targeting allowed for more daring forms of humor to appear on the medium, it also created space for comedy to reengage and dismantle the sense of sacredness that surrounded historical traumas. As a case study, it examines the ways that comedies in the post-network period (roughly 1980 to the present) have parodied the assassination of John F. Kennedy and related events. It uses varied examples of comedy's engagement with the JFK assassination from 1983 (*Saturday Night Live*), 1992 (*Seinfeld*), 1999, and 2009 (both *Family Guy*) to examine changing technology and demographic logics. These factors, along with others like the time elapsed since 1963, have allowed the representations of these events to not only grow more contentious but move from relative fringe programming times to the center of Sunday evening tent-pole positions. Ultimately, this chapter defines and engages with history in two senses. On the one hand, it shows how television's industrial developments throughout its history have defined the ways in which it can engage with sensitive topics. At the same time, these examples show how television began to negotiate national traumas and their politics through the lenses of parodic reimagining, a theme that will continue through ensuing chapters.

Chapter 2 examines cases where television comedy's textual history was edited in response to national trauma, demonstrating how that reflects larger changes in politics and discourse. In a larger sense, it also demonstrates how, despite the changes in the television industry discussed in chapter 1, changing historical circumstances can rewrite the rules of what may and may not be expressed. For instance, *Family Guy* aired a gag referencing Osama bin Laden in 2000. After 9/11, censors cut this bit from reruns and DVD releases. In these and other cases, comedy was vulnerable as a seemingly frivolous genre, which meant that it could no longer represent the moment of its production or airing in the same way it had previously. This reflected significant shifts in not only what could be discussed in the public sphere but also how Americans were allowed to remember the political and social history leading up to 9/11. This chapter also examines related moments, such as the way John F. Kennedy Jr.'s death functioned like a national trauma when editors cut references to him from an episode of *Sex and the City*. In that case, obituaries characterized him using similar discourses as were used for his father and uncle—a national hero and aspiring public servant. This marked a sharp departure from the way celebrity journalism had earlier characterized him, as a philanderer and object of a sexual gaze. Inasmuch as *Sex and the City* was a comedy text with heavy overtones of feminine sexuality, it was vulnerable to editing when discussion of JFK Jr. turned to more masculine nationalist as opposed to feminine private-sphere terms. In keeping with the theme of edited and censored discourses, this chapter concludes by examining the way that *South Park* tested established representational rules by satirizing censorship even as censors altered those precedents to rewrite the show's textual history in response to ongoing crises triggered by 9/11.

Chapters 3 and 4 focus on the ways television comedy negotiates emotional and factual meanings of national traumas. Chapter 3 argues that comedy plays an important role as a venue for "emotional nonconformity." Emotional appeals are significant to the building of national community around traumas and determine much of the ideology surrounding them. Inasmuch as humor dissipates and parody recodes earlier emotions and texts respectively, comedy acts as a significant site for reengaging and rewriting the emotional frame that defines national trauma. To demonstrate this concept, the chapter examines numerous sites of negotiation. In general, joking about and parodying these events allows audiences to recall them with a different emotional frame. But the manner in which shows do this has specific impacts. Self-consciously offensive comics like Anthony Jeselnik and Daniel Tosh provide examples for modeling the concept of emotional nonconformity in their engagement with relatively recent traumas like the 2017 Unite the Right rally in Charlottesville. It also examines the specific implications of parody, which as an imitative strategy is always in conversation with the pastness of other texts. News parodies like *Full Frontal with Samantha Bee* and *The Opposition with Jordan Klepper* question and otherwise mock fearmongering by news programs and others, dissipating the fear and training viewers to question such techniques. Additional shows like *Family Guy* and *The Sarah Silverman Program* mock retrospective and memorial programming as overwrought and corny, training viewers in camp approaches to these emotionally powerful texts. This chapter concludes by considering some of the political implications of comedy's ability to dissipate negative emotions, especially for issues like the war on terror and gun control.

Chapter 5 examines the phenomenon of popular history in the form of conspiracy theories. It argues that while political comedy and conspiracy theories represent similar ways of thinking about national traumas, these ways of narrating the past serve a range of political ideologies and subject positions. The conspiracy theory way of approaching national traumas represents a rejection of orthodox historical narratives. Considering their standing in culture more generally, American comedy is surprisingly concerned with these ways of reading history. In some cases, like that of Mort Sahl and somewhat more contemporary black-coded comedies like *Chappelle's Show* and *The Boondocks*, the paranoid view of history recreates the worldview of a certain type of critical political humor. Other comedies like *King of the Hill* and *South Park* satirize and ironize this approach to history, effectively supporting the orthodox view. More recently, as Donald Trump and others have brought conspiracy theories into the political mainstream, shows like *The Opposition with Jordan Klepper* have ironized conspiracy theories as a show of support for the concept of objective truth and orthodox history. Because they represent larger disagreements about the nature of a shared national history and political reality, these battles over common history are increasingly significant to national cohesiveness and political analysis.

The next two chapters present case studies in which comedy helped work through crises of ethnic identity in relation to larger American formations. Chapter 5 asks how African American–cast comedies responded to the 1992 Los Angeles riots, ultimately demonstrating how black talent was in a unique position to work through significant issues related to cultural authenticity and racial justice. As Herman Gray notes, changes in the television industry made black audiences a more valuable demographic for television in the early 1990s.[65] Network and cable responded primarily by greenlighting a spate of comedies, including *Def Comedy Jam*, *The Fresh Prince of Bel-Air*, *A Different World*, and *In Living Color*. The confluence of industrial factors with the particular crises of the Rodney King beating and Los Angeles riots meant that comedy was in a unique position to address these traumas. Yet, while television made these events national, discourse characterized them primarily as traumas to and of working-class African Americans. Inasmuch as the riots were tied to racial identity, these comedies frequently concerned who should be able to claim symbolic connections to the aggrieved community and how to properly perform membership in it. These shows responded to the riots and the traumas that sparked them by playing symbolic gatekeeper. On *Def Comedy Jam*, for instance, Martin Lawrence expressed feelings that poor Latinxs should not participate in looting even though African Americans could. Sitcoms like *The Fresh Prince of Bel-Air* and *A Different World* tested the racial authenticity of middle- and upper-class African Americans against the riots, arguing that these characters needed to perform a level of material and/or political commitment to claim membership in the larger racial community. In keeping with its sketch format, *In Living Color* was more mercurial. Initially, it attacked African Americans—including Rodney King—and other players who laid claim to the grievances in a display of comic cynicism. Eventually, however, the show developed a stronger sense of political commitment and inclusiveness by positioning the viewers themselves as members of a larger aggrieved community.

Chapter 6 is another case study involving ethnic identity. Like those that discussed the Los Angeles riots, post-9/11 comedies frequently concerned race. However, in focusing on those of Middle Eastern descent, as well as the associated categories of Muslims and terrorists, television comedy often positioned these groups as Others against which to define American identity. This chapter examines the ways that comedies reinforced and negotiated the construction of these post-9/11 Others in relation to American identity, arguing that these shows responded to issues of Islamophobia in the increasingly fractious and narrowcast environment by signaling their political stance to specific and sympathetic audiences. As Lynn Spigel argues, the post-9/11 sense of national unity was short lived as the reality of politics and culture meant that people returned to debate and specialized communities.[66] However, the massive impact of 9/11 meant that even as Americans returned to established patterns of a more siloed culture, they continued to work through concerns raised by those events. While many theories of comedy consider its role in building community, this function often depends on separating out individuals or groups for ridicule.[67] Building on these themes, this chapter examines the way that anti–politically correct comedians like Jeff Dunham and Carlos Mencia mobilized the image of terrorists and those of Middle Eastern descent not only to define their view of American identity but also to position themselves within the politics and economics of television. At the same time, other shows rejected the temptation to separate, instead using comedy to reintegrate the new Other. Sitcoms like *The Simpsons* recycled established plotlines in which a character unlearns prejudices in order to argue for a liberal-pluralist lesson on integrating Americans of Middle Eastern descent. It also examines the way that *The Daily Show* staked its claim to explicit left-leaning politics by engaging in public-sphere debates on these topics, using the "ground zero mosque" controversy as a case study. Finally, it looks more specifically at the way Arab American and Persian American performers responded to these issues in a comedy special titled *The Axis of Evil Comedy Tour*. It notes how they frequently used similar comic techniques as other television programs during this period, but with altered meaning due to the performers' ethno-religious identities.

While less focused on ethnic or religious identity as the previous two, chapter 7 continues to examine how subnational communities fit into the larger sense of the nation after a national trauma. Specifically, it demonstrates how, for Americans opposed to the Trump presidency and/or its policies, comedy's narrowcast address allowed it to create a trauma frame within which sympathetic viewers can make sense of recent events. This chapter notes how news has struggled to balance the ethics and business of journalistic neutrality with the seeming sense among portions of Americans that Donald Trump is himself a trauma. The 2016 election, the president's casual relationship with sexual assault, and policies like family separation all become fodder for a kind of emotionally engaged comedy that in many ways recreates the appeals to national trauma that television news has not fully adopted. For instance, late night comedies from election week 2016 borrowed and at times negotiated the rhetoric of national trauma. Sometime later, the feminist comedies *Full Frontal with Samantha Bee* and *Broad City*, respectively, fought against the routinization of news stories regarding—and used clinical trauma as a metaphor for understanding—Donald Trump's and Brett Kavanaugh's alleged but largely unpunished histories of sexual assault. Finally, the chapter examines how masculine comics Jim Jefferies and Jimmy Kimmel have themselves fought the normalization of apparently cruel policies, including attempts to repeal the Affordable Care Act and family separation, using overt performances of emotion.

In 2009, *Family Guy* imagined a world in which John F. Kennedy had been replaced by McDonald's mascot Mayor McCheese, setting up a gruesome sight gag that recreated the president's assassination in gory detail.[1] Showing this clip to a group of academics, I was surprised to discover how troubling certain audience members found this bit. Their reaction was likely in part due to the equating of presidential brain matter with hamburger (and that Jacqueline Bouvier-McCheese eats it), but likely also reflected a concern for its profane reimagining of sacred history. As one personally and professionally invested in contentious humor, I can understand such responses even if I have built a tolerance toward the kind of visceral reaction that some in my audience expressed. Nevertheless, what surprised me most was the extent to which this audience of culturally knowledgeable and hip adults found this troubling. It aired on broadcast television during prime time, after all. This vignette speaks to a number of issues analyzed in the following chapters. How is it, for example, that television got to the point where the Kennedy assassination became fodder for a gross-out sight gag during prime-time Sunday night programming? What does this say about the historical context in which such gags get decoded? How does parody play around with our factual and emotional relationships to history?

In examining industrial and aesthetic trends in television and meaningful events in America's last half century, this book concerns popular history as much as nationalism. However, nationalism leans heavily on popular understandings of the past in constructing a concept of shared culture, identity, and, well, history. To use the psychoanalytic trauma metaphor explicitly, television has gone through different periods of "latency" between the initial trauma and comedy's engagement with it. September 11 quickly became the subject for comedy, and the Challenger explosion never quite became a common topic for television comedy. The Kennedy assassination, however, was at first not a theme for comedy, but eventually appeared in the genre. By examining trends in audience conception and comic strategies, this chapter demonstrates how such humor moved from relatively safe jokes in late night to highly contentious humor airing during prime time.

National traumas at times produce moratoria, or periods of latency, to use the trauma metaphor, on certain types of comedy and humor and sometimes even humor in general. The most public hand-wringing over these issues in American culture occurred after 9/11, with numerous opinion pieces declaring it "the end of the age of irony."[2] Though declarations of irony's and comedy's death were hyperbolic, even those who dismissed the doomsayers had to admit that television comedies would have to adapt to new expectations over contentious and critical humor. Though Comedy Central continued to show its regular daytime reruns on 9/11, it was not without some concern. In explaining why the network had put *The Daily Show* on hold, Tony Fox assured the public that his network believed that there was nothing funny going on.[3] Eventually, of course, new comedies returned to the air, cautiously at first with Leno, Letterman, and Stewart pulling punches, while audiences, editors, and advertisers punished those like Bill Maher whom they perceived as stepping out of line.[4] After a time, boundary-pushing shows like *South Park* satirized elements of the response, but not without reinforcing some of the jingoism.[5] However, as Matt Sienkiewicz notes, the dominant style of comic irony shifted from relatively toothless to a more engaged, critical form.[6]

In the final counting, the moratorium on critical comedy was short lived. Public discussion of these issues might have even emboldened humorists as they vied for the respect and publicity that comes from pushing limits, even if some like Gilbert Gottfried got the backlash they courted.[7] How did American television get to this point? The worry over televised humor in 2001 was responding to a set of expectations regarding the state of television comedy at the millennial turn. On the other hand, while Lenny Bruce joked about JFK on the evening of the assassination, dead Kennedy jokes would have been unthinkable for 1963 television. Even as late as 1986, when sick jokes about the Space Shuttle Challenger disaster circulated orally, they were largely absent from Reagan-era television screens.[8] Television was apparently not perceived to be a site for this type of material until more recently.

There is a disconnect between the era of televised national trauma and the era of comedies engaging with them. Despite the Korean War, the failed Bay of Pigs Invasion, and other events, the first Kennedy assassination stands out as the most significant national trauma of the early television era, signaling the death, by many accounts, of the first television president and a turning point in the perceived legitimacy of television journalism. Of course, Kennedy was at least the third president to govern after the development of viable commercial television in America. However, as Mary Ann Watson notes, he cultivated a television-friendly image from the start, which certainly increased the emotional impact of his death.[9] Kennedy's youth and good looks contributed to his famous televisual victory in his debates against Nixon in the 1960 election, but so too did his self-conscious preparation for television performance in that arena. The president developed a friendly relationship with journalists over the years while his FCC's threats to increase regulation resulted in administration-friendly programming like *A Tour of the White House with Mrs. John F. Kennedy*.[10] The favorable coverage given to Kennedy and his family not only helped to support the public's positive opinion of Kennedy and his family, but also likely supported the public's parasocial relationship with them. That is, television's intimacy as a domestic medium and particular engagement with Kennedy supported his likeability and the public's sense that they knew him personally.

Barbie Zelizer also recognizes the extent to which the assassination itself supported this sense of Kennedy. Additionally, she notes the extent to which his assassination became a defining moment for journalism, television, and popular understandings of American history.[11] Additionally, while her book does not specifically discuss the role of funeral coverage in fostering a sense of emotional intimacy with the Kennedy family more generally, it repeatedly cites certain emotionally powerful images like Jacqueline and Caroline kneeling at the president's coffin and John-John saluting the procession. This preoccupation of coverage and Zelizer's argument that these were indeed powerful images indicate the extent to which they encouraged an empathetic approach to the family. Aniko Bodroghkozy examined the response of television viewers to the coverage of the assassination and funeral by reading their letters to NBC News.[12] Her research supports the sense in which coverage deeply impacted viewers as well as the extent to which they understood the family as if they were personally acquainted. For instance, one writer explains,

> I could not tear myself away, and as I can watch our TV from my kitchen, I took the task of baking rye bread rather than going out to the store, as I was in need of bread, but I really didn't want to get out of the house. I almost felt like I was in mourning for someone that was a personal friend.[13]

In these ways, television and journalism more generally helped foster a sense of the assassination as a national trauma, which was the culmination of television's larger support of Kennedy as a mythic figure.[14] However, parallel to the development of television as a medium for Kennedy to exploit grew a brand of so-called sick comedy that could discuss the assassination outside of and even counter to this sacred frame. This comedy belonged at first to nightclubs and LPs, taking some time before it could find a home on television.

THE GROWTH OF "SICK" HUMOR

In November 1962, impressionist Vaughn Meader released a comedy record featuring his take on the Kennedy family. Immensely popular, *The First Family* grew into the best-selling LP ever in any genre to that point and won the Grammy for Album of the Year.[15] When Lenny Bruce took the stage at Carnegie Hall on the evening of the Kennedy assassination in 1963, he sighed, "Boy, is Vaughn Meader fucked."[16] Of course, Bruce was correct. Meader retired his Kennedy impersonation, and his career never again approached any such success.[17] Formally, this is a joke of misattribution. Bruce's pity is directed at the wrong person. It also subtly points out the disparity between Bruce's own reputation for daring satirical humor and Meader's comparatively safe material. However, within its social and temporal context, it bears still greater meaning as an inappropriate joke about the inappropriateness of joking at that moment. While not terribly offensive or disrespectful in itself, the joke has nevertheless gone down in history as an act of legendary comic bravery.

Bruce helped shape a wave of what was dismissively referred to as "sick" humor widely defined with reference to everything from dead baby jokes to political satire, but almost always associated with the postwar era and, eventually, the postwar generation.[18] Ethan Thompson identifies a broad swath of comics from the 1950s and '60s labeled "sick" by virtue of their critical stance toward what was popularly understood to be the strained normativity of a culture marked by McCarthyism and suburbanization.[19] "It was in this distinctly *American* context of repression," writes Thompson, "that the new, sick comedy arose. The label of 'sick' was applied to a wide variety of comedians, from the overtly political material of Mort Sahl and satire of Lenny Bruce, to the confessional stand-up routines of [Shelley] Berman, and the loony antics of Jonathan Winters" (emphasis in original).[20]

While nightclubs acted as the incubators for their routines, Jacob Smith points to LPs as a particularly important medium for distributing these comics' material to the public.[21] Media historians generally point to the development of niche targeting as a governing strategy in broadcasting in the 1970s and 1980s, but Smith argues that LPs were engaging in such practices during the height of American broadcasting's consensus era in the 1950s and 1960s. In fact, evidence suggests that television and LPs functioned symbiotically:

> Comedy LPs were frequently understood as in relation to network television: at the time that comics banked on selling records through their television appearances, their records parodied television genres, presented material that the networks censored, imagined the future of broadcasting, and even represented modes of television viewing. Postwar comedy LPs were so intertwined with television that they were described by Philip Proctor of the Firesign Theatre as a form of "blind television."[22]

Besides the fact that LPs were a freer medium of expression, this snapshot into the relationships between these media is telling in other ways. While television comedy had been highly reflexive since at least the premiere of *Burns and Allen* in 1950, the impact of the medium on American culture increasingly drew parodies from comics of the era. When the baby boomers entered the industry as writers and producers, these parodic and reflexive tendencies would grow in broadcasting as well.

Along with audio recordings, magazines like *MAD* and *National Lampoon* grew as notable outlets for this mélange of satirical and offensive humor, expanding the outlets and distribution for this primarily urban comedy and influencing those that followed. *National Lampoon*'s February 1977 issue is particularly notable in this regard. Like *Family Guy*, the *Lampoon* posits an alternate history of Kennedy's assassination. In this version, although nobody shoots John, Jackie falls off the back of the car in Dealey Plaza and dies when a press bus runs her over. Portions of this issue offer self-consciously taboo humor: for example, Bloomingdale's paid tribute to Jackie by propping her corpse up in a store window, wearing the tire-marked pink Chanel suit in which she died.[23] John Kennedy is also the topic of off-color humor. In this alternative history, Vaughn Meader had turned *The First Family* into a series that was by 1977 in its twenty-third volume. Primarily concerned with Kennedy's sexual reputation, titles from Meader's latest LP included "Come-a-lot" and "You Can't Spell Kennedy without K-Y."[24] However, while clearly outrageous in those examples, this *National Lampoon* issue also critiques aspects of the administration. For instance, then in his fifth term as president, Kennedy shamelessly panders to youth culture. Rather than finding a moderate middle ground between the generation and income gaps, Kennedy's imperial presidency had simply flipped the structures of domination upside down so that wealthy conservatism had become the new counterculture. Evidently, there was space to be both taboo and at least somewhat politically incisive with such humor.

As the baby boomers grew in age, so did the influence of these types of humor. Not only did audiences and critics increasingly reward "sickness" with popularity, but within certain circles it was a badge of honor to unflinchingly address these topics in public. However, there is no bravery without danger, and as Bruce's numerous arrests on obscenity charges proved, this type of comic always runs the risk of "crossing the line." Bruce's reputation for the most part limited him to few television appearances.[25] On television, the 1963–1964 season's top comedies were *The Beverly Hillbillies* and *Petticoat Junction*. These were exactly the kind of "formula comedies about totally unbelievable families" denounced in FCC chair Newton Minnow's 1961 "Television and the Public Interest" (a.k.a. "Vast Wasteland") speech.[26] Despite the odd reference to contemporary culture, they were not exactly topical shows and certainly not likely to engage with a presidential assassination.[27] Although this strategy was not entirely totalizing, this was the era of consensus television, when the three networks self-consciously adhered to the strategy of "least objectionable programming" (LOP). Ostensibly intended to make television palatable to the widest possible audience, LOP, as the name implies, consciously avoided anything that would encourage people to change the channel. Offensive humor clearly falls into the category of potentially "objectionable programming." Although LOP was not entirely pervasive in this era—documentaries and dramas often proved more contentious—even relatively forward-thinking comedies like *Dick Van Dyke* and *Ernie Kovacs* remained relatively staid compared to what was occurring in other media. Of course, this tactic did not last forever, as shifts in network strategy arose from changes in audience conception as well as technologies like remote control and cable.[28]

Although prime-time sitcoms appeared fairly disconnected from the kind of comedy being produced in places like Second City in Chicago and the hungry i in San Francisco, comics such as Mort Sahl and Lenny Bruce were making appearances on television, though the former's more TV-friendly comedy afforded him more airtime. Tony Hendra points especially to *The Merv Griffin Show* as a friendly environment for innovative comedians in the 1960s. "The roster of young men and women assembled by producer Bob Shanks and an adventurous team of writer/talent scouts (including Tom O'Malley from the earlier Paar show) is impressive. There were not just the already established Boomer humorists, but Lily Tomlin, David Steinberg, Joan Rivers, George Carlin, Richard Pryor, Peter Boyle, and many, many more." Nevertheless, Hendra cautions against viewing *Merv* as a free-for-all: "Safe haven though it was, however, 'The Merv Griffin Show' was no place to be dangerous. It was, after all, television, and liberal though the producers were about taking passengers on board, no substantial rocking was allowed."[29] More daring forms of comedy would have to wait before they could flourish more fully on television.

ENTERING THROUGH LATE NIGHT: *SATURDAY NIGHT LIVE*'S ASSASSINATION PASTICHE

The fact that *The Merv Griffin Show* was the most likely place to find comics like Carlin and Pryor and yet avoided controversy demonstrates that American television comedy was unprepared to deal with Kennedy's death in 1963.[30] While American comedies would have to wait some two decades to even begin to address the assassination, television's acceptance of more controversial humor began to grow in the late 1960s and early 1970s as shows like those of producers Norman Lear, Bud Yorkin, and Grant Tinker demonstrated TV executives' growing valuation of younger, urban audiences. This so-called turn to relevance created a space in which comedies more bluntly addressed topics like civil rights and Vietnam, which had previously been handled more delicately if at all.[31] Despite its clear overtures toward a youthful market, the creative talent behind the turn to relevance was generally more veteran. Prime time was a bit too valuable and most baby boomers a bit too untested in the early 1970s for youngsters to take control.[32] With the arguable exception of *The Smothers Brothers Comedy Hour*, the first successful by-boomers, for-boomers show on US television was the late-night program *Saturday Night Live*.[33] Comedians from *National Lampoon* and the Second City, both institutions considered instrumental in the creation of postwar boomer humor, initially filled the ranks of *SNL*.[34] Not only were the not-ready-for-prime-time players brought up in a comic world that venerated edginess, but *SNL* marked a generational shift where comics largely could not remember a time without television. David Marc writes of *SNL*, "Having passed through the looking glass, comedians who had grown up watching television offered the first art to emerge from this definitive experience."[35] Of course, mass media existed before, but television's constancy and domesticity fostered a more heavily televisual sensibility, and the presence of a creative labor force weaned on the medium undoubtedly aided the growth of a more parodic television culture. It is thus unsurprising that the JFK assassination seems to have debuted as network TV comedy, as far as my research has uncovered, on *SNL* and to have been refracted through multiple parodic lenses.[36] Moreover, the framework in which these parodies unfolded not only directly quoted well-known television footage but also mocked traumatic news coverage as a form.

During the second wave of *SNL*, Eddie Murphy was its breakout star, and his signature impression was Buckwheat from the *Our Gang/ Little Rascals* comedies. Despite this popularity, Murphy eventually tired of playing the character and decided in 1983 to kill Buckwheat in a series of sketches that parody news coverage of national traumas. The routine's centerpiece uses visual language to paraphrase the well-known images of the March 30, 1981, shooting of Ronald Reagan and thus set up the dominant reading that it was primarily about a then-recent attempt on the president's life. In the footage of the Reagan shooting, the camera pans to frame the president walking from right to left as he smiles and waves to unseen people off-camera. Shots ring out, and the camera first moves closer to the ground and then quickly pans to reframe a scuffle in which a number of people pile on the shooter, John Hinckley Jr. In the *SNL* parody, not only are the actions nearly identical, so are the camera movements. Buckwheat walks from right to left, waving as the camera tracks him in medium framing. After shots ring out, the camera moves closer to the ground before quickly reframing to catch the scuffle of Buckwheat's assailant, John David Stutts.

Despite the direct allusion to Reagan, this bit also spoke to the respectively successful and unsuccessful assassinations of John Lennon and Pope John Paul II, both of which occurred within four months of the 1981 Reagan shooting. Considering that they variously represented the presidency, 1960s youthful optimism, and Catholic leadership, there were already strong symbolic connections between Kennedy's death and the recent rash of shootings. However, *SNL* cautiously strengthened these connections.

Unlike Reagan, Buckwheat dies in this narrative, nudging the allusion closer to Kennedy, along with Lennon. This routine also parodies news coverage more generally, allowing it to develop the conversation between texts even more. Portraying Ted Koppel, Joe Piscopo informs the audience, "Buckwheat was buried today and the entire world mourns." Footage of military parades and cannons firing underscore the absurd contrasts between Buckwheat and the sacred funeral rituals that occur when a significant world

Visual quotation in Saturday Night Live*'s parody.*

leader passes. It also alludes to televised and heavily viewed processions from Kennedy's funeral. "World leaders gathered to offer final tribute," continues Koppel's voice-over, accompanied by footage of Richard Nixon, Gerald Ford, Henry Kissinger, Nancy Reagan, and Princess Diana. Again, although twenty years had passed since the funeral of President Kennedy, that would have been the most familiar referent in 1983 for this kind of television coverage.

Although Buckwheat's shooting does not directly allude to Kennedy's, this sketch mobilizes elements of the Kennedy assassination as its pastiche plays on associations between Lee Harvey Oswald and Buckwheat's assassin, John David Stutts, also portrayed by Murphy. *SNL* draws parallels in both the way news investigated their past and the way both met their end. In one segment establishing Stutts's presumed guilt, he appears in a yearbook photo titled "Future Assassins of America." In it, Murphy poses with a rifle held at the same angle as Oswald in the iconic photo of Oswald with the assassination weapon.

More obviously, the sketch recreates the live broadcast of Oswald's murder, which occurred when Jack Ruby shot the suspect on his way to his arraignment. Quoting from *Broadcasting* magazine's description of the shooting, Barbie Zelizer notes how journalistic accounts of the event slipped between describing the event itself and describing its television coverage, as if there were no difference.

> "Oswald, flanked by detectives, stepped onto a garage ramp in the basement of the Dallas city jail and was taken towards an armored truck that was to take him to the county jail. Suddenly, out of the lower right hand corner of the TV screen, came the back of a man. A shot rang out, and Oswald gasped as he started to fall, clutching his side." . . . The juxtaposition of reality and the televised image, by which Oswald's killer was seen coming out of a corner of the television screen rather than the corner of the basement, paid the ultimate compliment to television's coverage of the event.[37]

As opposed to Kennedy's death, whose visual evidence would only trickle out to the public as still photographs and bootleg films over the course of a decade, Oswald's death was more visually available. Live television brought Oswald's death to viewers more immediately in 1963 and was an iconic moment in the "black weekend" that followed Kennedy's death.

Like *SNL*'s take on the Reagan shooting, the visual quotation is unmistakable. Men in suits stand on either side of Stutts as they walk down the hall, surrounded by a mass of reporters. A man emerges from the lower left corner of the screen wearing a fedora reminiscent of Jack Ruby's and fires on Stutts. Falling to the ground, Stutts rather nonchalantly says, "Ouch, I'm shot." Koppel appears back on the screen to narrate, "There you have it. John David Stutts, accused assassin of Buckwheat, has been shot right here before your eyes." By setting up Stutts as a parody of the alleged

Future assassins Lee Harvey Oswald and John David Stutts.

presidential assassin, *SNL* does not reproduce for viewers Kennedy's death but Oswald's, recreating what was likely for many a moment of televised justice done to Kennedy's assassin. That Oswald's shooting happened live on television justified this moment within the sketch's narrative; that

Oswald purportedly killed the president to an extent justified this moment within television culture.

This bit also mines humor by repeating violent imagery and ads that seem to come too soon after a trauma. Par for the course in terms of trauma coverage, SNL takes the repetition compulsion to satirical extremes in a critique of journalism's macabre obsession with the traumatic moment, suggesting that even august news could profane sacred moments. Its play of commercial sponsorship during times of national crisis offers a particular critique of a capitalistic impulse to ignore the solemnity of these occasions. Repetitive and intrusive to the point of humor, the ads themselves also contain commercial messages that further exaggerate their crassness. For example, the fictional "Texxon" not only interrupts but tactlessly adopts Buckwheat's postmortem voice to shill on behalf of the company. "Life goes on. And Texxon is there," announces a pitchman, "because Buckwheat would have wanted it that way."

While some viewers probably took offense concerning the recent or more distant shootings, the sketch also contained elements that reinforced the sacred framing in its critique of news tropes that, in this case at least, contrast expected decorum—though notably the critique of commercialism likely spoke more to the recent Reagan/Lennon/John Paul II coverage. Even so, Linda Hutcheon notes that irony runs the risk of recreating that which it means to criticize, so even in this case, SNL's ironic take on the profaning of sacred moments degraded the Kennedy legacy to some extent.[38] In terms of industrial and regulatory strategy, SNL could avoid flak compared to prime-time comedies of this period because it aired during the fringe of late night. The FCC declares this "safe harbor" time, which affords it more leeway than if it were in prime time.[39] Moreover, its strategies of simultaneously commenting upon and distancing itself from the assassination itself helped to soften its edges. Finally, SNL's playing with violence against Oswald and critiques of overcommercialized coverage obliquely suggested, if only in brief moments, that the sketch had sympathies with Kennedy and good taste.

Saturday Night Live's pastiche made light of a number of subjects, from then-recent shootings to television coverage of traumas. While not the primary target of the parody, the Oswald narrative connected it to the more sensitive issue of John F. Kennedy's assassination and allowed SNL to play without totally going there. Saturday Night Live, in general and in this particular case, represented an ideal site for dangerous humor in the early post-network era. Its talent and target demographics skewed young, and it was cordoned off in the late night slot, where fewer people would be offended and government regulators cared less about content. Racquel Gates argues in a larger study of Murphy's role on *SNL* that his purpose was in part to signify "'quality' and hipness, characteristics that defined cable and that networks desperately wanted to replicate."[40] In other words, *SNL* was an early adopter of narrowcasting strategies for network television, and Murphy's edginess in general, as represented by this sketch, fit into that strategy. As Bhoomi K. Thakore and Bilal Hussein note, *SNL* in the period of Murphy "was aimed explicitly at a younger, hipper, and smaller audience than the vast majority of network programming at the time."[41] *Saturday Night Live*'s followers, as far as assassination humor was concerned, would use similar strategies in ensuing years to avoid flak. At the same time, as narrowcasting increasingly came to rule the American television industry's programming strategy, comedies like *Seinfeld* and *Family Guy* could more boldly test the limits of good taste.

INTO PRIME TIME: *SEINFELD* AND THE MAGIC LOOGIE

As will be explored in more detail in chapter 4, national traumas like Kennedy's death and 9/11 serve as privileged events for conspiracy theorists. So when the pop zeitgeist turned to conspiracy culture in the early 1990s, *JFK*—both the 1991 film and the president—figured heavily. In its reexamination and questioning of historical narratives, *JFK* grabbed enough attention to "spawn," according to Renee Loth of the *Boston Globe*, "its own miniature industry of articles, documentaries, and spinoffs."[42] Loth goes on to comment,

> In an era where there [we]re few remaining taboos in mass entertainment, [director Oliver] Stone ha[d] obviously touched a nerve, and not just among those who wholly accept the Warren Commission's wobbly report concluding that Oswald acted alone. Even before he settled on a draft of the script for "JFK," Stone received the opprobrium of veteran journalists who had investigated—and dismissed—Garrison's claims. Dallas county commissioners, who now use the office space in the schoolbook depository building from where Oswald supposedly fired his fatal shots, denied Stone's request to film near the site four times.[43]

David Belin, a Warren Commission investigator, went so far as to call the film "a big lie that would make Adolf Hitler proud."[44] Despite controversy associated with the film and the possibility of ruffling feathers by joking at

all about Kennedy's death, *JFK*'s cultural ubiquity created a space in which his death became a reference point in prime-time comedy.[45]

Part of the *JFK* "cottage industry" noted by Loth, a 1992 *Seinfeld* episode offers a scene-length parody of Oliver Stone's film.[46] As resident goofballs Kramer and Newman explain that they "despise" baseball player Keith Hernandez because of an incident in which the ballplayer spat on them, *Seinfeld* flashes back to the incident with grainy footage connoting Stone's use of the Zapruder film in *JFK*. Similar to its source material's play with contrasting film stock, *Seinfeld*'s mise-en-scène cuts between a high-key video present and a grainy, filmic past in its parody of Stone's visual excess and use of the Zapruder footage. Ultimately, level-headed Jerry played Kevin Costner's Jim Garrison in order to debunk their story as the tale of a "magic loogie," visually recreating one of the film's famous

Seinfeld *parodies* JFK's *staging and film quality.*

courtroom scenes. There is little in the way of obvious political satire here. The magic loogie routine is a play on a popular media text evoking Frederick Jameson's notion of pastiche as "blank parody."[47] Building on these senses of the bit as a postmodern textual free-for-all, the parody developed out of the intertextual presence of Wayne Knight in both *Seinfeld* and *JFK*. As the actor explained, staff writer "Tom Leopold . . . was an assassination buff. When he went to see *JFK*, he noticed that I was in the movie and I was playing a character named 'Numa.' So the serendipity aspect of that added to the mix and I came back as Newman doing the same reenactment that I had done in *JFK*."[48]

The humor arises from contrasting the high sobriety of Kennedy's assassination with Kramer's being spat upon, as well as the president's mortal convulsions with Michael Richards's trademark spasmodic physical humor. According to Øyvind Vågnes, the pleasure of *Seinfeld*'s parody arises in part from its blatant refusal to engage in any clear didacticism or argument.[49] In borrowing both the film's verbal and visual language while avoiding the overserious trappings of the docudrama genre, *Seinfeld* revels in the fact that it explicitly avoids saying anything of substance about the assassination. In many ways, this is a comedy of misdirection, as both the film and the assassination were hot-button topics at the time. In fact, after all his parodic quoting, Jerry claims to have not seen the film *JFK*.

Discussing the possibility of its offensiveness, NBC executive Rick Ludwin recalls, "The audience howled to such an extent that the laughs actually had to be shortened in editing. But as I heard this it occurred to me that if a comedy show is able to wring comedy out of what is clearly a national tragedy, that this show had risen to another level."[50] As an NBC executive, Ludwin's opinions are influenced by his position and the esteem in which people hold *Seinfeld*. Nevertheless, his comments betray a set of assumptions about taste and quality that were perhaps not as widely held as this type of humor began to move from the margins to the mainstream. Between 1963 and 1992, joking about sensitive topics had grown less sick and more a sign of good taste. *Seinfeld*'s ability to dip into aesthetically challenging cinema about a national trauma and draw significant laughs had become a sign of erudite wit meant for a rarefied audience. Although airing during prime time, *Seinfeld* skewed young, urban, and liberal, especially in 1992, when it had yet to gain its eventual ratings dominance.[51] During the season in question, the program aired at 9:30 p.m. Eastern in between the adult-themed if juvenile-styled *Night Court* and *Quantum Leap*—itself a show often explicitly about working through historical trauma.[52] And on this night in particular, *Seinfeld* went up against the Winter Olympics, further whittling its audience to a demographic core.[53] Nevertheless, this was February sweeps, when networks try to gain a large audience, so the stunt casting of baseball player Keith Hernandez along with the possibility that controversy might draw viewers also exists. Judging by public reactions to *JFK*, *Seinfeld* potentially contained the seeds of controversy, but in part because of the type and size of the 1992 *Seinfeld* audience, the show's role as a comedy, and its parodic relation to the film, they never germinated into a clear moral panic. But neither did this episode appear to elicit significant negative reaction in syndication after the show had become a success, speaking to a mix of its skillful navigation of the issue, the leeway afforded comedy, and the differing role of reruns as opposed to original airings.

Both *Saturday Night Live* and *Seinfeld* treated their assassination parodies as events. In 1983, it became an overarching sketch that repeated throughout the *SNL* episode and also suggested other television events like the 1980 "Who Shot J.R.?" episodes of *Dallas*. While less overarching, *Seinfeld* devoted a full scene to its parody and broke with its typical stylistic language to note that its parody was significant. By contrast, *Family Guy*, a self-consciously sick show of more recent years, treats similar gags almost as narrative afterthoughts, using brief "cutaway gags" to push the envelope still further without dwelling much on the event or its play on it.

VERY OBJECTIONABLE PROGRAMMING: *FAMILY GUY*

Despite its apparent edginess, the magic loogie would pale in comparison to the ways in which parodists like self-consciously sick *Family Guy* played with this imagery later. In an episode from 1999, a short gag shows a child exiting a convenience store bragging, "Check it out; it's a John F. Kennedy Pez Dispenser!"[54] An errant bullet from off camera immediately shatters the plastic Kennedy head. The child then ominously consoles himself, "Good thing I still have my Bobby Kennedy Pez Dispenser." This is a sick joke to be sure, but a decade later, *Family Guy* went considerably sicker. In 2009, it replaced JFK's assassination with that of McDonald's advertising mascot Mayor McCheese in a gruesome sight gag.[55] The eerily accurate recreation stages the murder in the same way as the Zapruder film, shot at ground level with the car traveling from left to right. However, it forgoes the documentary footage's 8 millimeter graininess, instead portraying the events in *Family Guy*'s more typical high-key style. When the bullets strike, Mayor McCheese's exploding head is far clearer than JFK's in the Zapruder film. Additionally, to reiterate a point from this chapter's introduction, Jackie climbs on the back of the limousine not in an attempt to flee, but to gorge herself on the scattered McViscera. Beyond the obvious offensiveness of both bits, they subtly degrade the sacred construct of Kennedy by parodically equivocating him with relatively obscure childhood ephemera.

Despite these bits airing in prime time on a major broadcast network, the logic of television was so different from 1963 and the height of consensus television and "least objectionable programming" that a show like *Family Guy* could sell on a promise of, if not "most objectionable," then at least "very objectionable" programming. With the growth of the new networks and cable, the television audience became increasingly specific through the 1990s and 2000s. Add to that Fox's self-presentation as the edgiest network and *Family Guy*'s self-conscious riskiness, and the results were some of television's sickest and most iconoclastic comedic moments. In fact, reruns and late DVD releases cut the Pez dispenser gag, though it

Very objectionable programming on Family Guy.

has since returned in certain venues.[56] Against expectations, even *Family Guy* creator and showrunner Seth MacFarlane expresses regret over the Pez dispenser gag, suggesting that in retrospect, he has grown more conservative than the forces charged with limiting content.[57]

In addition to offering archaeological snapshots of each period's industrial logic, the examples of Kennedy assassination gags represent limit cases, on one topic at least, measuring the relative freedom of risqué humor on television and in culture more generally. Humor in this vein has political implications in that sacred figures—whether a martyred JFK or the post-9/11 Bush and Giuliani—were for a time beyond criticism. Since the mythic JFK crystallized in his death, to reimagine his death with a different affective frame is to begin to unravel the discursive construct that limits critical discussion of political and social history. Comedy operates as an important site to reignite a critical framework after sacred events have silenced or dulled those discourses.

To construct an event as a national trauma silences certain types of more conventionally political discourse. In the example of JFK, less triumphant moments of his presidency, like the Bay of Pigs invasion and his extramarital affairs, probably received less attention than if he had served a full term or two as president.[58] These gags neither soothe nor appear to celebrate resilience in the face of trauma. Despite their potential value in attacking the sense of Kennedy as a mythic figure, the examples above were not even strong instances of political commentary. They are mostly just edgy for the sake of edginess: a useful strategy for gaining key young demographics in the post-network era of television. However, within a television market freed to joke about national traumas, other comedy programs further degraded the mythological Kennedy in more pointed ways. Such jokes seem aimed less at shared memory or shock value and more at explicitly engaging with Kennedy's frequently, conveniently, and problematically ignored ethics and tactics. When the children of *South Park* attend a Bay of Pigs memorial dance without comment on the invasion, it simply reminds viewers of that tactical and strategic misstep.[59] More pointedly, *Simpsons* characters Mayor Quimby and Sideshow Bob offer satirical takes on Kennedy's personally and professionally suspect dealings. For instance, Sideshow Bob once stole an election for the mayor of Springfield by getting the votes of dead Springfielders and their pets, in reference to infamous voter fraud tactics undertaken in Chicago on behalf of Kennedy in the 1960 election.[60] While rhetorically valuable in their own way, examples like these came too late to engage in the immediate fallout of 1963. They act as a subtle reminder of history's complicated reality and discourage hero worship more generally. The acceptance of sick and satirical humor on television led to a faster turnaround such that in the case of 9/11, comedy programs tackled current events in more directly political ways more quickly. Additionally, and as other chapters explore, the time between tragedy and comedy appears to be even shorter in the current period.

While current forms of edgy comedy have roots in the mid-century and earlier, the extreme forms of humor were largely absent on US television during the era of network dominance. To some extent, general social factors like generational shift, the time elapsed since 1963, and broadly labeled permissiveness account for these examples' development of more shocking content. More pointedly, the network tendency toward ever more specific demographics allayed standards and practices, network, and FCC fears with the assumption that easily offended audiences would *not* be watching these easily offending shows. As business logic came to value a younger audience that it viewed as more socially aware, it began to open the doors to sicker and more engaged humor. Despite these historical changes, American television is hardly a free-for-all. As the edited JFK Pez dispenser joke shows, even relatively distant traumas maintain a sense of the sacred such that they can become sites of negotiation of acceptable comic speech. In the next chapter, I examine comedy censorship in terms of what it can tell us about television's temporality, how national traumas limit certain types of expression, and how comedies satirize censorship itself.

CENSORED COMEDIES
AND COMEDIES OF CENSORSHIP | *Chapter 2*

Although it never dared joke about the death of President Kennedy, *The Smothers Brothers Comedy Hour* remains a benchmark of daring political comedy on television. In aligning itself with countercultural movements in the late 1960s, it repeatedly commented on crises associated with mass demonstrations. In perhaps the most famous example, Harry Belafonte sings a medley of calypso songs while superimposed over footage from the 1968 Democratic National Convention and the riots that were occurring outside in the streets of Chicago.[1] Belafonte taps into the tradition of political protest in calypso music in part by singing "Don't Stop the Carnival," a song about protest, but also by altering the lyrics of additional songs in the medley to comment more directly on the situation at hand. "Humphrey, Muskie, McGovern, Eugene McCarthy split the party now nobody happy," he sings. "Tell the whole population we have confrontation. Let it be known: freedom's gone and the country is not our own."[2] This bit never made it to air but remains notorious in large part because of its censorship, receiving significant discussion from academics like Aniko Bodroghkozy and in documentaries like *Smothered: The Censorship Struggles of the Smothers Brothers Variety Hour* as representative of larger crises of authority in the 1960s.[3] The challenges faced by *The Smothers Brothers Comedy Hour* are neither unique nor limited to the late 1960s. As previous chapters have shown, even programming like *Family Guy* and Friars Club roasts, which sell themselves on edgy comedy, could have humor about the JFK assassination or 9/11 removed from broadcasts retroactively or preventatively. After a particularly damning documentary about Michael Jackson came out in 2019, *The Simpsons* removed a classic episode featuring the star from syndication and streaming.[4] Even *I Love Lucy* faced corporate censorship based on changing circumstances. CBS pulled the 1956 episode titled "The Ricardos Visit Cuba" from syndication after US-Cuban relations deteriorated following Fidel Castro's 1959 revolution, though it eventually returned.[5]

Television censorship can happen before an episode airs or in later distribution platforms like reruns, DVDs, and on-demand services. Bela-fonte's performance became fodder for later media texts like retrospective documentaries, suggesting the value of these moments in popular memory and for media content distributors. This is especially true in the cases where material becomes retroactively unacceptable due to intervening historical events, as occurs in response to crises as large as 9/11 and as minor as celebrity death. These cases demonstrate the value of censorship's varied purposes, such as avoiding flak, producing "value added" content for later iterations of television texts, and feeding the archival drive that fans demonstrate in their search for completionist histories of their favorite shows.[6] In other instances, comedies purposefully invite censorship in order to criticize it.

This chapter examines the significance of censorship and comedy around moments of collective trauma. It first looks at how censorship in the name of good taste can have significant political ramifications. In the case of 9/11, a major trauma, corporate censorship impacts orthodox political discourse. However, even relatively minor traumas such as the death of John F. Kennedy Jr. can draw censorship, exposing the ways in which conventions around issues like class and gender politics may be hidden or rewritten. This chapter concludes by examining the ways in which comedies like *South Park* use and invite censorship as a comic tool to imply profanity and reflexively expose limits to creative expression. In all, these battles over expressive freedom highlight the subtle ways in which national traumas alter the rules of discourse and what this means for collective memory and politics.

If, as this book argues, television and comedy are significant to the way Americans make sense of national identity and history, then the ability to control access to these critical discourses is vitally important. Owing to its perceived frivolousness and potential for offense, censors find a relatively vulnerable target in television comedy. As such, the genre not only serves as a common site for discursive policing, but also is usefully representative of these issues in society as a whole. It may not be terribly obvious that we can less easily question authority figures after terror attacks or as freely discuss our anxieties about class and gender after a celebrity dies, but when television explicitly prevents those discourses from airing, or removes them from reruns and other distribution platforms, the loss of these politically important discussions is more palpable. Of course, when comedies take up censorship as a topic, they more clearly highlight the issue's importance as well.

As discussed in the introduction, theorists note the significance of debate and shared popular memory to nationalism. Jürgen Habermas offers a model of public life predicated on the notion that debate constitutes a sense of community and played a significant role in the creation of modern nations.[7] Television studies work dating at least as far back as Horace Newcomb and Paul M. Hirsch's 1983 article "Television as a Cultural Forum" offers a similar dialogical ethics, arguing that healthy mass media culture offers access to the issues, debates, and histories that in many ways have defined American political and cultural life since the 1950s.[8] Benedict Anderson and others similarly note the significance of shared popular memory to national political life, so any alterations made to reruns, DVD releases, and streaming platforms mark an alteration to the public record that, as post-9/11 censorship demonstrates, limits access to political discourse and shared history.[9] In these senses, and in the examples that follow, elisions in popular access to media history constitute significant attacks on Americans' sense of national cohesiveness and identity. Moreover, because censorship carries with it such negative connotations, blocking or deleting sensitive material helps constitute a sense of trauma by demonstrating the perceived extremity of the event in question, a topic detailed more specifically in chapter 7.

COMEDY CENSORSHIP AFTER 9/11

Network and other censors alter television for many reasons and at any point during the production or distribution phase. Obviously, creative talent might be shot down in a writers' room or simply keep quiet about certain ideas.[10] Time also plays a factor in recutting television episodes. Programs imported from noncommercial systems like the BBC frequently have material cut to make space for advertising.[11] Even American shows often have material cut, and sometimes an entire program is subtly sped up to fit in more ads in syndication.[12] Obviously, as theatrical cinema releases move to television, they have material cut for both content and length, but as classic studio-era cartoons like *Tom and Jerry* aged, television syndicators censored, reanimated, or revoiced them to remove racist or other offensive material.[13]

As the example of racist cartoons and certain debates around the ethics of preserving the history of offensive pop culture indicate, the passage of time is a critical aspect of why some material is cut. In the case of *Tom and Jerry*, the shift in context from theatrical to television exhibition plays a role, but the larger cultural shifts around representational ethics are more significant. While racism and the long-term cultural responses to it represent their own kind of trauma, events like terror attacks and the deaths of public figures represent more sudden shocks and drive more immediate shifts in discourse. This phenomenon was especially on display after 9/11 as shows like *Family Guy*, *The Simpsons*, and *Friends* had scenes cut from initial airing as well as from reruns and DVD releases. For instance, in a bit from 2000, *Family Guy*'s psychotic toddler Stewie Griffin sneaks a cache of weapons through airport security, distracting the guards by dancing and singing "On the Good Ship Lollipop."[14] Retrieving his bag from the X-ray conveyor belt, he quips, "Let's hope Osama bin Laden doesn't know show tunes" before the shot reframes to show the terrorist mastermind performing "I Hope I Get It" from *A Chorus Line* as his suitcase full of arms passes through security undetected. Reruns and DVD releases cut this joke following 9/11, though it later returned in some editions.[15] Though the ostensible motivator for cutting it was decorum, it nevertheless silenced a critical discourse about Americans' foreknowledge of the terrorist. Although bin Laden had faded into the background of popular consciousness between the 1993 World Trade Center bombing and the 2001 attacks, there was significant debate about whether or not the federal government should have been more aware of the threat he posed. This was especially the case after May 2002, when CBS News broke the story of the August 6, 2001, presidential memo titled "Bin Ladin [*sic*] Determined to Strike in US."[16] Here, significant information regarding a then-active political debate disappeared. If, in a Habermasian model, debate actually defines modern political life and forms a sense of community, such elisions are significant problems for political and media culture.

While a vague sense of good taste drove the decision to censor *Family Guy*'s pre-9/11 bin Laden reference, respect for victims more clearly justified other examples of censorship. In a 1997 episode of *The Simpsons*, Homer spends much of a day in New York waiting to have a boot removed from his illegally parked car in the pedestrian plaza between the Twin Towers.[17] Throughout this episode, Homer expresses anger toward many features of New York: city government bureaucracy, ethnic food, and rude New Yorkers, to name a few. In part because of the Towers' prominence, but also likely because it did not fit with post-9/11 New York boosterism, the episode was removed from syndication packages for several years after the terrorist attacks. Even when it did return, it was missing one gag (that nevertheless appeared on the 2006 DVD release).[18] Homer attempts to remove the boot by biting the bolts holding it in place. A man in one of the towers yells, "Hey! When you're done with that, I got something up here you can bite on." Another man shouts from the other tower, "Hey, why don't you be polite, you stinkin' pus bag?!" Turning to Homer, he

Osama bin Laden knew show tunes on Family Guy *in 2000.*

explains how to get the boot off his car and continues, "Sorry about that guy; they stick all the jerks in Tower One."

Describing her experience reading the obituaries in the *New York Times* for all the 9/11 victims, Nancy K. Miller writes,

> Was it possible that no one who died in the attack on the World Trade Center was ever depressed ("They were always giggling"); self-centered ("Despite a hectic work schedule [he] took pains to put his family first," "She wanted to make sure everyone was happy"); without a passion ("He was also crazy about pop music from the 1950's and 60's"); had a career that seemed stalled ("He dreamed of becoming a recording engineer"); or sometimes found life not worth living ("He lived life to the fullest")? . . . I could not perform the translation, identify with these lives from which all traces of unhappiness were banished.[19]

Although different in many ways from the kind of erasures under investigation in this chapter, Miller points to a kind of purposeful forgetting that followed 9/11. In the simplified narrative of heroes and villains that followed the attacks, there was no room for victims who were less than perfect, just as there was no space to investigate the potentially complex motives of the "evildoers." The only jerks to have died that day were the terrorists.

In *Tourists of History*, Marita Sturken examines the role of kitsch in post-9/11 discourse, arguing that the ubiquity of items like teddy bears and children's drawings helped create a sense of national innocence.[20] This, she argues, prevented deeper critical examinations of the role of American foreign policy in fostering the resentment that leads to terrorism, since an innocent nation need not question its past actions. While operating in a different register, the deletion of a scene in which *The Simpsons* suggests that someone who worked in the World Trade Center could have been less than perfect certainly aids in this construct, since all the Americans who died that day had to be understood as innocent and/or heroic. If 9/11 created a discourse of national innocence, altering texts that suggest otherwise is a clear example of the ways in which censorship impacts how Americans understand the nation. While *Family Guy* and *The Simpsons* were censored retroactively, *Friends* had a scene cut before airing but after being shot. Meant to air less than a month after September 11, 2001, two of the characters struggle with airport security in a lengthy sequence. Waiting in line to get through the metal detector, fastidious Monica brags about never having set off the machine as sarcastic Chandler notices a sign reading "Federal Law Prohibits Any Joking Regarding Aircraft Highjacking or Bombing." In an act of miniscule comic rebellion, Chandler turns to a guard, quipping, "You don't have to worry about me, ma'am. I take my bombs *very* seriously." As he mugs to his wife in celebration of his cleverness, a security guard grabs Chandler and whisks him away. The narrative rejoins the couple in a windowless interrogation room where Chandler desperately defends himself.

> Look, this is ridiculous. I was just making a joke. I mean I know the sign says "no jokes about bombs," but shouldn't the sign say, "no bombs?" I mean isn't that the guy we really have to worry about here? The guy *with the bombs*? Not the guy who jokes about his bombs? Not that I have bombs, but if I did I probably wouldn't joke about them. I'd probably want to keep that rather quiet!

In response, the agents rifle through the couple's luggage, causing embarrassment as they discover Chandler's Speedos and frustrating Monica as they undo her careful packing.

The scene from *Friends* did not receive wide distribution until the release of the eighth season DVD set in the United Kingdom, where it was included as a bonus feature. Before the scene plays, the DVD offers a text scroll explaining its history.

> The following scenes were deleted from the episode "The One Where Rachel Tells Ross" and are being presented here for the

first time. The story involved Chandler joking with security at an airport and was to air two weeks after the events of September 11, 2001. In light of this, we decided to replace the original story. As part of the history of the show, we hope that the scenes can now be viewed in the spirit which they were originally intended.[21]

Of course, viewing these scenes "in the spirit which they were originally intended" is impossible. The context of September 2001 and what would have been a sickly ironic series of gags about terrorism and air travel ensures that this scene will be primarily "appreciated," if one can say that, with reference to 9/11. Yet these gags had increased in offensiveness to make their presence funny in new ways.

As it was with *Family Guy* and *The Simpsons*, the decision to cut this scene from *Friends* is also significant to political discourse. Among many other shifts taking place during that period, Americans saw notable erosion of civil liberties, especially in critical spaces like airports. Rachel Hall argues, "We remain willing to view what happens at the airport checkpoint as either necessary and therefore unchallengeable, or as lacking in gravity by comparison to the virtual threat of another terrorist attack and therefore not worthy of serious critique or political debate."[22] The loss of this scene from immediate post-9/11 discourse is complicated in relation to her argument. On the one hand, a comedy show making light of the difficulties of airport security would have seemingly supported the sense that the rigmarole of airport security is "lacking in gravity." On the other hand, this scene criticizes airport security for overreacting and overreaching. We all know Chandler posed no threat, and the loss of privacy represented by the examination of his Speedos speaks to larger concerns over the actions of a security state. Ironically, the message that one should be allowed to joke about issues of security was not allowed to air because it joked about issues of security.

Humor theorists frequently note the value of incongruity in making people laugh. Bakhtin saw the juxtaposition of high and low culture as a key component of laughter, while Bergson's image of the "mechanical encrusted upon the living" relies upon a similar contrast of ideas.[23] Bergson's ideas are especially relevant to the phenomenon at hand because recorded media touches upon his concepts of how people laugh at those who mechanically repeat actions despite changes in circumstances. To Bergson, seeing someone slip on a banana peel is funny because they did not adequately adjust to the conditions at hand. They should have either changed their gait to avoid the peel or at least managed to correct themselves in time to avoid falling after stepping on it. The theorist believed that our laughter expresses a human desire to correct those who are not fully aware of and responding to present circumstances. Examples of this kind of humor abound on television. The castaways on *Gilligan's Island* never seemed to figure out that they needed to imprison or kill Gilligan if they were ever to escape the island. Sideshow Bob stepped on rake after rake after rake, never learning the lesson that he should look down.[24] More subtly, examples in this chapter demonstrate the ways that characters "mechanically" reproduce behavior in inappropriate circumstances to make us laugh. For instance, sarcastic and wisecracking Chandler should know to tone down his quips when confronted with airport security. Yet he persists because he must continually live out his character type as wiseass. Government agents punish him to the audience's amusement. Recorded media, too, can take on this sense of the mechanical encrusted upon the living. Of course, a rerun is not literally a living creature, but in acting as a representation of a living being from the past, it can offer the impression of a living creature damned to habitually repeat some past action. Corny old reruns make us laugh in part because of the sense in which the characters act out of step with the present as we note the outdated conventions and aesthetics of dated television. Recontextualizing old media for new circumstances allows it to slip on the proverbial banana peel of new cultural and aesthetic trends and circumstances. However, national traumas often create significant new norms that make particular actions especially taboo. Moreover, these violations add a carnivalesque element by travestying the newly sacred topic. Viewers who might not have appreciated Chandler's inappropriate behavior at the airport might appreciate the macabre irony of the show's inappropriate behavior in a post-9/11 environment.

When shows inadvertently become darkly ironic in relation to traumas either major or minor, they can grow funnier, at least to an audience that appreciates morbid humor. Of course, there is other value in these examples. As noted in the introduction to this chapter, cultish completists and trivia buffs might appreciate the existence of this footage in different ways. Indeed, all three of the censored scenes were included on DVD releases, though *Family Guy* fans had to wait for the later *Freakin' Sweet Collection* before they could purchase an officially released version that included the bin Laden gag.[25] In any case, they provide value-added content that can get people to buy DVDs or create web traffic to a video sharing site, so cutting some material in some cases is a canny business strategy. However, not everything returns fully to the public record. As the next section demonstrates, even something as seemingly unimportant as a celebrity's death can permanently alter television's historical record.

"MINOR" TRAUMA, CENSORSHIP, AND CULTURAL POLITICS

Censorship of this sort is not always in response to major traumas like terror attacks and assassinations. Traumas need not engage issues as obviously political as federal agencies and national defense. In some cases, comparatively small traumas might bring edits or preemptions to comedies. In these cases, such censorship indicates the extent to which seemingly minor or short-lived traumas can take on the character of more memorable and significant ones. In this sense, television's decision to excise or recut content in response to certain events constitutes trauma. Deleting material demonstrates the extent to which television's gatekeepers consider it unthinkably inappropriate for public consumption and/or a threat to the bottom line. In the examples that follow, isolated severe weather events, household fires, and celebrity death do not immediately match the loss of life and property as events like Hurricane Maria or 9/11, but censorship suggests that it was too soon to deal with such weighty topics in comedy. In these cases, television's retroactive censorship indicates the extent to which those in charge of television content grow skittish over even relatively minor events. As with the 9/11-related examples, these cases prove significant to national culture in at least two ways. First, any elision of the collective memory and history represented by television is a loss in the defining collective experience of television viewing that characterizes a significant portion of our national life. Second, as was the case after 9/11, cuts are politically significant. The censorship of scenes in shows like *Friends* demonstrated how good taste and the desire to avoid flak might silence important discourse. The same can be true of these minor traumas, except that they offer insight into the more "everyday" politics of gender and class performance. As this section shows, discourses surrounding John F. Kennedy Jr. shifted significantly after his death, such that removing him from a scene in *Sex and the City* seemed to be a no-brainer. This was part of a larger shift to rehabilitate him from a figure with seemingly feminine attributes—often wielded against him in mocking tones—to a more respectably masculine figure in death. Cutting references to him in *Sex and the City* reruns was only the most obvious example of the subtle gender politics surrounding his passing.

Celebrity death is perhaps the most obvious example where seemingly minor losses turn into more major traumas in media discourse. However, other relatively minor events can elicit censorship on comedy television shows. For instance, episodes that dealt with natural disasters have had airdates delayed if a significantly destructive event occurred close to the planned airdate. The 2013 season finale of *Mike and Molly* features a tornado hitting Chicago. After a particularly strong tornado killed twenty-four people in Moore, Oklahoma, on the afternoon of the intended airdate, CBS preempted the episode, only to air it ten days later.[26] Similarly, in 2011, Fox had planned a crossover block of programming titled "Night of the Hurricane" that would link three Seth MacFarlane–produced shows by having characters on *Family Guy*, *American Dad*, and *The Cleveland Show* all encounter the same hurricane. Although initially scheduled for the evening of May 1, after the 2011 "super outbreak" of tornadoes hit the southeastern United States in late April, Fox delayed the programming event until October 2 of that year.[27]

More notably, *Beavis and Butt-Head* had an episode pulled from MTV's rerun schedules after the show came under fire for having caused a tragedy. In this episode, Beavis and Butt-head try their hand at stand-up comedy. Imitating a juggling prop-comic that had performed immediately before them, Beavis lights some newspapers, and eventually the whole club, on fire. A month later, this episode gained notoriety after it was blamed for inspiring a five-year-old to light his family home on fire, killing his two-year-old sister.[28] In an op-ed to the *Chicago Tribune*, the president and CEO of Maryland Public Television argues that this and other examples of children copying mass media amounted to a national crisis. "After this string of personal tragedies hit the media, there was a public outcry for regulation and laws that would hold networks and studios accountable for their programming decisions," he writes. "Video violence was labeled 'the No. 1 health problem in America.'"[29] Although this language is clearly hyperbolic, it metaphorically links *Beavis and Butt-Head* to more serious issues like the crack and AIDS epidemics. MTV responded by moving *Beavis and Butt-Head*'s time slot from 7:00 to 10:30 p.m. and editing references to fire out of existing and future episodes.[30] Although I contend in the introduction that television and mass media in general are the causes of "national trauma" in the sense that they define our experience of such events, public outcry in this case more literally blamed MTV for the trauma of a child's death. While each of these cases represents PR moves intended to limit blowback to the television industry, MTV's exaggerated response here was certainly due in large part to public perception of their culpability.

Celebrity death can also inspire similar censorship, often in ways

Sex and the City *presents the question, John F. Kennedy Jr. or Leonardo DiCaprio?*

that draw attention to the changes in discourse that accompany the loss of significant public figures. In a July 4, 1999, episode of *Sex and the City*, the oversexed character Samantha becomes intimate with a married man.[31] The man's influential wife uncovers the tryst and in retaliation uses her clout to have Samantha blacklisted in New York's high society. Samantha tries in vain to sneak, earn, and argue her way back into her former circles. After all other avenues failed, John F. Kennedy Jr. appears in backlit silhouette. As the voice-over explains, Kennedy befriends Samantha, restoring her to prominence within the socialite scene. Or so the story went on first airing.[32] Unfortunately, JFK Jr. died a mere twelve days after this episode first aired, having crashed his private jet en route from New York City to Martha's Vineyard. Sarah Jessica Parker rerecorded the voice-over for reruns and DVDs so that Leonardo DiCaprio had emerged as Samantha's new friend—though the silhouette still looks a lot more like John John than Leo. This change likely reflects an innocent sense of decorum, especially considering the fact that Parker had dated Kennedy in the early 1990s.[33] Nevertheless, the shift fits into larger cultural moves surrounding JFK Jr. that reveals a subtle sexism in the honor afforded him after death. Looking at the way the public discourse surrounding him changed, this is only the most literal attempt to rewrite the cultural scripts surrounding Kennedy so that a feminized, philandering joke in life became a masculine, loyal statesman in death.

JFK Jr.'s death took the form of a national trauma on television from the start. Round-the-clock coverage detailed the search and eventual memorial service for Kennedy on television. CNN noted the tendency for ribbons and makeshift memorials for events including the Oklahoma City bombing, the Columbine shooting, and the deaths of Princess Diana and JFK Jr.[34] Similar to the way 9/11's victims became spotless heroes, journalistic discourses commemorated Kennedy as having lived up to the serious, productive legacy associated with his father and Uncle Robert, whose deaths no doubt helped influence the understanding of Jr.'s as a national trauma. Introducing an episode of CNN's *Talkback Live* on the day of his funeral, the voice of a nun named Sister Adrian Barrett speaks over soft, mournful music and slow-motion footage of JFK Jr.[35] "I'm just sorry that we have to say farewell," she says. "I always hoped we'd see John Kennedy Jr. as president of the United States. I said a prayer for that, you know, that I'd live long enough to do that and now he beat me to heaven." Segueing into the live town-hall discussion show, host Bobbie Batista introduces the topic again: "Farewell at sea. The Kennedy family says goodbye to a favorite son. And the nation grieves for the boy they loved and the man they admired." In print, venerable publications like the *Washington Post* and the *New York Times* highlighted the apparent respectability of this beloved public figure, attempting to paint him as respected in both private and public spheres.[36] Obituaries significantly downplayed the extent to which negative stories circulated about Kennedy before his death, instead fabricating a more dominant discourse that was much kinder than that which accompanied Kennedy in life. Although expected of that form, memorials' respectful and mostly positive tone represented a significant shift from the discussions that dogged Kennedy through the 1990s, in which he existed primarily as a pretty boy and playboy, needlessly provocative, troubled in his personal life, and failed in his public ventures. Prior to his death, the UK newspaper the *Independent* encapsulated all of these aspects into an article ostensibly about the problems facing Kennedy's magazine, *George*. It begins,

> Last week somebody tried to rip off John F Kennedy Jr.'s shirt, and it wasn't his wife, Carolyn Bessette. Although she has had several public fights with the only son of the late President Kennedy, these latest fisticuffs took place in the New York offices of *George*, the glossy political magazine Kennedy began in 1995. JFK Jr's sparring partner was the magazine's executive publisher Michael Berman. Staff members say it is not the first time arguments over the contents of *George* have led to physical encounters between the two men.[37]

The article repeatedly shoehorns in references to Kennedy's good looks, noting for example his title as *People* magazine's "Sexiest Man Alive." Seemingly a backhanded compliment meant to suggest that Kennedy had gotten by on looks rather than intelligence, the piece's repeated gestures toward Kennedy's appearance act as a metaphor for their larger critique of *George* magazine's privileging of style over substance.

Although these critical discourses continued to some extent after JFK Jr.'s death, they were downplayed in favor of placing him within the more respectable legacy established by earlier generations of Kennedys. This kind of shift in discourse represents a purposeful misremembering in public discussions. Certainly few forget, and in private we may even chuckle at the way we used to mock the dead celebrity. However, these changes reveal deeper conflicts and assumptions about what a culture values and disdains. In this way, discursive shifts are significant in the ways they demonstrate how Americans refocus on some cultural values at the expense of others, reflecting and reinforcing larger senses of "American values." Comedy's sensitivity to such shifts again makes it vulnerable to erasures. Moreover, while *Sex and the City* was not particularly cruel to JFK Jr., it calls attention to more subtle changes that occur when comedies cease mocking figures like Michael Jackson or Joe Paterno in death. Similarly, if it was to be properly mourned, Kennedy's public image had to be adapted. Even if it was the producers of *Sex and the City* deciding to rerecord the section about him, it requires asking why *that* media text in particular was retroactively changed. Its status, both textually and demographically, as a feminine show draws attention to the fraught relationship between masculinity and public life for JFK Jr.

For those even loosely familiar with the program, *Sex and the City*'s bona fides as a feminine text are obvious. Jane Arthurs regards the program as unique among women-centered shows for its largely feminine focus. Up to that point, trends had hybridized masculine and feminine genres by allowing female characters to explore "the feminized, private world of personal relationships" within the masculine public sphere genres of crime and legal dramas.[38] Arthurs reads *Sex and the City* as uniquely appealing to a postfeminist audience in its remediation of the sitcom and glossy women's magazines. JFK Jr.'s implied appearance in an overtly feminine text seemed disrespectful after his death, a point that becomes clear from the larger discursive changes surrounding his star text. This move fits more generally with the hagiographic shifts that attempted to downplay the narratives that defined him in life. Kennedy was feminized as an object of the gaze (as a pretty boy) by his appearance in tabloids that narrated his life and marriage as public melodrama (an overtly feminine genre), and by his struggles and refusals to join the masculinized public sphere (failing the bar exam, struggling to establish *George*, and declining to become a politician).

JFK Jr.'s appearance within the narrative world of *Sex and the City* was short and lacked details, which likely contributed to the ease of cutting him. Nevertheless, the show subtly activated a host of meanings in the way they introduced him. He meets the character Samantha as both volunteer for a charity organization. In this episode as elsewhere on the show, charity functions are the domain of women in high society. So although playing on a more respectable aspect of his actual life, it feminizes Kennedy. More notably, however, is the fact that he appears to rescue Samantha, who represents an unrestrained sexual id within the program's narrative world. Especially considering that Samantha got into her social turmoil by getting too close to a married man, viewers were likely to infer that their relationship would result in a sexual pairing of some sort. Considering the Kennedy family's reputation for infidelity and the reports of marital troubles between him and Bessette, associations with Samantha that were comically suggestive one day turned unacceptable the next.

Moreover, placing Samantha in proximity to JFK Jr. suggests a reversal of the male gaze. This is characteristic of Samantha's encounter with men in general. "Samantha's guilt-free promiscuity is exemplary," explains Arthurs, "of the unruly woman, who inverts the power relations of gender and has sex like a man."[39] Kathleen Rowe's study of the unruly woman makes particular note that characters like Samantha are unruly in part because they reverse the male gaze.[40] Kennedy's star text plays a significant role here, too, as he was often figured as the object of a sexual gaze. When *People* announced his title as "Sexiest Man Alive," it used the desire by women to look at Kennedy as an organizing theme, beginning the first three paragraphs by ironically ordering women *not* to look at his body parts, implicitly suggesting that they should.

> Okay, ladies, this one's for you—but first some ground rules. GET YOUR EYES OFF THAT MAN'S CHEST! He's a serious fellow. Third-year law student. Active with charities. Scion of the most charismatic family in American politics and heir to its most famous name.
>
> Get your eyes off that man's extraordinarily defined thighs! What do you think, he strips down to his shorts for a game of touch football in Central Park so strangers can gape at them? They

are fantastic, though. Measure three, four feet around. Legend has it that if he lived in Tahiti, instead of Manhattan, he could crack coconuts with them.

Get your eyes off that man's derriere! We saw your gaze wandering back there. It is true that columnist Liz Smith has noted that the boy "has gorgeous buns," but you've got to remember: He has a mind too.[41]

The ironic reversal here, ordering women to focus on his mind instead of his body, glaringly suggests the extent to which nobody seemed to care about his forgettable mind when there were gorgeous buns to behold.

Also memorable along these lines was his role in the *Seinfeld* episode "The Contest," in which Kennedy is blatantly described as the object of a woman's gaze and masturbatory fantasy.[42] In this episode, the four main characters enter into a contest to see how long each can go without masturbating. Being a comedy, each character encounters exaggerated temptation: Jerry and Kramer have a woman undressing in full view of their apartment window, and George repeatedly witnesses an attractive female nurse sponge-bathing an attractive female patient in a hospital. Elaine, the only character attracted to men,[43] encounters John F. Kennedy Jr. at her health club and quickly gives in to her onanistic desires, despite the premise that women are better equipped to resist sexual urges. Interestingly, ancillary markets did not alter this episode. Having first aired in 1992 and regarded as a television classic—which has won numerous awards, including being named the best television episode of all time by *TV Guide* in 2009—this episode was too well ingrained in public memory to be altered after Kennedy's death.[44] But being more recent and only receiving a single airing, *Sex and the City*'s episode was more vulnerable, and thus the implications that Samantha might gaze at Kennedy likely played a role in the decision to reedit.

As the examples above indicate, there is something inherently funny about material that retroactively becomes too offensive for air. This speaks to television's general role in deciding and responding to what is and is not acceptable to national discourse, which is a significant aspect of its role in national culture. At the same time, television's inadvertent violation of these rules highlights the ways in which humor can draw our attention to largely unspoken rules about acceptable discourse when it comes to national traumas. Other comedy shows take advantage of censorship's comic possibilities by using or courting it for humorous and rhetorical ends. This chapter concludes by examining the way *South Park* provoked and used censorship to note larger challenges of making edgy comedy in a restrictive television industry.

PROVOKING CENSORSHIP

In the cases of censorship noted thus far, changing circumstances in the nonfictional "real" world impinged upon fictional texts, limiting expressive possibilities. Other shows have made such edits a topic for their comedy, inviting censorship of their anti-censorship rhetoric. In another example from *The Smothers Brothers Comedy Hour*, Tommy Smothers and Elaine May portray a pair of harsh censors in order to mock censorship itself.[45] Of course, censors cut the sketch. Perhaps the most public version of this kind of reflexive play occurred over a number of seasons of *South Park*, where creators repeatedly invited censorship from their corporate handlers so that they could criticize censorship as a response to national trauma.

In each of the cases from this chapter, attempts to hide or rewrite television history were incomplete (otherwise, this chapter would be impossible to research). In the case of the *Simpsons'* New York episode, enough time passed to allow the episode back into general syndication with one joke notably absent. In other cases—*Family Guy, Friends,* and *The Smothers Brothers Comedy Hour*—previously excised content became a way to add value to ancillary products like DVD releases. Still others, like *Family Guy* prior to its eventual DVD release, became a topic of conversation or completionist archiving practice among pop culture journalists and fans. So while silencing certain material may be political in some senses, the eventual reemergence of such discourses is not necessarily an act of defiance against hegemony. Responses may serve corporate economic interests or the cult fan desire to see and know all about a given text. But in at least one case, the battle over excised content took on the drama of an explicit battle over creative expression and cultural politics. Over the course of a number of seasons, *South Park* explored the comic potential of censorship in order to criticize censorious policies themselves. In so doing, this program performs in popular entertainment a similar form of media criticism as that which I undertake in this chapter. Interestingly, even when corporate censors kept aspects of this critique from the public, hacktivists accessed the content and brought it to light.

In 2005, Danish newspaper *Jyllands-Posten* published a number of intentionally confrontational cartoons featuring the prophet Muhammad in defiance of certain interpretations of Islam that prohibit such images. This stirred significant controversy, leading to an international crisis featuring widespread protests, some of which led to deaths, discussions about the role of offensive speech in liberal democracies, and the exacerbation of already tense relations between Westerners and Muslims worldwide. While this controversy erupted in Europe, it clearly fit into post-9/11 discourses pitting Islamophobic against liberal pluralist values, especially inasmuch as it exposed an apparent tension between desires for open expression and religious tolerance. Sensing a kindred spirit in *Jyllands-Posten* and an opportunity for the kind of provocation that is their trademark, the creators of *South Park* elected to make a statement with their program.

In a pair of episodes called "Cartoon Wars" from 2006, *South Park* responded with an extended allegory. In its narrative universe, the prophet Muhammad appears on rival cartoon show *Family Guy*. Although the representation is inoffensive besides showing the prophet's image, the fictional broadcast leads to worldwide protests and inspires threats from al-Qaeda. To make matters worse, *Family Guy* announces that it plans to show Muhammad a second time the following week. In response, Americans literally bury their heads in sand hoping to demonstrate that they are not watching the cartoon. Meanwhile, *South Park*'s *l'enfant terrible* Eric Cartman uses the controversy as an excuse to convince the television network to pull the episode. On the surface, he appears to be acting in good faith—preventing offense to Muslims and potentially violent reprisals. Eventually, however, Cartman admits that this is all a slippery-slope scheme to get *Family Guy* taken off the air. He says,

> All it takes to kill a show forever is get one episode pulled. If we convince the network to pull this episode for the sake of Muslims, then the Catholics can demand a show they don't like get pulled. And then people with disabilities can demand another show get pulled and so on and so on until *Family Guy* is no more.

Family Guy and *South Park* both rely on self-consciously offensive styles of humor, and in this episode, *South Park* uses *Family Guy* to explore its own relationship to Comedy Central's policies and its perceived ethical right to mock certain groups, if not with impunity then at least without network interference. In a move forcing the network to take a side, these episodes' plots blatantly invited Comedy Central's real-world censorship. As the first episode ends, it previews the next week's plot. Reaching a dramatic pitch, it makes the challenge explicit by naming Comedy Central, and not *Family Guy*'s network, Fox, as the final decision-maker. "Will the cartoon be allowed to appear uncensored? Will *Family Guy* be destroyed? Will television executives fight for free speech? Or will Comedy Central puss out?"

This comedy of ethics revolves around the creators' desire for unfettered expression on commercial cable television. Within the episode's narratives, heavyweights from the president of the Fox network to the president of the United States weigh in and ultimately decide that freedom of expression outweighs the desire to be free from fear, allowing the *Family Guy* episode to air uncensored. Ultimately, however, Comedy Central did censor the image of Muhammad, replacing it with a description of the events using sober white lettering on a black background, followed by the explanation, "Comedy Central has refused to broadcast an image of Mohammed on their network."

The decision to censor Muhammad proved especially interesting in this case, considering the prophet had appeared in previous *South Park* episodes as a member of a team of superheroes called the Super Best Friends and had even been appearing as a small background detail in a number of the show's opening credit sequences. This became a point for jokes in later self-referential 2010 episodes "200" and "201"—so named because they were the series' 200th and 201st episodes.[46] Exaggeratedly complex, these episodes' narrative revives a number of previous stories, centering on efforts to avoid mockery by the many celebrities that *South Park* had gibed in its first 199 episodes. Ringleader Tom Cruise explains, "Muhammad has a power that makes him impervious to being made fun of. What if we could harness that power?" Later, Cruise reveals his belief that Muhammad's power comes from a magic goo. The choice of Cruise as the mastermind here is also significant to *South Park*'s sometimes-fraught relationship with its parent company. After Comedy Central pulled a 2005 episode critical of both Cruise and Scientology, rumors surfaced accusing the star of threatening to cease promoting the upcoming *Mission Impossible III*, a film produced by Comedy Central's parent company, Viacom.[47]

Back in the episode's narrative, to avoid a lawsuit that would ruin the town of South Park, Cruise demands to meet with Muhammad. Since images of Muhammad are forbidden, the townsfolk worry that they will be unable to find the prophet. One of the boys reminds the town that, in fact, Muhammad had appeared in South Park (and on *South Park*). "Oh and what? And he was just out in the open where everyone could see him and nobody got bombed?" asks one resident sarcastically. Of course, this had indeed been the case as far back as July 2001.[48]

At the hall of the Super Best Friends, the boys meet with the other members of the group, most of whom are figureheads of major world religions, including Buddha, Jesus Christ, Krishna, Lao-Tzu, Moses, and Joseph Smith. A parody of the opening title sequence of Hanna-Barbera's 1970s cartoon *Super Friends* introduces each religious leader with an accompanying image, except that a black box with the word "censored" covers Muhammad. Two boys from South Park meet with the Super Best Friends to ask if they can bring Muhammad to their town. Jesus and Buddha explain that Muhammad can no longer make public appearances. The discussion quickly devolves into what sounds like a negotiation between *South Park*'s creative talent and corporate heads over their depictions of the prophet. Eventually, they settle on bringing Muhammad in a U-Haul trailer while additionally hidden in a mascot costume.

Under increasing demands by the celebrities to show Muhammad, the boys must reveal that, in fact, Santa Claus was posing as the prophet in the suit. These events occur during the second episode. However, in the week separating the two episodes, the restrictions on what could air had grown stricter and, in addition to blocking his image with a black square, the soundtrack replaced Muhammad's name with a bleep. Eventually, Tom Cruise steals Muhammad's power and a black box with the word *censored* appears over the star. However, a homophobic joke at Cruise's expense removes the box, showing that there was no immunity, for this star at least, from the show's satire.

South Park episodes commonly end with one of the characters announcing, "I learned something today . . ." generally followed by a fairly sincere, if on the nose, summation of that episode's moral lesson. In this case, one of the children, Jesus, and Santa Claus all join in what appears to be an in-depth speech, but it is bleeped. In total, the bleeped speeches take up a seemingly interminable thirty-nine seconds of screen time. Creators Parker and Stone made it clear that they did not intend for the audio censorship to be a meta-joke about censoring their attack on censorship; it was the decision of Comedy Central based on stated threats.[49] Between South Park Studios and Hulu, nearly every episode is available for streaming. The "nearly" qualifier is only necessary because a handful of episodes related to this issue do not appear online. Instead, although *South Park*'s website now tersely states, "We apologize that South Park Studios cannot stream this episode," it had previously more fully explained the issue:

> We apologize that South Park Studios cannot stream episode 200 [or 201] at this time. After we delivered the show, and prior to broadcast, Comedy Central placed numerous additional audio

bleeps throughout the episode. We do not have network approval to stream our original version of the show. We will bring you a version of 200 [or 201] as soon as we can.[50]

As of this writing, almost ten years after its original broadcast, the episode remains unavailable through these channels. Additionally, "Super Best Friends," the first episode to show Muhammad, also remains unavailable online through legal channels.[51]

Unlike in the above examples, this was an explicit attempt to insert politically sensitive material into episodes as a response to the protests over the *Jyllands-Posten* cartoons and later threats to the safety of Comedy Central employees. Unlike in examples of censorship discussed at the beginning of this chapter, Comedy Central did not just retroactively edit the images presented on air. It also changed the rules that governed *South Park* moving forward, causing a more heated controversy and more explicit engagement with the questions of how television's own sense of history changes depending on contemporary sensitivities. In response to the numerous issues brought up by this controversy as well as the actions of Parker and Stone, extremist groups, and Comedy Central, numerous parties expressed their support. Sympathizers ranging from other animated television show producers to political cartoonists to fans joined this effort. Most significantly to the discussion at hand, support came in the form of hacktivism, albeit delayed by years. Although "200" and "201" first broadcast in 2010, they began receiving renewed attention in late 2014. An internet user reportedly discovered a less-censored version of the episode on the South Park Studios servers that restored the final speech.[52] Its ironic message encourages violence as a way to stifle expression.

STAN: You see, I learned something today. Throughout this whole ordeal, we've all wanted to show things we weren't allowed to show, but it wasn't because of some magic goo. It was because of the magical power of threatening people with violence. That's obviously the only true power. If there's anything we've all learned, it's that terrorizing people works.
JESUS: That's right. Don't you see, gingers,[53] if you don't want to be made fun of anymore, all you need are guns and bombs to get people to stop.
SANTA: That's right, friends. All you need to do is instill fear and be willing to hurt people, and you can get whatever you want. The only true power is violence.

Muhammad visually censored as Stan delivers his bleeped speech on South Park.

This revelation led to further work by fans—with another version of these episodes (as well as the pair of "Cartoon Wars" episodes) appearing online in which users had reinserted the image of Muhammad as borrowed from the earlier "Super Best Friends" episodes.[54]

Depending on one's standpoint, these actions deserve varying levels of respect and/or praise. The ability to restore the politically and rhetorically meaningful "I learned something today" speech seems a worthier cause than merely reinserting the image of Muhammad, since the former is a more legitimate critique of the systemic issues at play. The best that can be said for the latter is that it sends the message that future attempts at censorship are bound to fail in the end. Nevertheless, these twin efforts at uncensoring bear significant meaning. Yes, they are somewhat important as a defiant gesture even if they accomplish fairly little. But more notably, they fit into a larger pattern described throughout this chapter in which information, to use the cliché, wants to be free. In the case of censored television material, it reveals the apparent desire to restore episodes to a state of originality. This desire can come from a variety of sources, including economic concerns, a search for originality for its own sake, a taste for macabre irony, or a show of support for the values expressed by the censored content.

In all these cases, censorship reveals the often complex temporalities that exist between production schedules, original airings, reruns, syndication, DVDs, digital distribution platforms like Netflix, and the *other* digital distribution platforms of legally dubious internet sharing, as well as the discursive construction of television texts and even the concept of originality itself. In a larger sense, these temporalities demonstrate the complex interactions that define popular memory and discourse in American popular culture and politics. While these forces are always in play to some extent, the intersection of sensitive topics related to national trauma with comedy's potential for offense and perceived low cultural status make it an ideal site to examine the ways in which national traumas can shift political and cultural discourses. These shifts in turn affect the way Americans understand their cultural and political history, which is significant to the way they understand themselves as part of a nation. If shared cultural memories and political discourses are two key ways in which Americans imagine themselves as part of the nation, then censorship in these arenas necessarily impacts American identity.

Chapter 7 picks up the issue of censorship as a comedic weapon, examining a 2017 episode of *Broad City* that censored the word *Trump* as well a companion internet browser extension that replaced internet text of the president's name with "Tr**p." However, the next two chapters shift focus from the more strictly historiographic questions of timelines and popular archives to issues of popular memory. While this chapter examined the way censorship literally alters records of television history, the next examines the ways in which comedy impacts the way we engage emotionally with memories of national traumas.

On the television show *Drunk History*, storytellers drink to excess while trying to recount significant moments from American and world history. Famous and semi-famous actors then play out these scenes, reflecting the speakers' drunken missteps and rambling in their performances. When *Drunk History* made the leap from a web series to Comedy Central, its first episode engaged with two moments of crisis from American history: Watergate and the Lincoln assassination. While not as significant to this book project as other, more violent and visible traumas from the more recent past, the use of these crises touches on some significant themes of this project. Among many others, it draws humor from the contrast between comedy's frivolity and deeply serious—some might say sober— topics. What *Drunk History* illustrates particularly well, however, is the sense in which history as an academic and pop academic discourse tends to come in serious tones. *Drunk History* is funny in large part because of this contrast between drunken comedy and serious history. History, at least the way it is usually discussed, is solemn to begin with, but as especially serious events, national traumas exaggerate this tendency even more. What happens then, when comedy engages the doubly serious discourses surrounding historical trauma?

Because its appeals to humor define contemporary comedy as a genre, any engagement with seemingly non-humorous topics necessarily results in tonal contrasts. In dealing with national traumas, comedy frequently involves displays of emotional nonconformity—whereby comics or comedy shows perform unexpected emotional responses to events that discourse commonly paints as causes for sadness, anger, anxiety, and so forth. Indeed, as Lenny Bruce demonstrated when he showed more concern for a hackneyed comic's career than for President Kennedy, unexpected emotional responses can themselves be funny. If, as this book argues, media culture defines national traumas in both their initial encoding and in their longer historical understanding as highly emotional events, comedy's tendency to perform against expectations is significant to the way the public understands and responds to them. Television comedy's ability to joke about John F. Kennedy's death is significant in part because it breaks with common discourse that understands him as a heroic mythic figure. Removing the gloss from the public's historical remembrance of Kennedy allows for a more honest engagement with the history of that presidency, including lessons that critical examination of policy missteps can teach. In this sense, comedy helps to demystify the ideological constructs that arise around national traumas. While chapter 1 examined how television comedy came to joke about the sensitive historical subject of the Kennedy assassination and chapter 2 examined more specific ways in which television remains a site of struggle over expression, this chapter looks more closely at the kind of emotional work undertaken by comedy in relation to national traumas.

Theorists of humor have long noted its role in easing or denying negative emotions and affect. Perhaps most notably, Mikhail Bakhtin writes, "The acute awareness of victory over fear is an essential element of medieval laughter."[1] Though Bakhtin's analysis here concerns physical displays in which, for example, celebrants destroyed physical images of hell, he points to a key characteristic of humor as affect. In defiance of the fear elicited by worldly governmental power and heavenly church power, comic celebrations not only offered a holiday from unpleasant emotions but also actively attacked and destroyed their representations through symbolic actions. Television comedy adopts a similar tactic. Media representations of national trauma are symbolic inasmuch as they live on screens as images. Television comedy also exists on a screen, but it frequently adds layers of symbolism in using fiction, parody, and other tools of the art.

Like carnival, contemporary comedies often perform fearlessness in response to seemingly scary things. In his essay "Horror and Humor," Noël Carroll argues that monsters and comedy both arise from a sense of categorical violation.[2] For instance, zombies and vampires simultaneously represent life and death—two otherwise mutually exclusive states. In the case of humor relying on incongruity, Carroll sees a similar (il)logic at play in that jokes can hold logical impossibilities in tension or even resolve that tension in preposterous ways.[3] The difference between horror and humor, then, is the element of fear. The removal of fear transforms the horrific into the comic. By this understanding, comedies can get laughs by diminishing the sense of threat from any source. This chapter explores these issues by examining comedies that model fearlessness in the face of threats, diminish the sense of threat from certain events, and even criticize other media texts for fearmongering. Of course, fear is not the only emotional response that helps define national trauma, and this model applies readily to sadness and other emotional registers associated with national trauma.

Though focused more on the internal workings of emotion as opposed to Bakhtin's more sociocultural approach, Freud offered similar thoughts. For him, humor is "the victorious assertion of the ego's invulnerability. The ego refuses to be distressed by the provocations of reality, to let itself be compelled to suffer. It insists that it cannot be affected by the traumas of the external world; it shows, in fact, that such traumas are no more than occasions for it to gain pleasure."[4] Here, Freud distinguishes humor from other types of funny material inasmuch as it puts individual suffering in perspective by appealing to a sense of larger issues. Freud's understanding of humor captures the sense that comedy puts emotional reactions to certain events in perspective. When comedy's disdainful mockery targets John F. Kennedy or others toward whom we would otherwise feel pity, it triggers laughter's emotional exclusivity, replacing the unpleasant experience of emotion if only for a moment. Furthermore, especially in cases of collective trauma, the temptation to make fun of these kind of rituals of suffering (in which individuals' connection to the traumatic event is virtual) invites laughter mocking the kind of automatic participation triggered by coverage of this sort, suggesting Henri Bergson's notion that laughter arises from perceiving unthinking habitual action in others.[5]

Popular memory can refer to a range of objects, from the way social practice reflects its own history to the ways members of a group remember particular events. Michel Foucault hints at some of the ways these different understandings cross over and inform one another. Elaborating on the notion of "popular memory" as the history passed along by the members and institutions of the masses, he offers the insight that history consists of more than mere facts.[6] While ambiguous on its legitimacy as a medium for renegotiating elements of history, he notes the importance of historical fiction films like 1974's *Night Porter* in fostering and negotiating affective associations between Nazism and eroticism. As this example makes clear, the ways in which societies understand the past are more complex than a simple list of facts regarding the past. Especially in the cultural milieu of history, emotion, politics, and ideology that arise from national traumas, affectively intense genres like comedy or erotica serve as a powerful and often ignored element of individual and popular history.

Foucault discusses the ways in which emotions project back in time to cast a different hue on past events, leaving it implicit that emotions significantly impact how we understand those moments in the first place. Certainly, Nazism inspired strong emotions in both its adherents and victims. Of course, the impact of emotions on how culture first records its popular history is especially obvious in cases like these, but these feelings color every experience, if at times only subtly. The introduction described how news coverage of national traumas prescribes particularly emotional understandings, using the hallmarks of melodrama. This arises not only from simplistic good-evil binaries and the powerful iconography of everything from destruction to people expressing emotion to memorials, candles, and teddy bears, but also from more formal tools like mournful music, still photograph montages, and close-ups. While these techniques are rare or entirely absent in typical television news coverage of everyday events, they are ubiquitous to the point of defining national traumas in television journalism, if not necessarily in comedy. It naturally follows that if these events are significant in part because of their emotional meanings, then any negotiation of such feelings also proves important.

COMEDY AND EMOTIONAL NONCONFORMITY

"I once told an ironically racist joke on television," explains Anthony Jeselnik in his 2019 Netflix special.[7]

> The next day I got a fan letter from a white supremacist in Jacksonville, Florida. Bone chilling. He just started praising me. "Thank you so much, Anthony. Thank you for not denigrating the great white race. Thank you for making fun of all the other races the way that it should be. And I can pay you $100,000. Come down to Jacksonville, Florida; do a private show just for me and my white supremacist buddies." I wrote him back right away and I said, "Absolutely not. You are against everything I stand for, you cheap piece of shit."

The structure of this joke is familiar—suggesting once again Lenny Bruce's concern for Vaughn Meader on the evening of JFK's death. In that case as in this one, the comics appear at first to have appropriate emotional responses. However, both comics surprise with punchlines revealing that the objects of their emotion are off. In keeping with his stage persona, Jeselnik here demonstrates exaggeratedly immoral concerns: in the face of neofascism, his priority is money, whereas Bruce was more concerned with a hackneyed comic's career than the president's death. Of course, this joke would more or less work for most, though certainly not all, American audiences during the television era. However, the rise in hate crimes, and particularly the events in Charlottesville in the summer of 2017, make this kind of emotional nonconformity starker and more shocking. At the same time, either joke allows for audiences to read it alternatively as supportive of Nazism or dismissive of Kennedy's importance, highlighting a key slipperiness that haunts humor in this vein.

Emotional nonconformity occurs when a text performs emotions that do not fit with cultural expectations.[8] Comedy is especially prone to this phenomenon since it is a genre defined in large part by the emotions associated with laughter, at least by contemporary understandings. Although comedians like David Letterman and Jon Stewart might have bowed to cultural expectations to perform sadness and anxiety after 9/11, humor's natural resistance to those feelings makes it a common site for emotional nonconformity. In fact, as I argued concerning examples from Lenny Bruce to Peter Griffin, it is often the contrast between expected and performed emotion that creates humor out of collective trauma.

Society expects cultural figures to follow rules of performance that include displaying particular negative emotions in response to trauma. Politicians and comedians alike face risks if they fail to act according to those standards. Donald Trump after Charlottesville, Bill Maher after 9/11, and Gilbert Gottfried after the Fukushima nuclear disaster all faced blowback of one form or another because they missed the mark expected by certain groups and gatekeepers.[9] Moreover, television's fear of public and regulatory blowback as well as the relatively centrist ideological position of ownership and labor usually prevent immediate displays of emotional nonconformity. Nevertheless, humor as a rhetoric gets some leeway to experiment with alternative responses, including performances of emotional nonconformity and rebellion. However, some humor-related subcultures, from online communities like Reddit's r/toosoon and r/imgoingtohellforthis forums to smaller social formations like friend groups, reward sick humor. Despite television's skittishness, the desire to appeal to these comedy cultures pushes some comedies to engage traumatic events in a comic mode, as *Family Guy* did with the Kennedy assassinations.

As noted throughout this book, comics whose material relies on shock value make frequent use of national traumas. The tones of mournfulness and respect create a useful set of taboos to violate by engaging them in a less respectful tone. In these cases, there is an expectation of particular emotional performances set by initial news coverage. For stand-up comics as well as comedies more generally, a performance of emotion that does not fit the appropriate frame can draw laughter. As the comparison of Jeselnik and Bruce indicated above, emotionally nonconforming performance might show the correct emotion but be directed at the wrong object (sympathy to the wrong person or anger at the wrong perceived misstep), but it can also include ironic rejection to perform clearly negative emotions in the face of horrendous events. Taken to the extreme, emotional nonconformity might even go so far as to ironically celebrate national traumas, as will be discussed in chapter 6 with regard to comic Carlos Mencia.

The ambiguous nature of emotionally nonconforming humor can produce success and controversy, as Daniel Tosh learned in 2012 when he clumsily joked about rape during a live set. While that particular example was rightly criticized, Jared Champion reads Tosh's most progressive work as existing in a space of ambiguity, particularly in his attempts to deconstruct overly simplistic moral binaries. Especially considering that the issues Tosh discusses in this register—racism, sexism, homophobia, and so on—are intense topics, emotional nonconformity is key to his ability to combine, in Champion's words, "the most progressive impulses with regressive language."[10] Tosh's performative engagement rarely if ever displays what would be considered appropriate emotions. However, Tosh's discussion of weighty topics using inappropriate emotional registers is key to his humor, as are his ironic takedowns of those that are more sincerely socially regressive.

In August 2017, neo-Nazi demonstrators clashed with police and counterprotesters in Charlottesville, Virginia. The iconic moment within the series of events occurred when a white supremacist drove his car into a crowd of counterprotesters, killing one and injuring nineteen. Shortly afterward, Daniel Tosh, on his show *Tosh.0*, referenced the event while commenting on a video clip in which a man lost control of his ATV, ramming into a group of onlookers. "Southern whites love reenactments," he jokes in a mock celebratory tone. "This is the battle of Charlottesville. [Audience moans.] I agree with you that joke's too soon."[11] Although there are multiple layers of humor in this joke, particularly in the contrast between Charlottesville's seriousness and the video's silliness, Tosh doubles back to sarcastically note that it was inappropriate to draw humor from this incident as he invokes the "too soon" metajoke. In this case, as in others, Tosh crosses the line, but does so to relatively progressive ends. Although white power groups protesting the removal of Robert E. Lee's statue in a public park set the events in motion, in drawing comparisons between the Civil War and the events in Charlottesville, Tosh makes more legible the racist undertones present in the nostalgia surrounding the Civil War and antebellum South. Simultaneously, he demonstrates the way in which his comedy is frequently about performing emotional nonconformity in relation to weighty topics.

Linda Hutcheon and theorists of polysemy more broadly note the potential for slippage in ironic speech.[12] While Tosh's progressive humor is fairly decipherable in this "battle of Charlottesville" joke, he has a history of telling more troubling jokes, including the aforementioned incident in which he responded to an audience member's assertion that rape jokes are not funny by asking, "Wouldn't it be funny if that girl got raped by, like, five guys right now?"[13] Tosh's ironic ambiguity even when appearing to argue for progressive ideas, along with his checkered history of telling more upsetting jokes, speaks to a larger tendency within emotionally nonconformist comedy. Jeselnik's joke about being more offended by the lowball offer than by the racial politics of his white supremacist fan also offers a reading that at best excuses rather than condemns the extreme right. Understanding this ambiguity is key to making sense of emotionally nonconforming comedy in relation to politics and history.

Of course, such humor is not limited to stand-up. In a 2007 episode of *Family Guy*, Peter converts to a satirically exaggerated version of post-9/11 patriotism.[14] Attempting to discount his credibility, Peter's dog, Brian, argues that Peter "didn't know what 9/11 was until 2004." Peter argues that he did indeed remember, prompting a cutaway in which Peter's wife Lois sits on the couch teary-eyed and surrounded by used tissues. Peter walks by, notices the television screen, and playfully taps her on the shoulder, quipping, "Ha! Must've been a woman pilot, eh?" This joke is more ambiguous than Tosh's and Jeselnik's in that it could conceivably support a reading of Peter being either an emotional nonconformist or merely stupid. If Peter is too dumb to know about or make sense of 9/11, this is a hegemonic joke with regard to nationalist ideology because, as an idiot, Peter acts as a counterexample. By that reading, the joke functions by playing on expectations regarding appropriate decorum in the wake of national trauma, and the audience laughs at him for his idiocy. Laughter acts as a performance of superiority, reinforcing nationalist ideology and presenting lessons in acceptable behavior. However, Peter's callous response to national trauma reads differently if one considers this character to be a jester or wise fool, who plays dumb in order to criticize others in a more Socratic mode.[15] His callous joke, made all the more inappropriate because it is such a bad joke to begin with, is then a performance of independent thought, rejecting the overwhelming social pressure to perform as a trauma victim in response to an event that he understands as more virtual than immediate to his experience. While the idiot reading presents him as unable to understand social decorum, the wise fool reading proposes, somewhat counterintuitively, that he is smart enough to play dumb. At the same time, while Peter rejects the idea of his own victimhood, he demonstrates this with an offensively sexist joke. So while he plays the wise fool in the realm of virtual trauma, he makes his wife and all women the butt of his joke, reforming, if ambiguously, a sense of his idiocy in the realm of gender politics and interpersonal interaction. *Family Guy*, and Peter Griffin in particular, creates much of its humor from blurring the lines between other fictions and its narrative reality.[16] As a stupid idiot, Peter perhaps mistakes reality for fiction. However, as a wise fool, he interprets 9/11 as a fundamentally virtual event that impacts him only to the extent that he allows it to, even if he plays the idiot in another sense.

PARODY AND PASTNESS

Emotional nonconformity is a performance strategy for edgy stand-up comics like Anthony Jeselnik and Daniel Tosh. While I typically use the term "performance" in this book to mean any action that creates meaning, the performative aspect of emotional nonconformity in this sense can have additional meanings. For one, it is notable, particularly in relation to polysemy, that comics like Tosh and Jeselnik can back away from their stage personas to claim that their "true self" conforms to emotional expectations.[17] However, although both of these comics and others do this to different extents in offstage communiques and moments of more personal candor performed on stage, they also use it as a strategy to reset their audience's expectations. Jeselnik did this when decrying his white supremacist supporter, using the expectation that he was attempting to explain away any racist overtones to his comedy before revealing his motivation to be greed. The other, more significant meaning of "performances of emotional nonconformity" is that they might not always be as nonconformist as they appear. While it is a cliché to praise comedians for "saying what we are all thinking," there is some truth to the idea that at some point, certainly more so as time goes on, reactions of grief in remembrance of national trauma might be more due to social pressure than to actual mourning. In this sense, comedy's ability to express feelings other than sadness and fear is significant in the ways it grants permission to audiences to compartmentalize and cease overidentifying with the emotionalized frame into which national traumas fall. Emotional nonconformity in comedy plays a significant role in altering the affective dimensions of popular memory.

"Must've been a woman pilot, eh?" asks Peter from Family Guy.

Besides the complex interplay of apparent genuine and stage personas for comedians, emotional nonconformity can also describe the performances of more fully fictional characters like Peter Griffin, representing in stark ways the broader comic strategies of post-PC comedies in relation to the culture's sacred constructs.[18] More in keeping with the question of comedy's relationship to popular history, the *Family Guy* gags' flashback structure highlights a significant aspect of this sort of humor in the way it engages the past. Jeselnik's and Tosh's discussions of then-recent events illuminate the ways in which emotional nonconformity reflects upon the past. However, examples like *Family Guy*—whether flashing back seven years to 9/11 or almost half a century to the JFK assassination—reflect the extreme end of a television trend that allows for offensive humor in order to appeal to specific audiences.

As a wise fool, Peter acts as a model for identification. Flashing back to 9/11, in order to reject the performance of national trauma expected of that moment, is political. His flippant attitude separates Peter from the hyperpatriotic crowd. Perhaps more importantly, it serves as an ex post facto rejection of the affects and emotions that dulled critical stances as well as the ensuing performances that many Americans undertook in those first weeks and months after 9/11. Especially as the Iraq War and perceived erosion of civil liberties in the wake of 2001 gave liberals and libertarians pause, early performances of national trauma came to seem like the actions of dupes preparing to give politicians permission to run rampant with increased power. This brand of patriotism is a central target of this episode's satire when Peter's eventual conversion to hyperpatriotism prompts virulent xenophobia. Indeed, since Peter's xenophobia primarily targets Mexican American immigrants, this satire has grown even more relevant as Donald Trump's rhetoric has relied on post-9/11 anti-Muslim and general anti-Latinx sentiment to push agendas.

The *Family Guy* episode's 2007 airdate mitigates the 9/11 joke's offensiveness to a large extent even if the joke's framing as a flashback places Peter's reaction in close proximity to the attacks. In less obvious ways, however, parodies always play with memory. By calling texts to mind and creating new meaning, parody affects its audience's memories. In this way, jokes about national traumas recode memories, not in the sense of factual understanding but in their connotative inflection. This speaks to neuroscientific understandings of memory. As Jonah Lehrer explains, "new research is showing that every time we recall an event, the structure of that memory in the brain is altered in light of the present moment, warped by our current feelings and knowledge."[19] Although Freud was concerned with the continuing effects of the past on the present, Jacques Derrida notes that he overprivileged the initial event to the detriment of a stronger understanding of memory.[20] Psychoanalytic trauma theorist Jean Laplanche argues along similar lines as Lehrer and Derrida, noting, "It is not the first act which is traumatic, it is the internal reviviscence of this memory that becomes traumatic."[21] While most models of memory suggest that recurring engagement can shift attitudes and reactions, these particularly unsettle the central importance placed on the original event and instead highlight the significance of each instance of remembering.

Using these approaches, media remembrances including early news coverage, anniversaries, and parodies grow more significant in their ability to call events to mind, provide evidence to corroborate or shift initial impressions, and alter the emotive inflection of memories and attitudes over time. In their claims to represent the truth of past events, traumatic or not, documentary and news coverage represent powerful tools for influencing popular and individual memory. In the privileged examples of national trauma, anniversary coverage and documentary programming become even more significant as we shift focus toward the act of remembering as opposed to the initial event. Even if the initial anxiety and sadness subside, these genres tend to renew displays of national trauma, reestablishing and strengthening those ideologically powerful scripts in relation to the events and the nation. For their part, dramatic fiction and fictionalizations tend to reinforce these events' dominant emotional frame.

For example, *Third Watch*, a drama about New York police, firefighters, and paramedics, kicked off its 2001–2002 season with a nonfiction tribute to real-life first responders and dedicated the majority of that season to 9/11-related story lines that largely reflected the reverential discourse of the period.[22] More recently, shows have engaged other types of traumas through drama, largely reinforcing their dominant framing. *Glee* and *13 Reasons Why* joined the long list of shows dealing with school shootings through drama, while *Madam Secretary* dealt with the Trump administration's family separation policy.[23] In the *Madam Secretary* episode, the titular secretary of state addresses reporters about her visit to a detention center. "What I saw was an affront to decency and an assault on our country's core values," she explains. "Children separated from their parents, in cages. Crying. Terrified. Lacking basic care." Though this character is fictional and describing events from the fictional narrative of the show, journalists or politicians could just as easily have used this language responding to real-world events under the Trump administration.

In cases like these, news media create history with a particular emotional tone of shock, horror, mournfulness, and reverence. News and documentary programs perform the genre's compulsion to repeat as they attempt to master traumatic events after the fact.[24] Factful and emotional work, from engineering analyses of faulty technology to interviews with victims' families, retroactively fills in knowledge gaps while generally reinforcing the initial emotional frame. Fictional and fictionalized dramas aim to fill in other gaps where the genres of news and documentary cannot. NBC's *Third Watch* offered a fictional account of first responders' post-9/11 recovery. Despite the ubiquity of cell phones, reports of school shootings may lack detailed footage because those taking pictures are hiding and removed from the sight of the perpetrators and because journalism is skittish about showing too much carnage. Images leaking out from childhood detainment camps are similarly limited, likely owing to their secretive nature and an awareness on the part of officials that videos and pictures would hurt their public relations battle. In response, shows like *Glee*, *13 Reasons Why*, and *Madam Secretary* place viewers "on the inside" of school shootings and family separation in the absence of quality footage, helping to fill in real or imaginary knowledge gaps in these significant moments.

As far as mass media representations are concerned, comedy in general and parody more specifically often serve as the first discursive sites to avoid or subtly shift the dominant mood. Even if Jon Stewart's and David Letterman's immediate post-9/11 humor proved fairly safe, moments of even slight levity allowed for cracks in 9/11's overwhelming emotional framing. Robert Turnock discovered that by the evening following Princess Diana's death in 1997, audiences in the United Kingdom turned to comedy television programming in greater numbers than on an average night.[25] This, his research revealed, was because viewers had grown exhausted by the emotional tone of news coverage over the course of the day and sought relief in the form of light entertainment. Notably, in this case, the audience actively searched for counter-programming for coverage of Diana's death. This of course complicates the meaning of "emotional nonconformity" since so many people used television in that way. Nevertheless, television texts that perform against expectation compared to larger public discourses certainly create meaning from the space between expectation and emotional performance. Moreover, if audiences understand performers and/or themselves to be acting against the expectations of public discourse, that qualifies as emotional nonconformity no matter how many people may or may not be actually acting in accordance with public discourse.

In the short term following a moment of trauma, humor serves as relief from the emotional exhaustion that can arise from dedicated television viewership of television news coverage. These moments play a role in television's process of moving past the overwhelming focus on the event at hand, but in doing so they point the way toward future revisiting.[26] Whether safe or contentious, hegemonic or counterhegemonic, to revisit events like these with a mirthful frame instead of a mournful one is to affect popular memory. Therefore, even if Peter Griffin's woman pilot joke did not inure him against hyperpatriotism, the joke lightens the mood of remembrance. In weakening the dominance of the sacred frame, if only for a moment, it reconstructs the events from outside its dominant emotional coding.

The tendency to rewrite emotional history is present at least to a limited extent in all humor regarding these events. But as opposed to other forms of humor, parody—as a representation of and way to play with other texts—serves as a particularly powerful tool. Comics like Jeselnik and Tosh as well as shows like *Family Guy* regularly reference national traumas in ways that are fairly apolitical except for their flagrant refusal to bow to the sacred framing. Other television shows have taken more pointed aim at aspects of sacred framing, variously mocking the emotional tone of journalism and fictionalized programming.

RESISTING JOURNALISTIC FEARMONGERING

In the days of *The Colbert Report*, its host parodied fearmongering news pieces with bits like "The Threatdown" and "Monkey on the Lam." As an ironic parodist of the infotainment style and persona, Colbert performed as a fearmongering blowhard in order to criticize television personalities and their tactics. More recently, *The Opposition with Jordan Klepper* revived this format on Comedy Central, taking aim at a newer generation of paranoid right-wing media exemplified by Alex Jones. As will be discussed in more detail in the next chapter, conspiracy theorists like Jones are ripe for parodic inversion by ironists like Klepper because much of the humor on these shows comes from willful misunderstanding and tortured logic. For instance, in the wake of the Marjory Stoneman Douglas High School shooting in 2018, student and other activists asked what could be done to protect students from gun violence. Klepper inverted this logic to ask what could be done to protect guns from student activists. In addition to echoing more traditional right-wing pundits like Laura Ingraham, who attacked students for protesting, Klepper also echoed the kind of fearmongering associated with more fringe political positions.[27] Despite the failure of a gun-control measure that had passed the Florida legislature only to be withdrawn fifteen minutes later, Klepper sounds the alarm: "This is it, gun lovers. I told you this was coming. This is the moment I've been warning you about. So delete your social security number, smash your phone with a hammer, then smash your hammer with a big phone, because we're going off the grid." Klepper makes a slippery slope argument, following unhinged logic to an absurd end. The camera angle rises in a crane shot, diminishing the host and making him appear powerless as his voice grows more intent and his fear grows more noticeable. "Suddenly, every gun store in Florida converts to a prenatal yoga studio, while Cory Booker sneaks into your homes to replace the TEC-9 under your pillow with a bag of nutritional yeast." This ironic rhetoric acts as a valuable corrective to ratings- and click-driven infotainment's penchant for fearmongering in general and its tendency to exploit the particular unpleasant emotions associated with collective traumas.

While not performing the same kind of ironic send-up of opinion journalism as Klepper and *The Colbert Report*, other comedy programs offer commentary on fearmongering news. For example, in a 2016 segment tracing the relationship between Fox News' fearmongering and Donald Trump's, *Full Frontal with Samantha Bee* examines the role of Islamophobia in the Republican Party.[28] Responding to a clip of Trump calling for a ban on Muslim immigrants, Bee notes,

> That xenophobic garbage didn't come from Republican Party leadership. After 9/11, President Bush set the tone by vigorously

defending people's right to walk around all Muslimy. . . . I honestly never thought I'd miss anything about George W. Bush. A Republican president [spoke out against Islamophobia] nine days after September 11. Nine days when most of us did nothing but cry, give blood, and buy flags.

She goes on to explain a belief that the shift from Bush's laudably tolerant view of Muslims after 9/11 to Trump's openly hostile one is partly the result of Fox News' appeals to "emotional non-stories" like the so-called Ground Zero Mosque controversy. While delivered in a humorous tone, Bee's commentary is not ironic like Klepper's. Hers is a direct attack on infotainment journalism's use of fearmongering to push a political agenda.

In a different form of parody, *South Park* attacked affective framing as well. It parodied Hurricane Katrina coverage along with fictional media in order to question the journalistic discussions from that period making connections between Katrina and climate change. In "Two Days before the Day after Tomorrow," two of the main characters accidentally drive a boat into and break a beaver dam, flooding the town below.[29] News coverage not only narrativizes the events as a national trauma but also unethically exaggerates the destructive fallout. Addressing his news anchor regarding the flood, a journalist reports, "I'm currently ten miles outside of Beaverton, unable to get inside the town proper. We do not have any reports of fatalities yet, but we believe that the death toll may be in the hundreds of millions. Beaverton has only a population of about eight thousand . . . so this would be quite devastating." As the crisis continues, the news continues to falsely report acts of looting, raping, and cannibalism while pundits blame George W. Bush, al-Qaeda, the town's mayor, FEMA, and global warming, ultimately showing that they care more about assigning blame than helping the victims. Eventually, experts settle on global warming as the true cause of the flood, prompting a massive fearful overreaction in which characters play out scenes from the eco-disaster movie *The Day after Tomorrow*. This aspect of the humor arises from the character's enacting disaster movie clichés despite there being no disaster—a mistake owed to their privileging emotionalism over rationalism. While the characters' reactions are to blame for the problems they encounter, journalistic fearmongering is the impetus of their overreaction. The gap between journalistic constructions of disaster and the lack thereof thus not only is the source of the narrative and much of its humor, but drives the critique as well. While sympathetic to Katrina's victims, this episode nevertheless laughingly attacks the news media with charges of exaggeration and misapplied blame. This did not simply break from the affective frame but satirized the news media and its punditry for its sensationalism in creating that frame.

RESISTING MEMORIAL TRAUMA

South Park primarily focused on journalistic fearmongering in its parodic attacks, but it also mocked the fictional film *The Day after Tomorrow* for engaging in what it portrayed as inappropriate histrionics over climate change. Though that film was more future oriented in its prediction of impending trauma, it along with *South Park*'s parody suggests the way that texts besides journalism and documentary continue and reinforce the traumatic emotional frame after initial news coverage. While a number of shows perform this work to limited extents, one episode of *The Sarah Silverman Program* is particularly instructive. This episode, titled "The Patriot Tact," exaggerates the kind of post-9/11 sitcoms (discussed in chapter 6) in which characters like Homer Simpson pursue racist hunches in order to instruct their audiences how not to relate to racial and religious Others. In addition to mocking television's half-hearted attempts to combat xenophobic fear, the *Sarah Silverman* episode takes aim at memorial art and in so doing instructs audiences in camp approaches to it.

In this episode, the main character, Sarah, rushes to judgment when faced with people who resemble Osama bin Laden—so much so that she attempts to run innocent victims down in the street. After hitting a bin Laden lookalike with her car, friends and victims alike forgive her, justifying the action as necessary in a post-9/11 world. Sarah continues to hit men over and over again, each time finding victims who look less and less like her intended target except for having some kind of beard. After each mistake, more and more people turn against her until Sarah finally promises that she will not attack anyone else, no matter how much he may look like bin Laden. Eventually, of course, she comes across a man implied to be the actual bin Laden. True to her promise, Silverman allows the terrorist leader to escape. In a final speech summing up the rightness of her decision, she states, "I could have caught him and I could have killed him. But I also would have killed the hope of killing him, you know? I think that's what America needs: hope. The hope of murdering someone foreign that we can all hate together, as a nation. As one nation."[30] In regard to this larger narrative arc, Silverman undercuts the sitcom's penchant for simple didacticism. Her racism is so ridiculously exaggerated, it seems less directed at actual post-9/11 xenophobia and more at moderate-left attempts to correct such behavior. Her repeated attacks on those who do not look like bin Laden, culminating in her apparent mercy on the actual terrorist, enters into a reflexive hall of mirrors. This satire of satire suggests the endless negation that, according to Peter Sloterdijk, underlies postmodern cynicism.[31] However, *The Sarah Silverman Program* also engages earnest targets: specifically, remembrances that habitually reinscribe the emotional framing of national trauma.

As those around her recognize Sarah's pattern of attacks, she comes up with another plan. "I'm being persecuted," she explains, "because the people of this town don't remember 9/11. . . . I'm gonna make sure the people of [this town] remember the horrors of 9/11." The result is a play titled *Never Forget: A Tribute to 9/11*. Two men appear on stage as the towers. As the play gets underway, a third actor jumps on stage with arms outstretched, announcing, "I'm an airplane." Overly dramatic piano music punctuates the scene as the plane chases the buildings around the stage. Denoted by his antenna, the North Tower asks, "I'm just a nice building; why are you so mean?" On-screen audience reactions are mixed. Responding to Sarah's pride at "opening [his] eyes to the horrors of 9/11," one character, the ever-serious Jay, responds, "Your play has opened my eyes to the horror of your play." Another patron shushes him, implying her deeper investment in Sarah's memorial theater. Jay's offense is the result of his habitual humorlessness, but the woman who shushes him is clearly too accepting of this overwrought spectacle. The ideal television viewer—the one laughing at this—responds appropriately to cheesy remembrances. Laughing at corny, manipulative art is an act of emotional nonconformity against understanding these moments in history through the negative emotions of trauma. It is a refusal to be re-traumatized.

Sarah's hyperpatriotic attempt at melodrama brims with camp value. Her idiotic effort to make an emotionally touching play serves as a comedy set piece mocking remembrance itself as hopelessly corny. Setting up memorial art, already given to kitsch according to Marita Sturken, as an object for camp enjoyment not only rewrites the affective frame of the initial event but also subtly instructs media consumers in camp attitudes toward sacred history.[32] In her "Notes on Camp," Susan Sontag spends a handful of passages explicitly discussing the relationship between camp and humor in ways that illuminate this scene.

> The whole point of Camp is to dethrone the serious. Camp is playful, anti-serious. More precisely, Camp involves a new, more complex relation to "the serious." One can be serious about the frivolous, frivolous about the serious. . . . One is drawn to Camp

An overwrought memorial play on The Sarah Silverman Program.

> when one realizes that "sincerity" is not enough. Sincerity can be
> simple philistinism, intellectual narrowness. . . . The traditional
> means for going beyond straight seriousness—irony, satire—seem
> feeble today, inadequate to the culturally oversaturated medium
> in which contemporary sensibility is schooled. Camp introduces a
> new standard: artifice as an ideal, theatricality.[33]

This description goes a long way toward describing emotional nonconformity more generally, but Sontag, and indeed camp sensibility more generally, privileges overwrought emotionalism as something worth laughing at. Perhaps more than in other examples, *The Sarah Silverman Program* presents a camp performance for enjoyment. This runs against Sontag's preference for naive "pure camp" as opposed to that which is produced with the intention of serving a camp appreciation. Of course, the fictional character Sarah is naive in her production of this play, but the show as a whole intends it for camp appreciation. However, while this play-within-a-play functions on one level as a camp object, it doubles as a camp reading of the type of overly sincere art it satirizes.

THE POLITICS OF EMOTIONAL NONCONFORMITY

Jonathan Gray argues that reflexive parody teaches media literacy.[34] When comedy critiques television itself, viewers internalize the problems that comedy exaggerates to humorous ends. If *The Sarah Silverman Program* taught camp ridicule as a critical media literacy strategy in response to memorial programming, similar readings can be made for parodies of news and opinion programming like *The Opposition with Jordan Klepper* and less ironic critique of fearmongering journalism like that of *Full Frontal with Samantha Bee*. The political implications of audiences who are more resistant to these kinds of messages are clear within the larger context of this book's discussion of the relationship between disasters and nationalism. Appeals to emotion, memorial coverage, and other aspects of television culture coming under fire in these programs are significant elements to the nationalism that national traumas form and reinforce. To weaken them is to weaken that particular form of nationalism. However, there is more at stake here politically than crude nationalism.

"One could tell the story of the Bush administration," writes Sasha Torres, "as a series of more or less successful efforts to provoke and press into service the unwieldy affective intensities mobilized by 9/11."[35] As Torres points out, emotions and appeals to them by politicians were incredibly important to post-9/11 politics. Although causes are obviously complex, it is difficult to imagine the two wars in the Middle East, loss of civil liberties, reelection of George W. Bush in 2004, and election of Donald Trump in 2016 occurring without the anger, sadness, and fear spawned by those events. Moreover, while Barack Obama branded himself with more positive, "hopeful" emotions, President Trump has even more boldly harnessed emotions of fear and resentment in his rise to power. If comedy's engagement with 9/11 served in part to dampen the emotional intensity of Americans' memories, it also eroded support for these policies and politicians.

However, the comic response to trauma is not necessarily progressive by nature. As noted in the introduction, even before school shootings once again became a major agenda item following the 2012 Sandy Hook Elementary School shooting, *Family Guy* was goofing on those events by way of Columbine in ways that likely tempered viewers' emotional involvement. The show also responded with ambiguous humor to the Trayvon Martin shooting, though it also criticized the racism of the criminal justice system. In response to the many mass shootings that occurred during his tenure as president, Obama began to make it a point to fight against the routinization of gun violence in media and collective culture. "The reporting is routine. My response here at this podium ends up being routine," he told reporters in 2015. "The conversation and the aftermath of it. We've become numb to this."[36] The implication is that the emotional impact of gun violence, whether tied more explicitly to the politics of the gun control or Black Lives Matter movements, requires an emotional engagement for positive change to occur. This argument has become more common even though progress on gun control remains slow, as mass shootings continue in places like Las Vegas, Parkland, Dayton, and El Paso. While there is potential value in performing emotional nonconformity and easing the emotional intensity of national traumas, the political ethics of this comedy vary greatly depending on the political impact of the emotions that result from national trauma.

My analysis in this chapter has mostly discussed emotional nonconformity as a way to trigger critical framework because it negates the audience's connection to the emotions that underlie nationalism. However, national identification is a stubborn and complex thing. Allowing viewers to reengage national traumas from a more comfortable emotional position is unlikely to fully negate the powerful emotions associated with national trauma, but it acts as a way to continue to reengage these privileged national events. And even if mass-mediated comedy erodes the possibility for collective action, it does so to mass audiences, supporting inaction at a collective level. Comedy's impact then remains national.

If emotions are a crucial aspect to the way popular history makes sense of national traumas, then any reengagement with such events that can shift their emotional understanding is significant. Comedy and humor, in their ability to deny negative feelings and replace them with neutral or positive ones, hold the power to leave audiences more rational in their approach to politics, but also less caring. Even so, it does this at a national level and while addressing large numbers of people about ostensibly national events. The next chapter shifts the discussion more squarely to comedy's engagement with the factual understanding of history by examining conspiracy theories as battles over official historical narratives.

CONSPIRACY THEORIES
AND COMEDY   *Chapter 4*

In 2018, Roseanne Barr posted a tweet insinuating that former Obama adviser Valerie Jarrett was a member of the Muslim Brotherhood and comparing her to an ape. The firestorm leading to Barr's firing from her successfully rebooted show focused mainly on the racism of the ape comparison. By contrast, pundits paid little attention to the idea that an Obama adviser was working for the Muslim Brotherhood, a conspiracy theory clearly caught up in post-9/11 Islamophobia. However, in the feeding frenzy of stories that followed this uproar, entertainment journalists pored over Barr's Twitter history, uncovering a number of additional conspiracy theories. Among many others, Barr supported the ideas that both 9/11 and the Boston Marathon bombing were "false flag" operations, as well as the contention that Marjory Stoneman Douglas shooting survivor and gun-control advocate David Hogg gave a Nazi salute at the 2018 March for Our Lives rally.[1] While many earnestly condemned the star, late night comedians had fun mocking her within larger historical and political contexts, with Jordan Klepper, in character as a right-wing conspiracy nut, arguing that ABC only canceled her show because she was a Trump supporter. It could not be because of the racism, he argued, "because Roseanne has been writing racist tweets for forever."[2]

As this story indicates, some comedians have strong sympathies with conspiracy theories, while others use the opportunity of the low cultural standing of conspiracy theorists and theories to mock them. As Roseanne's partisan loyalties and the comic response suggests, these relationships have important political implications. However, 2018 was not the first era in which conspiracy theories have been significant in public discourse, nor is Roseanne the first comic to subscribe to them. Besides terrorist attacks and mass shootings, other national traumas like John F. Kennedy's assassination and Hurricane Katrina are privileged events for conspiracy theorists. Patrick Leman argues that this results from "major event–major cause reasoning."[3] People tend to form conspiracy theories around these events because the alternative "presents us with a rather chaotic and unpredictable relationship

89

between cause and effect. Instability makes most of us uncomfortable; we prefer to imagine we live in a predictable, safe world, so in a strange way, some conspiracy theories offer us accounts of events that allow us to retain a sense of safety and predictability."[4] Because of this mostly fallacious way of understanding national trauma, conspiracy theories form a substantial part of the discourse that surrounds such events. Inasmuch as the popular view understands these as faulty logic promulgated by delusional loners, conspiracy theories are also much-maligned ways of thinking.

Arguing against the tendency to dismiss conspiracy theories without considering their cultural implications, Mark Fenster reads these phenomena as representative of a populist mistrust of power.[5] Fenster does not defend all conspiracy culture as prosocial or factual, but nevertheless points to examples like the separation of governmental powers and antitrust laws as the brainchildren of conspiracy theorists. Political satire frequently also contains the kind of populist libertarianism Fenster sees as common to both the US Constitution and conspiracy theories. However, such celebrations of conspiracy theories as essentially anti-authoritarian ignores their usefulness for both preying upon and stirring up resentment against those in positions of less power. Like many tools of resistance, conspiracy theories can also benefit hegemony when deployed by the powerful.

As *Seinfeld*'s take on Oliver Stone's *JFK* demonstrated in chapter 1, the widely denigrating view of conspiracy theories and theorists makes them a ripe target for ironic satirists. Besides *Seinfeld*, examples abound from one-off conspiracy episodes on shows like *South Park* to long-lived characters and series like Dale Gribble from *King of the Hill*. At the same time, there is a brand of sincere political comedy that reflects Fenster's view of conspiracy theorists' populist mistrust of power, represented by comics like Mort Sahl and Dave Chappelle. These examples demonstrate how comedy acts as a key site for these battles over contested history. While such debates over who gets to define truth are self-evidently important, these are especially noteworthy for national identity due to national traumas' significance to a sense of popular history and national self-understanding.

MORT SAHL: "KYNICAL" CONSPIRACY COMEDY

Similarities exist between conspiracy theorists and a certain type of political comedian. Both mindsets represent a fundamental mistrust of the institutions of power and in so doing fit a contemporary understanding of cynicism. Peter Sloterdijk cautions, however, that true cynicism is pessimistic to the point of apathy and thus has little hope for exposing truth or corruption.[6] Earnest conspiracy theorists invest in a search for truth and instead run closer to the "kynical" viewpoint championed by the philosopher. Despite possible associations between figures like Oliver Stone and a postmodern view of truth as relative, kynics assert a vision of the world governed by singular truth. In a political era governed in part by conspiracy theorists and multiple truths, the ability to define a singular truth is a powerful tool. Sloterdijk uses the ancient Greek Diogenes, a Cynic philosopher prone to laughter at the expense of power, as the basis of kynicism.[7] Jonathan Gray offers a more contemporary example in his reading of *The Simpsons'* politically engaged yet world-weary style.[8] Gray develops these ideas largely in relation to *The Simpsons'* viewing community, but it is easy to see in his study of the show's parodic satire of sitcoms, advertising, and news that the program often concerns media power and its ability to frame and affect domestic, economic, and political issues. While cynical rhetoric carpet-bombs the world in criticism, kynical rhetoric is a laser-guided missile. It is still destructive, but it aims more exclusively at worthy targets.

Mort Sahl is a curious example of a kynical comic turned conspiracy theorist. By 1960, he had established his career to the point that *Time* magazine placed him on the cover, declaring him "the patriarch of a new school of comedians" that included Mike Nichols, Elaine May, Lenny Bruce, and Jonathan Winters.[9] While careful to maintain his image as an iconoclast, Sahl nevertheless went to work writing jokes for the 1960 Kennedy presidential campaign.[10] However, his comedy remained critical of Kennedy both during and after the election, at least until late 1963. This kind of relationship with electoral politics, both engaging so directly with a political campaign and remaining critical of the president he helped elect, reveals Sahl to be both highly and earnestly engaged in politics.[11]

There were signs that Sahl's popularity began to wane due to broad trends resulting from decreased demand for political humor and sharp satire after Kennedy's death.[12] However, most narratives of Sahl's career, including his own autobiography, point to a more important factor in his retreat from the spotlight: his becoming a Kennedy assassination conspiracy theorist.[13] As part of his work on a syndicated television program, Sahl traveled to meet Jim Garrison (the subject of Oliver Stone's *JFK*), who by 1967 claimed to have solved the mystery of Kennedy's shooting.[14] The CIA, by Garrison's account, killed the president because of his efforts to end the Cold War and weaken the agency. Garrison deputized Sahl, who, funded from his own pocket, delved into the investigation. These years proved particularly difficult for the comic. Not only was he spending time and money investigating instead of performing, but his reputation and performances as a paranoiac prevented bookings and disappointed audiences. Of course, by Sahl's probably not entirely false account, those who disagreed with or wanted to silence his opinions on this matter, including powerful members of the entertainment and political world, torpedoed his career. But in any case, the trauma of the assassination germinated into a marked shift in Sahl's career and performances.

When Sahl performed, his routines increasingly focused on the assassination. Audiences grew tired of his repeated performances reading word-for-word from the *Warren Commission Report* and staging sketches quoting government testimony.[15] Holding the comic up as a prototypical post-Kennedy conspiracy theorist while explaining his downfall, John Leonard in 1978 wrote in the *New York Times*,

> He went strange after the assassination of John Kennedy. And in that sense, too, he was a stand-in for the children of the 1950's. It suddenly seemed that we were no longer the pampered children of the Enlightenment, getting better every day. Until that particular assassination, there was a European way of thinking about conspiracies (there has to be a conspiracy, because it would absolve the rest of us of guilt) and an American way (there can't be a conspiracy, because then there's no one to take the rap). Mort Sahl went European all the way into the swamp wevers [*sic*] of the mind of New Orleans Attorney Jim Garrison.
>
> And the talk shows stopped wanting to hear him go on about the grassy knoll, the two autopsies, the washed-out limousine, Lee Harvey Oswald's marksmanship, Jack Ruby's friends. He wasn't funny. He was also, eventually, unemployed, and bitter, as he made clear in his memoir, "Heartland."[16]

Although vindicated to some extent by the eventual public mistrust of the *Warren Commission Report* and more provable conspiracies like Watergate, Mort Sahl remains something of an anomaly in the relationship between political humor and conspiracy theories, at least among white comics.

Sahl's kynical approach to comedy and his commitment to Kennedy conspiracy narratives also set him apart from many of his followers, especially those who approached conspiracy theories from a more ironic perspective. Sahl's dedication to uncovering what he considered the truth betrays a worldview that precludes a relativistic understanding of truth. He rejected that cynical approach and sacrificed his career in the process.

This attitude contrasts that of many of his followers in both comic and political arenas, who found different uses and approaches to conspiracy theories in later decades.

BLACK CONSPIRACY THEORIES AND COMEDY FROM THE MARGINS

Roseanne Barr's ethnic identity helps to explain, if not condone, some of her conspiracy theories in recent years inasmuch as they are tied to real historical persecution suffered by Jews. While Sahl did not explicitly tie his conspiracy theories about Kennedy to suspicions of anti-Semitism, then-recent and longer histories of Jewish persecution may well have been a factor in training Sahl to be suspicious of government power turned toward nefarious ends. Conspiracy theories tend to circulate more readily among minority communities. This is true in part because groups subjected to actual murderous and persecutory conspiracies have good reason to be paranoid. Moreover, conspiracy theories represent efforts to make sense of persecution that those in positions to write authoritative history may not explore. Despite the serious consequences of this way of thinking, the discourses of conspiracy theorists often take a playful tone, allowing theorists to test ideas in the "just kidding" mode of humor. African American comedies and comedians like *The Boondocks* and Dave Chappelle work in this mode, making sense of traumas in relation to black identity using conspiracy theories.

In 1996, journalist Gary Webb published a series of articles alleging that a significant amount of the cocaine fueling the 1980s inner-city crack epidemic were turned into profits for the CIA-backed Contras.[17] Worse yet, he argued that both the CIA and the Reagan administration knew of these developments and not only turned a blind eye to the problem but also shielded domestic crack distributors from prosecution so as to avoid interrupting the flow of money back to the Nicaraguan counterrevolutionaries. While mainstream press sources largely dismissed Webb's journalism, it gained traction within African American communities.[18] Regarding the way media framed black communities' responses to Webb, Fenster believes that critics, of whom there were many, "conceded that the black community may have good historical reasons to be paranoid, of course, but they all rejected the notion that this excused its inability to distinguish fact from conspiratorial fiction."[19] For his part, Jeffrey A. Hall believes that the discursive formation of black communities as full of gullible "conspiracy mongers" demonstrates the way cultural and racial hierarchies determine who gets to construct the truth.[20] While not precisely a national trauma in the senses of suddenness and ubiquitous media coverage, the tale of Webb's work and its reputation among black communities and the mainstream press speaks to the ways in which ideas circulate and compete among and between cultures and subcultures. Nevertheless, even in this case—in which respected leaders like Maxine Waters, the chair of the Congressional Black Caucus, offered support to this narrative—those who construct and adhere to authoritative history more often than not dismiss or belittle believers.[21]

Historians regularly highlight the importance of humor for African American communities dealing with inarguable conspiracies like slavery and Jim Crow. Records on this oral tradition are understandably spotty, but in the postwar period, Dick Gregory stands out as an early comic-turned-conspiracy-theorist comparable in outlook to Sahl. Sympathetic commentaries by those like Mel Watkins and Bambi Haggins characterize this turn as the result of his commitment to black civil rights and later social justice movements.[22] More dismissive critics like Daniel Pipes, however, characterize comics like Gregory as part of a larger problem of conspiracy theories that circulate in black communities dismissed as "the sophistication of the ignorant."[23] Like Sahl, Gregory's success as a comedian diminished after becoming more vocally engaged in such discussions. Unlike Mort Sahl, however, Gregory more actively moved away from comedy of his own volition in order to focus more fully on civil and Indigenous rights. However, somewhat more contemporary black-appeal comedy programs on television manage to more fully marry comedy and conspiracy theories, albeit while displaying some caution in their willingness to stand fully behind such claims.

Comic speech often takes the form of play, meaning that it stands outside the regular rules of discourse.[24] Peter Knight notes the extent to which conspiracy theorists self-ironize their own conspiracy theories, engaging less in sincere belief and more in "as-if" scenarios that waver between the poles of total belief and disbelief.[25] This playful stance is in part a defense against dismissal as an unhinged paranoid but also accounts for much of the practice's pleasure. In this sense, they act in the "just kidding" mode, in which the speaker can make claims without necessarily having to defend or even fully stand behind them. Comedies and comics that take this approach are less earnest than Sahl, though they stop well short of fully rejecting conspiracy theories.

The animated series *The Boondocks* uses this mode, rejecting some conspiracy theories while entertaining others, exploring these issues through a mix of parody, satire, exaggeration, and sincere explication. For example, in an episode titled "The Trial of Robert Kelly," the show engages with theories about the framing of black celebrities, arguing that such ideas act as crutches and tools for delusional fans and opportunistic lawyers.[26] In another episode, conspiracy theories seem more plausible as the main character—Huey, a radical leftist—becomes the target of a government agent. However, it is unclear to both the character and the audience whether his "white shadow" is real or the result of a paranoid delusion.[27]

Regarding conspiracy theories on national trauma, *The Boondocks* supports some reasonable mistrust of official accounts. The pilot episode establishes Huey's character primarily through his plan to scandalize a white, upper-class garden party by grabbing a microphone and saying, "Jesus was black, Ronald Reagan was the devil, and the government is lying about 9/11." The joke is not in Huey's statements but in the contrast between his hope that this would outrage his audience and the reality that Huey merely impressed them with his articulateness. By all indications, Huey believes these statements. Since he is honest to a fault, intelligent, suspicious of poor logic, and the audience's primary surrogate, the program's authorial voice supports these claims.

In another example, Huey introduces an episode by describing aspects of Hurricane Katrina's impact on New Orleans. "On August 29, 2005," he begins, "Hurricane Katrina struck the Gulf Coast of the United States. Several hours later, residents of New Orleans' Lower Ninth Ward reported hearing loud explosions. Then the flood came. In the days and weeks that followed, the nation watched and wondered, how could it have all gone so wrong?"[28] This introduction connotes journalistic language, down to his qualification that the "residents . . . reported hearing loud explosions" as well as the editorial flourish summarizing a common public reaction to the disaster. As Huey speaks, images of the disaster illustrate his narration. First, the animation shows a high-angle shot of flooded streets with residential houses poking above the water. Imitating the ubiquitous helicopter flyover shots of the disaster but lacking other visual hallmarks of coverage like lower-third chyrons, it nevertheless bolsters the narrator's journalistic tone, setting a character of truthful objectivity. The next shot is of a family crawling onto furniture inside a house in order to escape rising water. While not referring to any particular shot or type of shot from news coverage, this speculative scene demonstrates a story that the viewer could imagine having happened but would have escaped news cameras' view. This adds a layer of pathos by illustrating an imagined instance of personal suffering that was likely to have happened even if it does not refer to any specific image or story.

While ambiguous, Huey's mention of explosions puts this sequence in dialogue with conspiracy theories that levees protecting poorer areas of New Orleans were purposefully destroyed in order to take pressure off those protecting wealthier neighborhoods.[29] In addition to the journalistic images, *The Boondocks* offers speculative images of these "reported" events. The portion of this sequence noted in the third and fourth panels in figure 4.1 is ambiguous. This shot occurs during the portion of the narration in which Huey describes residents hearing explosions, implying that the sound prompted their reaction. However, the fourth panel, which shows the levee

The Boondocks *visually quotes hurricane coverage before using animation to more speculatively witness the effects of Hurricane Katrina.*

breaking, immediately follows the shot of the residents reacting to the sound. While Huey's narration only speaks of witnesses that heard explosions, the editing could be read as an eyeline match. An eyeline match implies that the fourth panel is a point-of-view shot, privileging the victims' senses of sight over hearing. While there is a sound effect that could be either an explosion or a levee breaking from other causes, it is relatively quiet and obscured by the ambient sounds of the storm. This distinction proves important, as the voice-over only refers to audio witnesses. It would presumably, following evidential hierarchy, privilege the more trustworthy visual witnesses if this were in fact the moment it means to describe. Additionally, if this means to illustrate a possible vantage point of a witness to any such explosion, the point-of-view shot explains the lack of visual witnesses, in that anyone close enough to see such a violent collapse would not have survived to report it. However, the authority given narrators to interpret visual evidence in news and documentary as well as this character's more specific position of authority over truth and interpretation on *The Boondocks* suggest that this image represents witnesses to the reported explosions. This sort of introduction is a stylistic and narrative anomaly for *The Boondocks*. First, it is a rare instance of humorlessness for this comedy. Additionally, even in episodes dealing with current or historical events, it uses such exposition primarily to set the stage for "what if" scenarios and fictional interactions between the characters, actual people, and historical events.[30] In the rare cases where there is more straight exposition, as when one episode describes singer R. Kelly's legal troubles to set up a joke about television news hyperbole and an elder character misunderstanding the term "golden shower," it serves to fill in viewers who may have missed the relevant story.[31]

For the most part *The Boondocks'* humor expresses an earnest belief in objective truth, even if that truth is not readily available. Other African American comedic talent is more fully committed to discourses that intersect at conspiracy theories' alternative histories and comedy's playful modes. In his 2017 comedy special, *Deep in the Heart of Texas*, Dave Chappelle wonders aloud, "Isn't it weird how there's a disease that just starts in 1980, and it doesn't kill anybody but niggas, fags, and junkies? Isn't that a fucking amazing coincidence that this disease hates everybody that old, white people hate? I think either God is white, or the government hid that shit in disco balls. Only fun people get AIDS."[32] Part of Chappelle's return to comedy after near silence for fifteen years, this bit hearkens back to a longer tendency in his career that included his role as "Conspiracy Brother" in 2002's *Undercover Brother* and work on *Chappelle's Show*.[33]

In a 2003 sketch from *Chappelle's Show*, the comic uses well-known conspiracy theories from black communities in a sketch. He explains,

> We've been getting a little flak in the press. I don't know if you
> guys have seen some things that were written calling us controver-
> sial, which I was surprised by. That's the thing about being on TV,
> you just never can say what you want to say, man. Because if I said
> everything I thought it would just freak America out. You wouldn't

want to hear a young black dude saying half the things I be think-ing. The only way people would listen to the stuff I think is if a pretty white girl sang my thoughts. And I actually happen to have a pretty white girl here![34]

For the remainder of the sketch, Chappelle remains mostly silent, instead communicating through messages written on note cards for the pretty white girl to sing in her gentle espressivo.

Although it acts as a commentary on who in society gets to speak what, the humor of this bit arises primarily from two sources: the perceived contrast of a pretty white girl singing Chappelle's contentious opinions and the outrageousness of those opinions. The humor serves as an alibi for Chappelle to express non-PC or otherwise unacceptable homophobic and sexual speech ("Gay sex is gross. I'm sorry, I just find it to be gross. Unless of course it's lesbians.") and racism ("All Chinese people look alike."). But the alibi of the humor also serves as a vehicle to express reserved belief in certain conspiracy theories through the woman's singing. "Crack was invented and distributed to intentionally destroy the black community. AIDS was too. The police never looked for Tupac and Biggie's murderers. Fuck the police." Throughout the bit, Chappelle smiles mischievously, blunting the impact and indicating that he is not entirely serious about these statements. These factors cast some doubt on the seriousness of the earlier statements as well as some of the later, more blatantly offensive ones, marking the comic's belief in the veracity of his own claims as ambiguous.

Comparing *The Boondocks* to Dave Chappelle's work reveals the ten-sion between comedy's truth-telling and playful functions. While none of the texts are as willing to display the dedicated sincerity of belief that Mort Sahl or Dick Gregory did at times, *The Boondocks* invests more in the possibility of truth in its claims, whereas Chappelle is more agnostic. Chappelle's rhetoric is not a full-throated endorsement of the US govern-ment's role in either the crack or the AIDS epidemics. It is polysemically open, allowing those attuned to ironic approaches to these topics to read into it what they will.

RIGHT-WING CONSPIRACY THEORIES AND THE COMEDIC RESPONSE

While useful for subaltern groups in particular, tools of resistance includ-ing conspiracy theorizing are often equally available to groups of higher or more ambiguous status. The explosion of conservative talk radio in the

1980s and the growth of the internet in the 1990s created fertile ground for the contemporary popularity of right-wing conspiracy theories. While freer to test the limits of free speech than his FCC-regulated counterparts on terrestrial radio, Alex Jones is a direct outgrowth of Rush Limbaugh's format. While it may not have been the only factor, the right-wing grievance culture represented by these figures both benefits and informs Donald Trump. Obviously, the likes of Trump and Limbaugh are in positions of power, but the power relationships between adherents to such theories are not as simplistic as the leaders' status might suggest. This way of viewing the world obviously draws support from a more diverse socioeconomic range, although racial diversity among subscribers is likely limited. That is to say, while conservative conspiracy theories likely appeal primarily to whites, their appeal cuts across class lines to members of the working class. The same could of course be said for the relationship between successful black comedians and working-class adherents to such theories, except that Donald Trump is significantly more powerful than the likes of Dave Chappelle. Moreover, the reality of support for conservative conspiracy theorists complicates an overly simplistic view of how the politics represented in these theories articulate race, class, and power. Finally, examples of recent conservative conspiracy theorists demonstrate the extent to which they act as self-conscious entertainers, even approaching the level of fictional personas.

Although less obviously, Limbaugh and Jones express conspiracy theories using techniques similar to the playful, "what if" register used by Chappelle. Rush Limbaugh's 1990s television show functioned as a comedy program. Taped in front of a live studio audience, Limbaugh performed crowd work, introduced comedy sketches, and mocked politicians to audible laughter from his audience. Then as now, while Limbaugh earnestly promoted Clinton-related conspiracy theories, he peppered humor into this rhetoric. In 1995, his radio show played a parody song called "Whitewater Blues" in which a Bill Clinton impersonator admitted to the misdeeds that Limbaugh continued to promote even as late as 2019.[35] More recently, Alex Jones's lawyer characterized his client as "a performance artist," in opposition to Jones's ex-wife's claim that his on-air statements prove that the host is an unfit parent.[36] While Limbaugh's brand of political thought might have shown a face of seemingly good-natured humor to the world, at least on television, the dangerous effects of the far-right conspiracy mongering would show its face later in the 1990s after the Oklahoma City bombing and the subsequent coverage of militias. So even if some of these ideas originated from a more playful mode of speech, overly sincere audience members appeared to take their belief too far. As such, they were ripe for mockery in other texts.

King of the Hill emerged from this milieu in 1997 with a character named Dale Gribble, who is a mostly right-wing anti-government white conspiracy theorist. While Dale never goes as far as trying to blow up a federal building, his distrust of the federal government and frequent dalliances into conspiracy theories clearly place him in dialogue with the militias and domestic terrorists that came to prominence over the course of the 1990s. Of course, this being a relatively light comedy, Dale is always too cowardly or incompetent to cause significant harm. Nevertheless, he is one of the most absurdly exaggerated conspiracy theorists on television. At the same time, because of his relatively realist characterization and thirteen seasons in which to develop, Dale is complex for the sitcom genre. While full of contradictions—at once paranoid and naive, selfish and devoted—this character most often plays the sophisticated ignoramus decried by Pipes. A 2005 episode of *King of the Hill* puts Dale in conversation with history vis-á-vis his paranoia and conspiracy theories.[37] In a twist on his character, Dale goes from his usual paranoid suspicion of government power to a pro-government position that turns his paranoia against fellow citizens. Rather than minimizing character flaws related to his paranoia, then, this episode especially highlights their purpose within the show and importance in relation to larger political issues.

In this episode, Dale attempts to put his son to bed by reading the *Warren Commission Report*, which he calls "the greatest fairy tale ever told." Revealing a measure of ignorance in response to his son's question, Dale admits that the book's appendix "has been keeping the kitchen table from wobbling all these years." Upon retrieving it, he discovers that some of his details had been inaccurate, causing Dale to question his understanding of the Kennedy assassination. From here, this becomes a comedy of parodic inversion as Dale's paranoid worldview crumbles in favor of a more ortho-dox understanding of history. Dale's shock that "the government could be right" manifests in poor self-care and expressionist flourishes like angled framing and rapid camera movement showing his unsettled inner perspec-tive.[38] Dale travels to Dallas in order to reestablish his conspiratorial view of history but is distressed to find further evidence supporting the *Warren Commission Report*. After hearing the obviously problematic ideas of local pamphleteers, Dale has a complete breakdown. At his emotional nadir, a police officer approaches the former conspiracy theorist. A swell of music along with a close-up from Dale's point of view on the officer's American flag pin signal a final metamorphosis from paranoiac to patriot.

Dale's transformation is not from the fringe to a more moderate position, however. The comedy of inversion takes a new angle as Dale appears back in his home neighborhood wearing a ludicrously patriotic costume that includes an Uncle Sam top hat and a T-shirt that reads, "America: Love It or Leave It." "If the government was right about Kennedy," Dale reasons, "they must be right about everything." In a B-story, masculine Hank's driver's license lists him as female. This development and his unsuccessful attempts to navigate the bureaucracy that could solve his problem both mortify and frustrate Hank. His troubles come into conflict with Dale's newfound belief in government infallibility as, when forced to take sides, Dale uses his binarist logic to figure that Hank must be a woman. "You tell me what's crazier," he demands, "that the government's free cheese contains surveillance devices to monitor America's underclass, as I once believed, or that you're a woman, as I now believe." As this conflict builds, Dale increasingly confuses Hank's frustration for dangerous anti-Americanism, causing the new patriot to contact the Department of Homeland Security. With this action, and his expectation that he could speak with Secretary Tom Ridge, Dale makes explicit his complicity with cultural and governmental post-9/11 paranoia, a position that serves hegemonic interests. While his allegiances may have shifted, his wrongheaded paranoia remains. Luckily, when an FBI agent arrives to investigate Hank, he explains that while it is illegal for him to profile anyone, Hank does not fit the profile. This dig at the underlying racism of post-9/11 security measures and the pretense toward hiding said racism is about as politically satirical as *King of the Hill* ever got.

Following episodic sitcom conventions, Dale eventually comes to his senses and accepts Hank's gender, apparently toppling his newfound trust in the government in time for the following week's episode. Nevertheless, the point connecting his anti-government conspiracy paranoia to his pro-government security paranoia remains. Dale's conspiracy theories, whether directed at the government or at Hank, are equally laughable. While his belief in Cold War conspiracy theories like Area 51 gets him into trouble in other episodes, this one paints his faith in the JFK assassination conspiracy as relatively harmless. By contrast, his conversion to post-9/11 hyperpatriotism places his best friend in danger. One aspect of this episode's message is to make equivalent the obvious lunacy of Dale's usual paranoia and the seemingly more commonplace, though usually more understated, paranoia over post-9/11 threats. However, *King of the Hill* takes this argument a step further as it suggests that paranoia in fear of the government is healthier than that which is allied with it.

Poor self-care and cinematic flourishes show Dale detaching from his worldview on King of the Hill.

King of the Hill mobilizes the paranoid styles of culture and moving images in order to attack the conspiracy theory mindset itself. Whether as an imagined victim or more active ally of the United States government, Dale's willingness to engage in Cold War–era or post-9/11 paranoia is idiotic. In the more patriotic iteration of his psychosis, Dale becomes a too-willing participant in post-9/11 regimes of official power. Thus, despite a line of thought most notably argued by John Fiske that beliefs in conspiracy theories are naturally resistant methods of understanding history, *King of the Hill* argues that this mindset can be turned in favor of hegemonic power structures.[39]

While *King of the Hill* demonstrates the danger of excessive paranoia toward either the government or its apparent enemies, the *South Park* episode titled "The Mystery of the Urinal Deuce" more directly explores the effects of such narratives as myths of governmental power that foster a sense of political impotence, questioning the Fiskian understanding of conspiracy theories.[40] However, this episode makes its point in an interestingly roundabout way: by imagining the source of paranoid conspiracy theories as a government conspiracy in itself. On the one hand, this is a parodic play on the kind of abstruse narrative and logical style of conspiracy tales. On the other hand, in making the apparent misinformation of 9/11 conspiracy theories a conscious method of control, it allows characters to explain how it acts as a method of discipline in a Foucauldian sense.[41]

South Park's narrative form in this episode owes a debt to fictional conspiracy mysteries that revel in the paranoid style as plot developments uncover increasingly surprising levels of power involved. As the school counselor labors to discover who defecated in a school urinal, Cartman suggests that it might be "a conspiracy, like 9/11." Cartman's classmate and primary target of ire, Kyle, questions his logic, prompting Cartman to make the populist claim that since a quarter of Americans believe in an alternate version of 9/11, conspiracy theories must have some validity. After performing exhaustive research, Cartman presents it to his elementary school class.

> For show and tell today I have brought my shocking PowerPoint report on the truth behind the 9/11 attacks. We are told to believe that the fire from the jet fuel melted the steel framing of the towers, which led to their collapse. But did you know that jet fuel doesn't burn at high enough temperature to melt steel? We were told the Pentagon was hit by a hijacked plane as well, but now look at this photo of the Pentagon. The hole is not nearly big enough and if a plane hit it, where is the rest of the plane? So now the inevitable question: if terrorists didn't cause 9/11, who did? Remember that there are in fact two towers. Two minus one is one. One, one: eleven.

Cartman's argument shifts from what seem to be legitimate concerns over the official 9/11 narrative to nonsensical numerology, leading him to accuse Kyle of masterminding the attacks. Cartman caps this increasingly absurd

Cartman "proves" Kyle's guilt on South Park.

argument by exhibiting his most damning evidence: an image of smoke from the towers, falsely and amateurishly "computer enhanced" to prove Kyle's guilt. Directly satirical of the conspiracy mindset, Cartman's attack on Kyle, the show's most prominent Jewish character, also critically references the anti-Semitism common to many conspiracy theories, especially those related to 9/11.

Under increased scrutiny from his schoolmates and the CIA, Kyle enlists his friend Stan's help in clearing his name. Seeking out the help of a 9/11 "truther," Stan and Kyle discover a conspiracy theorist whose disheveled hair and living space offer insight into the disordered mind behind his blemished face. The truther explains that 9/11 was a gambit in the US government's "false flag" policy, which manufactured national trauma in order to justify foreign wars. Kyle's skepticism turns to alarm as the truther hands him anthrax samples just as a SWAT team breaks down the door to arrest the trio. Taken to the White House, they encounter a parodic George W. Bush far removed from the bumbling idiot portrayed in most comedy shows of the period. The president explains, "We know everything. We control everything. We've all worked very hard to keep our involvement in 9/11 a secret, but you just had to keep digging." After executing the truther, Bush explains that the conspiracy was indeed about justifying the wars in the Middle East for the sake of controlling the world's supply of oil. In a nod to Dick Cheney's infamous hunting accident, the vice president attempts to shoot the boys but instead hits a fire alarm, allowing Stan and Kyle to escape. Making a bus transfer in Chicago, Kyle questions the ease with which they escaped the White House. Then they spot the truther, alive. In chasing him down, they encounter an older man who knows the actual truth. "All the 9/11 conspiracy websites are run by the government," he explains. "The 9/11 conspiracy is a government conspiracy. . . . For a government to have power, they must appear to have complete control. What better way to make people fear them than to convince them they are capable of the most elaborate plan on earth?" Bush and company appear and mount a meager defense before quickly giving up. Asked why they do not simply tell people the truth, Bush responds, "We do that, too, and most people believe the truth, but one fourth of the population is retarded." Obviously harsh, in addition to being politically incorrect, in its use of the word "retarded" to describe conspiracy theorists, *South Park* highlights its commitment to orthodox historical narratives. Cleverly literalizing a pop-Foucauldian model of power, Bush describes conspiracy theories here as a power-laden discourse of false helplessness. Obviously *South Park* does not aim to convince anyone that the government is actually planting these stories, but the point about such narratives of power acting as a form of social control remains.

In this way, while critical of the mindset they represent, *South Park* allies with the likes of Mort Sahl, Dick Gregory, and *The Boondocks* in its support for the concept of objective truth. Comedies and comedians like *King of the Hill* and Dave Chappelle appear comparatively agnostic and playful with such issues. In these cases, comedy's engagement with conspiracy theories responds to crises over the status of truth in relation to national traumas. More recently, the 2016 election, Trumpian rhetoric labeling the legitimate press as fake news, and Trump associates like Kellyanne Conway and Rudy Giuliani floating ideas like "alternative facts" all contribute to the sense that American culture is in the midst of a crisis over the status of truth. In response, left-leaning political comedians reassert the concept of objective truth, often using ironic speech.[42]

South Park and *King of the Hill* argue that conspiracy theorizing was not only a tool of counterhegemony or the left. Although Oliver Stone's *JFK*, among some other popular texts, aligned conspiracy theorists with the left or perhaps outside of the traditional political spectrum, there is a strain of conservative politics in conspiracy theory.[43] As in the early 1990s, right-wing media have again brought conservative conspiracy theorists like Tomi Lahren and Alex Jones to more widespread prominence. For these hosts, who are major power players in some right-wing circles, conspiracy theorizing composes a significant amount of their material if not the bulk of their airtime. Even more notably, the election of Donald Trump placed a vocal conspiracy theorist in the White House.[44]

Efforts to delegitimize this recent iteration of conservative conspiracy theorizing through comedy have gone on for a few years. Both Jon Stewart's and Trevor Noah's *Daily Show* have taken shots at such figures. *The Colbert Report* often made use of the tortured logic of conspiracy theories, and *The Late Show with Stephen Colbert* similarly parodies Alex Jones. Borrowing the Colbert model of spinning off a *Daily Show* correspondent's persona to mock right-wing media personalities, *The Opposition with Jordan Klepper* made the culture of right-wing conspiracy theories its primary satirical and parodic target. Though only lasting a year, it nevertheless represented the most concentrated source of this type of comedy, which has become common across the politically satirical television market. Most obviously an attack on Alex Jones and *Infowars*, a central joke of the show's premise is that Klepper considers himself a member of "the opposition" even though his conspiracy-minded approach to the world seems to support those in power.

In an interview with *Deadline Hollywood*, Klepper explained that the show originated from a piece he did on *The Daily Show* interviewing Trump supporters who were getting their news from "far-right fringe sources":

> So as we were building the show, we wanted to satirize that point of view and this sort of fake news world, the world of Steve Bannon, the world of Alex Jones. We were surpassed by the speed with which the world of conspiracy and paranoia caught up with the real world; we thought it would maybe take a few years to get here. Donald Trump was someone who was a birther and stoking the flame of conspiracy. Right now we are in the middle of Spygate and an attempt to delegitimize news altogether, and you see Sean Hannity now turning practically into state-run media.[45]

While conspiracy-mindedness is a theme in every episode of *The Opposition*, a 2017 episode covering the US government's release of additional documents related to the Kennedy assassination illustrates this theme especially well.[46] Although it aired on October 23, Klepper introduces the show by wishing his viewers a Merry Christmas while wearing holiday-themed clothes and standing next to a video screen showing a burning fireplace. A video montage crosscuts between iconic images from Christmas movies like *It's a Wonderful Life* and news and opinion pieces explaining that the government is unsealing Kennedy documents. One reporter explains, "For the conspiracy theorist, this final trove of documents is Christmas Day." Donning a tinfoil Santa hat, Klepper describes how in the wake of Oliver Stone's *JFK*, Congress set a deadline after which the last of the Kennedy documents would be released unless stopped by the president. This gives Klepper the opening for a zinger: "If Donald Trump wants to get these documents out into the public, what he has to do is nothing. It's brilliant. Getting nothing done is his strong suit." Klepper's joy turns to concern as he interviews the fictional host of *The Alpha Free-Thinking Conspiracy Hour*, who warns him that "the whole point of the JFK assassination plot is that we know what they are not telling us. So if they tell us, what do we know? . . . If this thing goes down, so goes crop circles; so goes chemtrails; and dare I say so goes Benghazi." While situating this particular discussion around the JFK assassination, Klepper manages a dig at more contemporary, right-wing conspiracy theories like Benghazi, tying it to more clearly outlandish ideas like crop circles and chemtrails. Though he does not explicitly call out Trump's conspiracy theories in this sketch, he manages a dig at the president's effectiveness. Moreover, this is part of a larger attack on the right-wing conspiracy theories that have served Trump in his political career.

In the era of Trump, when a conspiracy theorist is the most powerful person in the world, the comic trope of mocking conspiracy theorists as unhinged lunatics has become more significant. As *The Opposition* made clear, the language of postwar conspiracy theorizing since the first Kennedy assassination is available for humorous interrogation of national trauma and its fallout. However, it has also become one of many satirical tools with which to respond to the politics of the Trump era. Klepper's is, of course, not the only comic approach to Trump, whose political career owes a debt to trauma-related conspiracy theories. In chapter 7, I delve deeper into the phenomenon of comedy in the Trump era to consider the ways in which comedy has become increasingly significant in defining some events as traumas. The next chapters, however, continue examining the role of comedy in negotiating the relationship between ethnic minorities and American identity in the wake of national traumas.

On April 29, 1992, Los Angeles erupted in an outburst of pent-up anger that would cost dozens of lives and upward of one billion dollars in damage.[1] Although many factors contributed to these events, the uprising was ostensibly in response to the light punishment doled out to four police officers whose savage beating of unarmed motorist Rodney King had been caught on videotape and played ad nauseam on television to Angelenos, Americans, and others across the world. By the September following the riots, African American television shows had responded across a range of comedy subgenres. Stand-up showcases like *Def Comedy Jam* proved a significant venue for monologues on the riots, while more narrative forms like *The Fresh Prince of Bel-Air*, a sitcom, demonstrated a more dialogic approach. Programs coded with working-class cultural signifiers, like *In Living Color*, existed alongside more middle-class fare like *A Different World*. While far from a complete view of these issues or opinions on them, these and other programs proved key in "instruct[ing] audiences about citizenship, politics, the law, and social interaction from the perspectives of minority communities," features that Rebecca Krefting identifies as critical to the significance of comedy.[2]

Despite differences in form and style, however, a number of themes ran throughout the episodes that touched on the riots. Issues of racial inequality and civil rights expectedly dominated, along with discussions of police and black-on-black violence. As with national traumas more generally, these shows also focused on matters of community and inclusivity. Unlike in some other examples, however, the riots and the larger problems they represented appeared to belong to some, not all, Americans. Black-cast comedy programs repeatedly addressed these issues by playing symbolic gatekeeper, articulating who could and should lay claim to the grievances represented by the riots and instructing those who were justified on how to respond. As a comic ritual, then, comedy proved significant in negotiating the relationship of an aggrieved subnational community to the nation as a whole.

The riots themselves began a few hours after the verdict, and while the worst of it occurred in the predominantly black South Central part of the city, disorder spread wide across Los Angeles's urban sprawl and beyond to include parts of the San Fernando Valley and even San Francisco. Amid the growing unrest, striking media images and sounds complemented footage of the Rodney King beating. Inverting the scenario of white police attacking black motorist King, a group of young black men pulled white truck driver Reginald Denny from his vehicle, beating him in full view of a news helicopter. Representative of disharmony between minority groups, Korean American shop owners defended their property with firearms. Two days after the verdict, Rodney King pleaded to cameras, "Can we all get along?" These iconic moments, wrought with emotional impact, echoed through the culture, including in parody by shows like *In Living Color*. As those examples indicate, television took an active role in trying to prevent further disorder. News not only covered events but interviewed celebrities, like Arsenio Hall and Edward James Olmos, who implored rioters to stay home. KNBC Los Angeles also aired the finale of *The Cosby Show* with the express purpose of getting people off the streets. (It is unclear how many rioters were swayed.)[3] After days of disorder, the riots ended, but television's engagement did not. Television eventually moved into a retrospective period that reengaged the riots from a broader range of programming including documentary, drama, and comedy.

Television was in a unique position to respond to the Rodney King riots as compared to similar past events like the 1965 Watts riots. While police abuses and civil unrest were not new in the early 1990s, television had undergone a change. Since the 1960s, the industry had invested in shows featuring African American talent. The success of programs like *Good Times* and *The Cosby Show* with white audiences certainly played a role in this shift, but Herman Gray points to the more significant factor of audience fragmentation.[4] Networks saw higher-income white audiences invest in cable and VCRs, while black audiences remained more beholden to over-the-air content, making African Americans a key demographic for networks by the early 1990s. Rather than developing black-coded shows across a range of genres, representational progress occurred primarily in comedies like *Def Comedy Jam*, *The Fresh Prince of Bel-Air*, *A Different World*, and *In Living Color*. More than any time before or since, black creative talent on television was in a position to address both African American and wider audiences about the crisis of black citizenship represented by the King beating and ensuing civil unrest. This work was in comedy, which necessarily affected the way television framed and dealt with these issues.

In her study of black television in the 1990s, Kristal Brent Zook discusses the ways these shows represented intraracial difference, "present[ing] the possibility that racial authenticity could be negotiated rather than assumed."[5] Zook identifies these narrative concerns as a result of *The Cosby Show*'s uncoupling of blackness and poverty along with the diversity of representation that was newly possible with the increasing numbers of black characters on television. However, because of their role in representing blackness to American audiences of all races, these shows proved especially important in negotiating the relationship between the riots and African Americans in the cultural forum of television.[6] Bambi Haggins notes in her book on black stand-up comics that although the humor represented in her study arises from African American experience and speaks in particular ways to black audiences, public performance makes it available to a broader range of audiences.[7] Taking my cue from her study of performance, this chapter necessarily, if largely implicitly, considers not only the way these shows appear to address a black audience but how they function in the "crossover" environment in which these shows operated. This is in part a necessary admittance of my perspective as a white scholar, but also a consideration of how—to elaborate on the concerns of J. Fred McDonald, Beretta Smith-Shomade, and others—even in this era of increased black representation on television, black-cast television necessarily operated inside of a national discourse that assumes a white perspective.[8] Although this chapter is not especially concerned with authorship, it bears noting that the shows under consideration represented varying levels of African American control. *A Different World* and *Def Comedy Jam* consistently featured black producers, while black talent struggled with white producers and executives for representational control behind the scenes of *The Fresh Prince of Bel-Air* and *In Living Color*.[9]

Instead of focusing on industrial histories of representational control, this chapter examines the way television articulated a particular subnational group in terms of a televisual national community, as described in the introduction. In service of these formations, African American comedies of this period frequently articulated concepts of racial authenticity in relation to the riots. As scholars including E. Patrick Johnson, Stuart Hall, and others note, "authentic blackness" is a social construct and therefore both arbitrary and slippery.[10] Zook details how comedies like *Fresh Prince* demonstrate authenticity's performative nature when black yuppie Carlton "successfully mimics, performs, and constructs 'blackness.'"[11] In glossing over the wider diversity among African Americans, argue Stuart Hall and Herman Gray, popular culture of this period presented black legitimacy as synonymous with working-class black identity, especially as articulated through images of black criminality.[12] For the most part, the shows in this chapter acknowledge the assumption that working-class markers signal authentic black identity. Understanding the riots as expressions of poor African Americans thus easily fits them into established discourses of authenticity. In response, some comedies reinforced this articulation of race, class, and the riots. More often than not, however, they negotiated the role of race and/or class in relation to concepts of credibility and the riots by alternatively accepting and troubling aspects of these constructs. By negotiating these events in terms of authenticity and belonging, black-coded comedy programs repeatedly used their platforms to discuss who could lay symbolic claim to the grievances that sparked the riots and what their responsibilities should be in the wake of this national trauma.

DEF COMEDY JAM AND RACIAL GATEKEEPING

In the early 1990s, *Def Comedy Jam* was probably the best-known outlet for edgy black humor.[13] Compared to the relatively blunted comedy available on broadcast and basic cable networks, HBO's showcase gave comics the opportunity to work bluer than other outlets. HBO's subscription model and regularly large viewing audiences meant it likely drew a "crossover" audience that included black and other viewers.[14] Nevertheless, the stand-up comics, branding, rhetoric, and on-screen audience, as well as a host of other factors, code this show as authentically black. Racial difference is a common theme in stand-up comedy and on *Def Comedy Jam* in particular. The topic took on heightened resonance when placed in the context of the Rodney King beating and the Los Angeles uprising. A number of comics discussed this topic from the perspective of who did and did not get to participate in the riots. For instance, Angela Means joked that her boyfriend dumped her because she was light-skinned and he was afraid to be seen with her during the riots.[15] As the most frequent host of the show, however, Martin Lawrence acted as the most important comic voice on *Def Comedy Jam*. When he spoke on these issues, his was an authoritative voice. Drawing some seemingly good-natured distinctions between races, the routine in which Lawrence discusses the riots at greatest length mainly jokes about how white people grew scared of him following the uprising.[16] He specifically notes a lone white man in his otherwise all-black audience, greeting him with a mock-friendly tone before complimenting the white man for his bravery. As the comic points out, the riots redrew racial difference in sharper contrast. This gesture toward "Mr. White Man," as

Lawrence addresses the audience member, is an acknowledgement of the kind of gatekeeping that goes on in and around African American culture even as it welcomes the apparent outsider into the space of black comedy.

Martin Lawrence was not so welcoming when it came to participation in the riots, however. This routine criticizes those who he believed lacked a legitimate cause to participate in the uprising.

> We are all gonna rise as a motherfucking people, aren't we? [Applause] We will rise! Because you know as well, they made it seem like black people was doing all that looting and stealing and shit. I'm not gonna lie, I got me some shit. No, no, but it wasn't black people who was doing all that shit. It was the Mexicans. They just didn't show that. And the Mexicans didn't even know what the cause was about. They just saw the opportunity to get some free shit. Seriously, a Mexican came up to me, [in an exaggerated accent] "Yo, my friend. This is fucked up. This should never fucking happen. The way they beat Rodney Dangerfield was fucked up. This is fucked up."

While he performs with a smile on his face, Lawrence's routine is somewhat venomous. Recreating but redirecting a common critique of black looters, the criticism of Los Angeles's Mexican American population, complete with an exaggerated accent, argues that certain opportunistic looters lacked legitimate anger over the King verdict. These people, he argues, simply saw an opportunity for material gain. News and entertainment programming repeated these critiques, typically focusing on black looters, but the comic here twists that logic away from a criticism of African Americans to instead condemn any looter who is not black. Lawrence's routine was not the only comedy text to explore issues beyond a simplistic white-black binary, though discussions of Asian or Latinx American conflicts and roles were typically footnotes to a conflict primarily characterized by black anger toward white society. John Caldwell supports Lawrence's complaint, noting how television news largely ignored the many white and Latinx looters.[17] Lawrence's monologue is exceptional not only because it paid roughly equal attention to both Latinxs and whites, but also because it acted as a televisual corrective by presenting looters as more racially diverse than did television news. At the same time, it participated in the gatekeeping by reserving the moral right to loot for African Americans like Lawrence.

Other comedies explored below argued for racial alliances built around class. Lawrence argues the opposite. Though the Latinx Americans he mocks are presumably members of similar socioeconomic strata, he maintains that their looting and rioting are illegitimate. Lawrence, on the other hand, by his very presence on stage, offers evidence to suggest that he had at least a moderate level of economic means. Nonetheless, he admits to looting. When Lawrence draws up the rules of symbolic and associated victimhood as well as the rights of individuals to make up for injustices, race trumps class. At the same time, *Def Comedy Jam*'s coding as working-class culture along with the assumption that Lawrence has at least a middle-class income level suggest an openness to this form of blackness. This and his one-way conversation with Mr. White Man shows Lawrence enacting both sides of the integrationist-separatist dialectic that Johnson identifies as critical to arguments over black authenticity.[18] However, the racial gatekeeping on display distinguishes more sharply between minority ethnicities regarding who has the right to participate, actually or symbolically, in expressing grievance against a racist society.

While primarily antagonistic, Lawrence's performance argues for in-group solidarity and uplift as he predicts their "rise as a motherfucking people." This relates to his gatekeeping efforts since othering necessarily reinforces group cohesion. In a moment where distinctions between black and white were perhaps too obvious to merit much attention, Lawrence sought another target. Lawrence positions himself as a member of the underprivileged class due to his presence on *Def Comedy Jam*, performative style, use of blue language, overall persona, and claim to have participated in looting. Nonetheless, he signals a sense of uplift ideology more closely associated with the black middle class. Unlike traditional ideologies of uplift, however, whose methods hinged on the success of middle-class African Americans leading the way for the rest, Lawrence's hopes relied on violent demonstrations.[19]

Obviously, there is a clear distinction between the more "authentic," Chitlin' Circuit–influenced *Def Comedy Jam* and the middle-class sitcoms of the early 1990s. Whereas *Def Comedy Jam*'s performers had more free- dom to express a set of views that might well have made middle-class and white audiences nervous in the early 1990s racial climate, sitcoms like *The Fresh Prince of Bel-Air* and *A Different World* either ignored the discourse of anger or put it into dialogue with more moderate, and more hegemonic, voices. Of course, these differences are in part attributable to industry structure and regulation—*Def Comedy Jam* would never have played in network prime time.

As far as programs go, *Def Comedy Jam* was unique among early-'90s comedy in its bold expressions of anger and relatively unfettered speech, even when compared to seemingly similar programs like BET's *ComicView* and Comedy Central's *Comic Justice*. More generally, stand-up comedy's comparatively monologic rhetorical style contrasted the more dialogic forms that characterized the narratives, conflicts, and styles of sitcoms and sketch comedies.[20] *Def Comedy Jam* represented the work of many different creative artists in that four different comics performed their own material on every episode. Yet, the branded images associated with Def Jam Records and HBO as well as the milieu of style, politics, and performances of authenticity pressed those who dealt with these issues into a relatively narrow position from which they could explore the King beating and riots. This is not to argue that such expressions were dishonest or overly calculated, only to point out the economic and social factors that help shape mass-mediated expressions of black culture. Those same economic and social factors allowed television in the early 1990s to engage this particular crisis from the perspective of black-coded comedy. While such factors also affect all of the examples below, they offer different modes of engagement again shaped by the expectations of genre and form. In reaching different audiences with different addresses, each had a role to play in defining different groups' symbolic connections to the riots.

THE FRESH PRINCE OF BEL-AIR AND CRISES OF AUTHENTICITY

The Fresh Prince of Bel-Air was a fish-out-of-water sitcom that asked what would happen if J. J. Walker of *Good Times* moved in with the Huxtable family. Streetwise black teenager Will leaves Philadelphia to join his Aunt Vivian and Uncle Phil, along with their three children and butler, in wealthy Bel-Air, California. The conflict between Will's street-smart, working-class upbringing and his new family and surroundings provide much of the show's narrative and humorous content. Kristal Brent Zook notes how *Fresh Prince*'s male characters "engaged in ongoing struggles to redefine black authenticity."[21] In a typical episode of *Fresh Prince*, Will served as a symbol of working-class blackness—a role made all the more obvious in comparison to the square and at times insufficiently black family members. However, the riots suspended the show's typical formula, initiating or serving as thematic background for crises of black identity for Will and his Uncle Phil. South Central, its residents, and even the anger demonstrated by the riots are so markedly and authentically black that even homeboy Will seems like a poseur by comparison. In resolving these conflicts, "Will Gets Committed" takes a didactic role in demonstrating how African Americans of aspirational classes should relate to the issues raised by the riots and thereby earn their symbolic association.[22]

Somewhat like Martin Lawrence, who implicitly argued for intraracial inclusion across class positions, *Fresh Prince* argues, albeit more explicitly, that African Americans of all classes could join in the sense of group identity crystallized by Rodney King and the riots. However, *Fresh Prince* suggests that this is an earned right rather than a given. Beretta Smith-Shomade views Will in this series as the symbol of authentic blackness against which to measure other family members.[23] In this episode, however, a family visit to a predominantly black neighborhood to help clean up after the riots places Will's blackness under suspicion. Faced with the significance of the riots and seemingly more authentic African Americans, Will's class position appears relatively more upper class. Yet the episode rehabilitates his position in relation to the more convincingly authentic working-class blackness through the creation of interclass alliances.

This episode is in keeping with E. Patrick Johnson's assertion that "often, it is during times of crisis (social, cultural, or political) when the authenticity of older versions of blackness is called into question. These crises set the stage for 'acting out' identity politics, occasions when those excluded from the parameters of blackness invent their own."[24] His book notes a complex dynamic of understanding blackness in which, although notions of legitimacy typically function to delimit and exclude, performances of blackness also create spaces for inclusion, if only implicitly. Indeed, discourses of exclusion cannot help but reinforce a sense of in-group cohesion. As Andy Medhurst points out in his study of English comedy, mocking those who do not fit with a group's sense of self-identity reinforces that group's sense of itself and creates a ritualized sense of cohesion.[25] While this episode does some work in this area, it more explicitly demonstrates how those with liminal inclusion in the in-group identity, by sharing some but not all of the seeming characteristics of authenticity, might earn their way more fully into the group. The crisis represented by King and the riots creates a more personal crisis of black identity for two characters in that their relatively privileged class position places them outside of a seemingly more authentic working-class identity. At the same time, the sociocultural trauma represented by racism generally and the destruction of the riots more specifically offer opportunity for those of higher class positions to prove their legitimacy by offering material commitment to improve the station of working-class African Americans.

Despite the inclusive argument in the larger narrative, certain characters must be excluded from categories of authenticity. As the family begins work cleaning up "the old neighborhood," Will and Carlton, his preppie cousin, compete to demonstrate legitimacy to neighborhood residents. Carlton, for example, attempts in vain to perform street cred, hailing a passerby in his overly proper manner, "Yo, my brother. When the going gets tough, the tough get going. It's Hammer time." Carlton's square performance of inauthentic blackness typically allowed Will to appear more credible by comparison. Will attempts to exploit Carlton's nerdiness in this scene, but the strategy only works for so long. After apologizing for his cousin, which helps establish the sense that he can communicate with "real" African Americans, Will makes a friend. Noah represents unquestionable legitimacy through his Africa-shaped pendant, dress, speech, and politics. Will and Noah express shared disgust toward people who do not "understand what went down." In response, Noah complains, "Most of those fools aren't coming back here anyways. A few more months, everybody's conscience will be cleared; things will be back to status quo." The friendship grows until Will squirms his way out of further commitment with excuses of schoolwork and dating. After Will protests that he was coming back, Noah responds, "No you're not, man. I bet you feel pretty good about yourself, don't you? I mean you come down here, do the right thing, and then you go home patting yourself on the back because you helped out the poor folk." Will responds, "Yo, I'm from Philly. We had to save up to be poor. Why you sweating me, man?" "Because," Noah lectures in a serious turn,

> you're just like all the rest of them. You come down here in the X cap and the cool Doc Martens and you're all "dope" and "word to your mother" and you think that makes you committed. Let me tell you something: this ain't no game, and if you think that it is, maybe you should go home because you're not welcome here. Tell Dan Quayle I said, "What's up?"

Although both young men share stylistic signifiers of authenticity, Noah accuses Will of lacking substantive commitment. Despite his protests, Will's claim to inner-city poverty and its associated coolness comes under fire by someone with more cred. Will's commitments to Bel-Air are stronger than to his past and race. Noah trumps Will's blackness.

After shaming Will, Noah abandons him in a low-rent apartment. A Latino man enters with a baseball bat and, having mistaken Will for a looter, threatens to "knock [his] head off." Responding to Will's calls for help, Uncle Phil enters and recognizes the man as Hector, their former

Noah and Will perform authenticity through a handshake on The Fresh Prince of Bel-Air.

landlord, grocer, and friend. The family acquaintance apologizes for the mistake, explaining that he had "been a little jumpy" due to repeated robberies. Hector is a symbol with which *Fresh Prince* negotiates the relationship between black Angelenos and other minorities. Unlike in Martin Lawrence's routine, nobody explicitly states Hector's race, though his name, his vaguely Spanish-as-a-primary-language accent, and his use of Spanish to describe Will's "muy grande orejas" clearly mark him. As a property owner involved in the violent defense of his property, Hector stands in for the more common image of a Korean American shop owner. However, his most important role is to reaffirm Will's authenticity after he suffers his most acute crisis of black identity. Even in the riot-torn neighborhood, Hector demonstrates, Will can still pass for a threatening young black man. After Uncle Phil recognizes Hector as his old friend, however, Hector represents hope and harmony for the varied races coexisting in the neighborhood.

It is in this role that Hector serves as the impetus for narrative resolution. Throughout the episode, Uncle Phil had worried aloud that his wife had gotten bored with him. Once established as an old family friend, Hector asks if Uncle Phil is "still fighting for little guys like [him]." "Well I'm still fighting," Uncle Phil responds, "but it's corporate mergers, mostly," embarrassed to own up to his life choices. Hector takes his leave and the discussion triggers a flashback. The family is poor in this scene, showing a past in which they were more authentically black. Explaining to her daughter why they cannot afford newer toys, Aunt Vivian explains, "With all the free legal aid your daddy gives, we can barely cover expenses, but there are more important things in life than fancy clothes and big houses." Uncle Phil had been committed to the black community in which they lived, giving his time at the expense of his family's material well-being. In the flashback, work interrupts family time when an important law firm calls to offer Uncle Phil an interview. Upon hearing the news, the children celebrate, imagining their privileged futures. Uncle Phil lectures them, "Even if I do get this job, nothing changes. This is our home and this community is part of our family. And I'll never turn my back on it." A cross-fade returns to the present, where Uncle Phil continues the thought: "Yeah, we had some good times in this old place . . . and we made some very good friends here, but we haven't kept our commitment to them or to this place." Leaving the old neighborhood and forgetting his commitment had caused Uncle Phil to lose his legitimacy. The flashback highlights Uncle Phil's lost blackness.

Although the memory primarily indicts Uncle Phil, Will responds to it by pledging to find Noah in order to plan a schedule for further volunteerism, thus soothing his cognitive dissonance. Common for a sitcom of the period, and especially for very special episodes, the promises and relationships formed during this narrative do not carry into the future. However, at least one element of this story continues. Uncle Phil's greatest fear is that his lost blackness has caused his wife to cheat on him. Supporting his fears, Vivian acts evasive and distracted throughout the episode. Once alone with his wife, Uncle Phil resolves his identity and personal crises.

UNCLE PHIL: I sold out. I did everything I said I wouldn't do: became a high-powered lawyer, bought that house in Bel-Air, and never looked back.

AUNT VIVIAN: Philip, honey, you shouldn't feel guilty about your success. Baby, nobody gave you anything. You have worked hard for everything you've got. You've been generous and you've contributed to a lot of causes.

UNCLE PHIL: It takes more than just writing a check. I've lost myself. I've lost my fire, my passion. You're right, Vivian, I've become dull and predictable.

AUNT VIVIAN: Philip.

UNCLE PHIL: I want to be the kind of man you fell in love with. I want to be open to risks. I want to take chances.

AUNT VIVIAN: Oh Philip, do you mean it?

Aunt Vivian embraces Uncle Phil. He coldly pushes her away and accuses her of infidelity. Revealing that her recent absences were for doctor visits, Vivian admits that she is in fact pregnant. Uncle Phil faints, the crowd cheers, and the credits roll.

While the riots in this episode of *Fresh Prince* serve different purposes for different characters, both Will and Uncle Phil face crises of black identity spurred by the uprising. Will's change of heart over his commitments resolve his internal conflict as well as his episodic narrative arc. This was of course not a new concept in the understanding of class relations in African American communities, despite Johnson's assertion that crises frequently create new ways to perform authenticity. It is, however, presented as new within the logic of *The Fresh Prince of Bel-Air*. While Will's credibility had never been questioned and Uncle Phil's had been fairly well established up to this point, new circumstances called for new ways to reestablish their blackness. However, the narrative logic of the sitcom led to odd resolutions, undercutting its message. The attempted lesson claiming that symbolic connection to disadvantaged African Americans requires sacrifice and commitment is laudable. In the longer narrative, however, this episode only gives an easy solution that mirrors Noah's earlier criticism of those who perform working-class blackness without long-term commitment. In this case, while this episode sets up a longer-term engagement, the serial narrative drops this story element and only occasionally returns to the more serious issues of underprivileged African Americans.

While his new friendship with Noah causes Will's crisis, it is barely interpersonal. That is to say, while Noah acts as the catalyst for Will's exploration of these concerns, his is fundamentally a personal narrative about his relationship to the socioeconomic class and space in which he grew up and which he continues to perform. Uncle Phil, however, ties the loss of social commitment to the imagined dissolution of his marriage. The personal is political here, but hardly in the sense that the phrase is usually invoked. The riots give rise to Uncle Phil's guilt over forgotten commitments and social responsibilities, but he most acutely expresses them in his cuckold anxiety. In an odd narrative logic, then, the resolution of this personal conflict through reaffirmation of heterosexual reproduction stands in for the more political and social aspects' resolution. The pregnancy continues, but future episodes largely forget these social and political narratives, ironizing the message and title of "Will Gets Committed."

A DIFFERENT WORLD AND CENTER-LEFT LEGITIMACY

A Different World had a number of elements in common with *The Fresh Prince of Bel-Air*. Both sitcoms aired on NBC, achieving significant "crossover" success by building on the legacy left by *The Cosby Show* at that network. While *Fresh Prince* added variation to the theme of an upwardly mobile black nuclear family by adding a fish out of water, *A Different World* spun off from *Cosby*, serving as a vehicle for Cliff Huxtable's daughter, Denise. Following the first season departure of Lisa Bonet, however, *A Different World* became more of an ensemble show, focusing on the varied faculty, staff, and student body of the fictional historically black Hillman College. Like *Fresh Prince*, *A Different World* explored intraracial difference. However, the wider cast of characters and the academic environment, which encouraged thoughtful Habermasian debate, allowed a more multifaceted and intersectional engagement with the riots and associated issues. While *A Different World* similarly examined the topic of how privileged African Americans can and should relate to the riots, it did so through characters from a wider variety of sociopolitical positions.

In this episode, two central characters relate the story of how their honeymoon in Los Angeles coincided with the riots.[26] At the end of the previous season, streetwise intellectual Dwayne had married Southern bourgeois Whitley, completing the show's stock will-they-or-won't-they? narrative arc. As the new season commences, returning and new students gather to hear the story of their honeymoon, which took place in Los Angeles during the riots. This sets up a flashback structure in which the audience sees Dwayne and Whitley's experiences in Los Angeles, but continually reverts to the narrative present so that Hillman's diverse black population can discuss these events and issues. In so doing, characters make sense of themselves in relation to the riots and make explicit arguments about how African Americans in general should and should not respond. Ultimately, the message is similar to that of *Fresh Prince* in that all African Americans have some symbolic purchase on the grievances represented by the riots, but its lessons differ. *A Different World* argues for a moderate leftism, demonstrating the appropriate ways to be angry and mocking those that it deems too radical.

Early in the honeymoon, before the riots begin, Whitley and Dwayne debate the jury's trustworthiness in the trial of the officers who beat Rodney King. Whitley believes that the jury will convict the police officers. "This is not 1965 in Selma, Alabama," argues the recent bride, using the couple's good treatment in "the finest of stores" as evidence. As was often the case in these shows' discussions of the riots, class is a central question in what it means to be black. After Whitley says that "it's not as hard" as it once was, Dwayne responds pessimistically, "For who, Whitley? Most black folk never get a chance to test your theory in those boutiques of democracy. And the brothers in South Central got it a lot harder." "Well just because I don't spend my life walking around with this cloud of oppression loom-ing over my head," responds Whitley, "doesn't mean I'm not concerned, informed, and aware." Of course, retrospectively, Dwayne is correct in his cynicism about the jury's decision. Whitley's confidence does not appear to be meant for ridicule, but her experiences will test her faith in these systems and she will experience a political awakening before the end of this two-part episode.

The couple separates, and each explores an area of Los Angeles related to their character. Dwayne drops Whitley off at a boutique mall so that he can drive to South Central in order to pick up Lakers tickets. While in his rented car, Dwayne hears the news of the police officers' acquittal. Frustrated, he parks and exits his car in order to regain his composure. This gains the attention of a passing squad car. Acting out a comic good cop-/-bad cop routine, one of the police officers harasses Dwayne while demonstrating stupidity and cowardice. For instance, while Dwayne clearly poses no threat, the bad officer orders him to drop his weapon and place his hands on the nonexistent roof of his convertible. Meanwhile, his well-meaning partner attempts to moderate the bad behavior. In the end, the officer tries to explain to Dwayne that their lives are frequently threatened as police officers, to which Dwayne sarcastically replies, "I guess that makes us brothers." This scene makes Dwayne representative of larger social narratives. Although they did not beat him, Dwayne's harassment at the hands of the LAPD puts him in conversation with Rodney King. He responds with mild verbal aggression but ultimately cooperates when faced with police violence. At the same time, the more moderate police officer attempts to explain away bad behavior using a common discourse about the stress experienced by police. As a lesson to the audience, Dwayne rejects this rhetoric.

Despite proving that his "cloud of oppression" is justified and gaining greater right to be angry over LAPD abuses, Dwayne resists the tempta-tion to grow too radical or participate in looting or destruction, despite opportunity. In a later scene, he encounters a crowd threatening to rob and destroy a pair of small businesses in a predominantly black neighborhood.

In this fairly humorless morality play, the primary victims are a pair of storeowners, one African American and one immigrant Chinese American.

> BLACK STORE OWNER: It ain't right what you all are doing. I came from the ghetto too. Just like you.
> RIOTER: Man, get out of my way.
> BLACK STORE OWNER: You call this black power?
> MR. HUNG: I see video. Police officers guilty! Guilty!
> RIOTER: What about the Korean grocer that killed Latasha Harlins because she thought she was stealing juice?
> MR. HUNG: I am not Korean. I'm Chinese!
> RIOTER: It's the same thing, man! (Audience laughs)
> DWAYNE: Hey brothers, come on now. I know what you're thinking. It was messed up, but this ain't gonna bring her back. Think about it for one second.
> RIOTER: Give me this! (Pulls a boom box from an adolescent's hands)
> ADOLESCENT: Hey man, that's mine. I just stole that.
> RIOTER: This is for Latasha! (Throws the boom box through the window of Mr. Hung's store)
> BLACK STORE OWNER: Where you gonna shop tomorrow? How you gonna hold up your heads?

This scene constructs the riots as a battle between classes as much as races. It references the more palpable tension between African and Korean Americans—a conflict brought into sharp relief in the real case of a Korean American shop clerk fatally shooting black fifteen-year-old Latasha Harlins, whom she had mistakenly thought was stealing a bottle of orange juice. Dwayne intervenes to calm the threat, placing him at the intersection of working- and aspirationally middle-class African Americans and reflecting his character's background having grown up poor in Brooklyn before achieving success through education. Because he can convincingly express anger verbally but takes a more moderate position against violence, Dwayne symbolically and successfully stands between the representatives of the working and middle classes. The show codes Dwayne as legitimately black despite his upward mobility, allowing him to represent both interests. At the same time, it argues that store owners like these should invest in the health of black communities and be considered off-limits as targets. This episode treats Dwayne as a good example of how to respond to the riots and the wider issues they represent. Obviously, the South Central residents threatening the store owners offer a counterexample.

Spatial blocking represents class alliances on A Different World.

Amid the flashbacks, the episode also returns to the narrative present of Hillman College, which allows *A Different World*'s more regular characters to present comparable lessons. Dwayne and the other wise characters continue to represent responsible moderation in this environment, but there are notable other counterexamples at which the show invites laughter. After Dwayne relates his story of police harassment, for instance, he explains that the police retreated from the most dangerous areas. Radical freshman Lena expresses her disdain for the police, inviting other characters to mock her.

> LENA (Sarcastically): Oh yeah, they could have gotten really hurt.
> KIM (Angrily): Hey, you are not aware of the pressures policemen deal with. Now my dad was shot in the streets before these riots, Lena.
> CHARMAINE: Yeah, they have a hard job. I mean if Chief Willie Williams were here right now, I'd give him a kiss.
> LENA: Yeah, kiss them so they kick you back. You can't trust anybody in a uniform.
> [. . .]
> COLONEL TAYLOR (Dressed in a military uniform): Lena, it's not the uniform, it's the person behind the uniform.

This conflict between responsible middle-class and more radical positions played out similarly multiple times. These discussions do not argue that these characters' feelings or commitments are illegitimate, but that their extreme rhetoric is. Unlike in *Fresh Prince*, where middle-class positioning cast characters' authenticity under suspicion, there is relatively little here to suggest that anyone is less credibly black than anyone else. Yet, there is a sense that performances of blackness connected to authenticity may be associated with wrongheaded political ideas.

As the most militant student, Lena plays the comic idiot, reflecting Bergson's beliefs that humor arises from discovering flawed logic and that group laughter shames an individual who does not follow their mores.[27] This happens when one character mimics Lena's overwrought, angry performance before tearing down her calls to violent action. Later in the same scene, Lena claims to be "tired of voting for the lesser of two evils." Of this, the ever-respectable Colonel Taylor asks, "When did you vote, honey? Last time we had an election you were what? All of about fourteen years old?" In both of these instances, on-screen characters as well as the studio audience join in mocking laughter of Lena's extremist politics. Dwayne's authenticity gives him the ability to speak authoritatively to these issues. By contrast, Lena's misguided attempts to claim the anger represented by the riots makes her less credible.

In addition to radical Lena, *A Different World* presents many other characters for identification, from the respectably Afrocentric Shazza to Ron, who comes out as a Reaganite in this episode. Still, the narrative seems most concerned with giving voice to the left-leaning centrists like Dwayne, who take more measured views of their experiences. The character Freddie is particularly telling in this regard, as she surprises her friends in an early scene by abandoning her "Tracy Chapman" look in favor of a conservative business suit so that she can "be taken seriously" and study "the system in order to change it" as a lawyer—claims met with approving cheers from the studio audience.

Whitley encounters gatekeeping most obviously in this episode inasmuch as Dwayne places her blackness under suspicion when they discuss the trial verdict. In the sense that she is bourgeois and black, her character faces similar questions of legitimacy as Will and Uncle Phil from *Fresh Prince*. Yet, neither Colonel Taylor nor Ron the Republican have their bona fides questioned, suggesting that it is more Whitley's naivety and her class awareness that need correction. After her discussion with Dwayne, Whitley ends up in a boutique mall as televisions convey the news of the verdict. Whitley responds with disbelief, but another black woman played by political lightning rod Sister Souljah lectures her from a more strident position: "Girl, please. They can beat us, kill us, do whatever they wanna do and get off. Just like they always have. . . . Stop worrying about integrating and being accepted and start thinking about building. For yourself. For our people. So that we can provide a future for our children." Despite associations with more radical politics that this episode largely criticizes, Souljah's star persona as a hip-hop artist and political activist gives her character credibility as she proposes community building as a response to racism. While Whitley appears suspicious of these calls to action, her experiences in the next few scenes convert her to a more active political position.

Without transportation and frightened for her safety, Whitley takes refuge in the mall and witnesses a number of wealthy white women looting an expensive shop. As they do so, the women complain about prices and employees who "breathe down [their] neck[s]," adding, "We all know who does the stealing." Another responds, "They should stop complaining. They bring it on themselves." Emerging from hiding with her anger boiling over, Whitley scares the women away, shouting, "They who?! Who is 'they?' What about you? What are you doing about the problem?" This scene makes a point similar to Martin Lawrence's, that some looters were simply opportunistic and had no legitimacy participating. More importantly, however, it proves significant to Whitley's journey.

Whitley fully realizes her political awakening with help from an unlikely source. After a white homeless man offers her a plastic bag in order to help keep her warm, they develop a quick friendship, though it is tainted by her classist request that the man sit downwind. Out of desperation more than actual confusion, Whitley asks, "What's happening?" giving the elder man the opportunity not only to historicize the events but also to argue for identification across and between races and classes. "What always happens? Every generation same thing: St. Louis, Chicago, Watts, Newark! And it's not just about color, you know? Oh no. It's about being invisible like me. And when you're invisible you have to shout! Otherwise, people don't notice you and that's what's going on in this city! People are shouting! You have to shout or you'll go crazy!" After some encouragement, Whitley learns to shout, signaling that she has connected with justified anger despite her class. Moreover, the show afforded her poor white friend legitimacy by virtue of his class. At this moment, a television reporter approaches the pair. Mistaking Whitley's class, the reporter asks for "the homeless response to the riot." Whitley seizes the opportunity, berating the journalist for failing to cover these issues properly before turning to the camera and demonstrating, both literally and figuratively, that she learned to shout.

Whitley's transformation earns approval from her comrades at Hillman and applause from the studio audience, signaling that her anger is legitimate and earned. Notably, the most significant figure in her transformation, the white homeless man, was unlike her in both class and race. While the appropriate action for Dwayne was to stand with the forces of uplift represented by neighborhood small business owners of different races, Whitley discovers wisdom from a poor white friend. At the same time, overly radical characters like Lena and the rioters earn rebuke from the more respected characters in this series. According to *A Different World*, the right to participate in the grievances represented by the riots, while certainly connected to racial identity, has more to do with performing responsibly moderate responses.

IN LIVING COLOR: NIHILISM TO ENGAGEMENT

Like *Def Comedy Jam*, *In Living Color* presented itself as hip-hop television. Despite the prominence of Jim Carrey as a breakout star, it was coded as young, black, and urban. Because of this, *In Living Color* could have easily been open in its expressions of solidarity and sympathy with rioters. It was not at first. As discussed in the previous chapter, comedy has a reputation for cynicism that discourages political engagement.[28] Certainly, the politically engaged comedies throughout this book offer counterexamples to this critique, but the variety of black appeal comedies working through the riots in 1992 meant that apolitical cynicism appeared on the dial alongside more principled fare. Although *In Living Color* eventually took clearer stands on these issues, its initial response engaged in politically apathetic cynicism by criticizing anyone connected to the riots. At first, then, the message subtly proposed that nobody has a right to earnestly claim grievance in relation to the riots. Eventually, however, it criticized police abuses more specifically, offering perhaps the most radically inclusive message of any show in this chapter.

According to Herman Gray, "*In Living Color* discursively enacts a cultural politics of representation that settles around a position of ambivalence."[29] Gray offers further insight in quoting show creator Keenen Ivory Wayans as saying, "You know, the thing is that parody for black people is a new thing. . . . It's hard for black people to understand that you're just making fun of them. If you're in the lime-light, you become fair game. Whatever is public, is public."[30] As a parody, and a primarily black-coded one at that, *In Living Color* represents a second-order imagining of mass-mediated black culture. Wayans's quotation above suggests feelings of responsibility as a satirist ridiculing culture. In fact, staff conflicts and external criticism arose from this tension.[31] However, attacking those who were upset by the Rodney King beating was a fraught strategy.

Relating black culture's sense of oppositionality to Bakhtin, Stuart Hall notes, "The carnivalesque is not simply an upturning of two things that remain locked within their oppositional frameworks; it is also crosscut by what Bakhtin calls the dialogic."[32] In this case, *In Living Color*'s dialogism not only voices many subject positions but turns criticism back against the apparently oppositional black culture. As this chapter has shown, this was true of other shows, as when *A Different World* criticized radical political positions. However, *In Living Color* does so without a clear ideology, middle class or otherwise, to replace the discourses it attacks—at least not in the first episode following the riots. Gray is correct in noting how *In Living Color*'s nihilism sets it apart from its contemporaries in the fall of 1992. Although comedy allows for this kind of ambivalence, none engaged in it to the extent that this show did. *In Living Color* uses comedy to brutalize essentially every significant public and symbolic figure associated with these events.

All but one of the sketches from the first episode of the 1992–1993 season is about the riots in some way.[33] Although dealing with the uprising, *In Living Color*'s tone and message skews away from that of other shows in its willingness to mock sacred cows. While possible to read some politics into these sketches, the type of didactic public sphering of other shows is notably absent. In fact, the only satire in this episode dealing directly with electoral politics is a Ross Perot sketch that does not mention the riots at all. Otherwise, the show takes aim at multiple targets related to these events. It mocks clear victims like Rodney King and firefighters, and attacks those living in poor neighborhoods for demonstrating along with politically engaged celebrities. On this latter point in particular, it mocks Edward James Olmos's laudable efforts to calm rioters and clean up, characterizing his actions as more about publicity and personal gain than social commitment.

Some sketches use recurring characters to engage the riots. For instance, "Bonita Butrell" was a recurring neighborhood gossip character played by Kim Wayans, who in this sketch sat on a bench as looters and protesters scrambled and marched by. Two-faced and hypocritical, Bonita first criticizes the rioters as "heathens taking everything that ain't glued to the ground," before picking up a boom box dropped by a passing looter. The rest of the sketch repeats the joke that Ms. Butrell compliments people to their face but counters it as soon as that person is out of earshot. After recognizing a young man taking a television, she offers a huge smile and the justification, "Don't feel bad about taking it because I know you ain't stole a single thing in your whole life." As soon as the young man runs off, she turns to the camera, leans forward, and grows serious as she corrects herself: "That's a born thief right there. When his mama gave birth to him, he ran off with the placenta." Critiques of looting as illegitimate political expression were a common theme repeated by Martin Lawrence, *A Different World*, and others. However, while those other performers and programs frequently stated or at least implied that there were better, more legitimate ways to express political frustration, Bonita Butrell undermines any such reading by shifting her attacks to those practicing more traditional political speech. As a woman marches by chanting and holding a sign reading "No Justice, No Peace," Bonita shouts after her, "Hey Denise! Look at you, girl, regular little politician. And I hear you, baby: no justice, no peace." Again shifting her demeanor to tell the real story, she addresses the camera, "More like no twenty dollar bill, no piece." This joke repeats itself three more times—savaging a Korean restaurant owner, a news reporter, and "Ms. Jenkins," presumably an "upstanding" member of the community like Bonita. While the primary target of this sketch is Bonita herself, the jokes also tear down a host of types associated with the riots and black communities more generally. This sketch is an example of highly cynical humor in that it satirizes without offering alternatives.[34] If any action the residents of black neighborhoods might take—looting, demonstrating, being a victim, reporting, and/or being a respectable figure—are all worthy of attack, what else is there to be done? There is no legitimate response to the trial or riots other than mocking resignation.

Though less thoroughly nihilistic in their treatment of actual figures involved with the riot's discourses, other sketches from this episode are comparably cynical and more iconoclastic, such as one that mocks newly canonized secular saints Rodney King and Reginald Denny in ways that touch on the same taboos discussed in chapters 1 and 2 regarding the Kennedy family and 9/11 victims. Parodying a public service announcement, this sketch allows the pair to directly address the camera. The pair stands arm in arm to deliver a message begging people to stay in their cars. This is somewhat critical inasmuch as it is absurd to compare exiting a vehicle with more typical PSA dangers like drug use. However, the laughs come primarily from displays of their injuries. Both characters show the marks of their beatings in speech and gesture, but the respective emphasis upon each comes in different ratios. While nervous and jumpy on the surface, David Allen Grier performs Rodney King's physical trauma verbally. His difficulty maintaining a train of thought and using appropriate metaphors

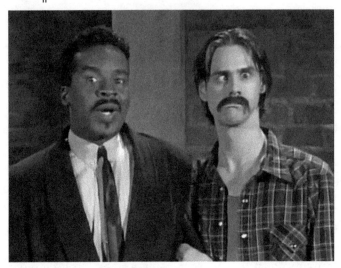

Victimhood mocked on In Living Color.

indicates psychological and perhaps physical trauma to the brain. "It's not whether you win or lose," King states, before a confused look overtakes his face and he continues, "Is it over when the fat lady sings? Can't we all just get along?" More jokes repeat in this way throughout, and King always ends with his misquoted "catch phrase." While apparently struggling in his own verbal capacity to some extent, Carrey's impersonation of Reginald Denny primarily concentrates on physical trauma even as it ignores most of the extensive permanent damage to Denny's face and body.[35] In addition to a crossed eye and crooked jaw, he pauses his speech to squint hard or violently shake his head. While neither quite gained the status of hero, media of the period mostly portrayed King and Denny as innocent victims and worthy of pity. This sketch not only mocks them but specifically focuses on the marks of their victimhood as its primary vehicle for getting laughs. It mocks the victims for their victimhood. Considering the going discourse surrounding these men, this was a surprisingly irreverential take. More significant because these two men are symbolic representatives of all people with grievances, the negation of their legitimacy acts as a wider assault on any such claims. If we laugh at Rodney King's victimhood, claims to associated and systemic victimhood also become laughable.

The first post-riots *In Living Color* episode surprised with its rejection of network television's sentimentality and its general refusal to participate in the orthodox scripts of binarist good/bad constructions expected of African American and other television programming of the period. However, later

The biggest threat to the boys in blue, as depicted by In Living Color.

in the season after other shows largely forgot about the riots and their immediate causes, *In Living Color* returned to these issues as the trial over whether police had violated King's civil rights got under way. A February 1993 sketch depicts Stacey Koon, the ranking officer at the scene of the King beating, as a racist cop guilty of abusing his power.[36] In that sense, it presents a clear, expected critique of the most notable symbol of police abuse, though in a literal sense it shows Koon as a lone bad actor. However, the second sketch to explicitly critique Koon takes a systemic view of the problem, imagining a police academy training session led by the sergeant wherein he demonstrates technique by sadistically beating, macing, biting, and choking his recruits.[37] Even more significant than training police to abuse their power, however, is the way that this sketch implicates viewers in their role as witnesses through mass media.

Koon attempts to train the recruits how to identify threatening suspects on a firing line. This bit relies on the training exercise in which officers quickly assess the potential danger of people represented by cardboard cutouts. Following a rule-of-threes structure, Koon dismisses threats from men with knives and guns before revealing that the "much bigger threat to the men in blue" is "the bastard with the camera." After the recruits empty their weapons into the camera operator cutout, Koon explains, "Take him out and you can waste everybody else at your own leisure." Koon continues his attacks on cameras. Before the sketch ends, he breaks the fourth wall by realizing that the viewers saw the entire training session. Addressing the camera directly, he asks, "What's this? What do you think you're doing? You think you can just come in here and film police officer's training, is that it? This is top secret, mister! I'm gonna have to give you a little warning." With that, Koon smashes the camera lens with his nightstick.

At its most basic, this is a cleverly reflexive way to end the sketch, but the viewer's position is significant. The attack locates viewers as victims of Koon's abuse, which situates them as members of a larger community of the aggrieved. If earlier sketches negated even King's victimhood, this sketch is a more inclusive and community-building gesture. Koon's sudden awareness of the gaze positions the viewer simultaneously as observer, citizen, and audience member. As an observer, the viewer has the power to threaten police abuses. Like George Holliday, who videotaped the King beating, and more recent documenters of unwarranted police violence, the observer-viewer interrupts and threatens those who abuse power. Similarly charged with vigilance in the public sphere, the citizen-viewer is responsible not only in the particular situation of obvious abuse, but also in ferreting out systemic problems as represented by a poorly run police academy. Finally, and perhaps most crucially for *In Living Color*'s self-importance, the viewer's position as a member of a television audience facilitates participation in a public sphere. The act of watching satire threatens figures like Koon. This was true enough, in fact, that Koon's attorney spoke out against both *In Living Color* sketches, suggesting that they posed a significant threat to his client.[38] In this way, the sketch breaks down the gates of symbolic participation. Everyone is implicated.

In Living Color, along with a host of other black-cast television shows from this era, was in a unique position to make sense of the riots, using humor to articulate the ways in which people of different subject positions can and should relate to the riots. Contemporary instances of police abuses against African Americans as well as the Black Lives Matter movement and other examples of civil rights protests echo the events of the early 1990s. The ubiquity of cameras has heightened the exposure of such abuses, and comedy continues to engage them. However, increased audience fragmentation means that while shows like *Black-ish* and *The Rundown with Robin Thede* discuss these issues, they are necessarily to smaller, more targeted audiences. Moreover, the twenty-four-hour news cycle and political polarization resulting in part from media fragmentation means that neither these shows nor the events they discuss can have as much impact as did the events and television shows of 1992. Gatekeeping and instruction continue as rhetorics, but television technology and industry practice act as gatekeepers themselves, limiting those exposed to such messages.

In 2005, Comedy Central aired a stand-up special featuring a group of Arab American and Persian American comics titled *The Axis of Evil Comedy Tour*.[1] As one might expect, the comics registered complaints about their treatment in post-9/11 America, discussing topics from media representations to the increase in hate crimes. Calls for greater acceptance of Muslim and Middle Eastern Americans into the larger American culture frequently punctuated these routines. More surprisingly, these comics also mocked Middle Easterners and Americans of Middle Eastern descent. Jokes of this nature ranged from Dean Obeidallah's self-deprecating comments about Arabs "smelling like lamb" to discussing the existence of terrorists in Muslim communities. In its concern with Middle Eastern identity in post-9/11 America, the special served as a microcosm of larger discourses about Islam and those of Middle Eastern descent in post-9/11 television comedy.

In the wake of 9/11, comedies frequently discussed those of Middle Eastern descent as America's new Other. With the increased fragmenting of American television markets, these shows staked out different positions in the fractious cultural politics of the time. Appealing to a more conservative strain of audience, comics like Carlos Mencia and Jeff Dunham leveraged the increased xenophobia using comedy that mocked those of Middle Eastern descent. In so doing, they reinforced a sense of American identity defined against the Other. On the other hand, comedies like *The Simpsons* and *The Daily Show* spoke to a more liberal pluralist sensibility by criticizing Islamophobia and rehabilitating those of Middle Eastern descent as fully American. Although these discussions were largely taking place among those of non–Middle Eastern descent, television also made space for programming like *The Axis of Evil Comedy Tour*, which drew from and commented upon the same discussions about American identity as television more generally. These comedic battles demonstrated the extent to which American national identity was defined with and against those of Middle Eastern descent in post-9/11 America.

While the cliché that 9/11 changed everything was partly true, there were also continuities between it and earlier periods and traumas. In magnitude and kind, 9/11 was different from the other traumas examined in this book. Like the Los Angeles riots, however, discourses of racial conflict defined much of the coverage as those of Middle Eastern descent came under heightened scrutiny. At the same time, narrowcasting also defined much of television comedy's longer response to the riots. But although narrowcasting allowed a relatively focused group of black-cast television shows to address the riots in comedy in 1992, narrowcasting would allow for a wider array of subject positions to address Middle Eastern identity after 2001. *The Axis of Evil Comedy Tour* notwithstanding, most of this humor came from those who were neither Muslim nor of Middle Eastern descent.

In the case of post-9/11 comedy, humor responded to what appeared to be an ongoing threat from Muslims and Middle Easterners at home and abroad. There is, of course, a longer history of using racist comedy to propagandize against perceived foreign threats, including titles like "Bugs Bunny Nips the Nips" and "Hare Meets Herr," both of which *South Park* references in an episode where Cartman plays Bugs to Osama bin Laden's axis foe.[2] While not clearly about negotiating Americans of Middle Eastern descent, this episode plays on strains of Islamophobia and Orientalism, mocking the Other in a display of humorous cultural chauvinism common across a range of post-9/11 comedies.[3] Hamid Naficy notes the importance of similarly derisive humor in America's relation to Iran in the wake of the 1979–1981 hostage crisis, which represented a threatening mix of despotism, Islam, and anticolonial attitudes.[4] While bin Laden replaced Khomeini on toilet paper sheets and in parody songs, the enormous cultural imprint of 9/11, among other factors, meant a larger and more varied television engagement with the Middle East, its people, and its diaspora. Additionally, while the taking of American hostages in Iran necessarily focused attention on another part of the world, the domestic nature of the 2001 attacks caused American Muslims and those of Middle Eastern descent to come under heightened scrutiny that often threatened and/or denied their status as fully or authentically American. General cultural suspicion along with more official federal responses from agencies like the FBI and FAA echoed the kind of xenophobia directed at Japanese Americans in the wake of the Pearl Harbor attack in 1941. This chapter demonstrates how comedy constructs and negotiates, as well as ritually abuses and rehabilitates, the apparent Others that arise in the wake of national traumas.

ISLAMOPHOBIC COMEDY IN THE CONTEXT OF POLITICAL
CORRECTNESS

"Political correctness" already had a history by the time of the Los Angeles
riots, but the cultural trend denoted by this term continued to develop and
expand during the period intervening those events and 2001. In *Political
Correctness: A History of Semantics and Culture*, Geoffrey Hughes explores
the history of the term as well as many of its implications.

> *Political correctness* became part of the modern lexicon and, many
> would say, part of the modern mind-set, as a consequence of the
> wide-ranging public debate which started on campuses in the
> United States from the late 1980s. Since nearly 50 percent of
> Americans go to college, the impact of the controversy was wide-
> spread. It was out of this ferment that most of the new vocabulary
> was generated or became current. However, political correctness
> is not one thing and does not have a simple history. As a concept it
> predates the debate and is a complex, discontinuous, and protean
> phenomenon, which has changed radically, even [since the late
> 1980s]. During just that time it has ramified into numerous agen-
> das, reforms, and issues concerning race, culture, gender, disability,
> the environment, and animals rights (emphasis in original).[5]

Hughes continues, offering a complex history of the way an explicit academic attempt to "sanitize the language by suppressing some of its uglier
prejudicial features" transformed into a more implicit set of codes pre- and
proscribing certain actions and forms of communication. To detractors like
Doris Lessing, the threat of being labeled politically incorrect acts as a
form of "mental tyranny . . . manifesting as a general intolerance."[6] Political correctness in the television industry is likely the result of two primary
factors. First, it reflects a genuine ethical concern of a largely left-leaning,
metropolitan, college-educated creative labor force. At the same time, to
the extent that rules of conduct might help to avoid scaring away viewers
and advertisers, the strictures also reflect a business strategy. However, television is made up of many players and seeks a variety of audiences. Since
comedy is particularly given to testing the limits of acceptable speech, it
has consistently acted as a site of negotiation over political correctness.

   As the 1990s popular understanding of political correctness rose to
cultural prominence, both cultural conservatives like Lessing and comics of
more varied political leanings grew nervous regarding their ability to speak

with impunity.[7] So while these attitudes may have helped usher comics like Andrew Dice Clay out of the limelight, hipper comedies like *Seinfeld* and *The Simpsons* narrativized the apparent struggles of straight white males to navigate the new cultural sensitivity.[8] By the late 1990s, more self-conscious rejections of political correctness on shows like *South Park* and *Family Guy* appeared on broadcast and cable. At the same time, stand-up comics like Carlos Mencia worked comedy clubs and television's fringier cable and late-night sites as the apparent successors to Don Rickles, playing on their ability to say in comedy routines what could increasingly not be said elsewhere.

This thumbnail sketch of comedy in the 1990s suggests that those who negotiated, ignored, or flaunted the developing rules of political correctness served a wide swath of demographic markets from young adults to fans of older, more Borscht Belt–inspired comedy. While crises of racial identity like the O. J. Simpson case informed these comedic debates throughout the 1990s, 9/11 inflected the conflict differently. But as these nebulous standards acted as a subtle dominant governing many areas of public life, certain television texts could differentiate their product by testing or flouting the rules. So while there was a perceived air of multicultural tolerance by the turn of the millennium, 9/11 created an Other defined in large part as a minority culture, religion, and ethnicity. In its ability to navigate issues of sameness and difference within culture, comedy proved to be a privileged discourse in navigating these seemingly oppositional desires.

Though comics like Don Rickles and others had been pushing similar buttons for decades, self-consciously anti-PC comedians and comedies from the right-wing Jeff Dunham to the mostly leftist Bill Maher show *Politically Incorrect* broke the rules as a way to build comic credibility. Thus, after 9/11, Muslims and Middle Easterners became prime targets for comics who wanted to demonstrate their edgy rejection of political correctness while ingratiating themselves to those who self-identified as more truly American. In comedy especially, the clashes of cultural and religious toler-ance, nationalist anger, anti-PC backlash, and humor's ability to negotiate such issues created a particularly telling milieu where these debates could be argued and examined like they could in no other television genre or cultural discourse.

MIND OF MENCIA: UPDATING ANTI-IMMIGRANT COMEDY

In the opening monologue of the first episode of *Mind of Mencia*, host Carlos Mencia paints himself as an anti-PC bad boy primarily through his attacks on Muslim Americans:

I'm gonna make fun of everybody. I get Muslims pissed off. [adopting an Arabic accent] Why are the American people messing with me? [returning to his voice] Because Achmed, it's your turn! America's a giant game of tag, somebody's always "it," and guess what, Achmed? You're it. Here's what happened; a lot of people don't understand. September 11: bad day in American history, great day for blacks and Hispanics, greatest day in our generation, because on that day, white people accepted us as Americans. Before that, we weren't Americans. Then on the eleventh, the buildings collapsed; they showed the pictures of the hijackers. When they showed those pictures, Maria, Loquisha, Carlos, and Tyrone walked up to Achmed and went, "Tag. Your turn!"[9]

Lanita Jacobs-Huey's ethnography of black comedy clubs after 9/11 demonstrated a common commitment to emotional nonconformity among African American comics, joking that Arab Americans were the new African Americans.[10] These jokes argued that since Americans of Middle Eastern descent were the new most hated ethnic minority, the position of others would rise in relation. Multiple comics of different ethnicities echoed this sentiment in the years following 9/11. For instance, Arab American comic Dean Obeidallah willfully misinterpreted the joke to mean that Arab culture was now cool, imagining that teenagers would be "dressing Arab, wearing a traditional Arab headdress tilted to the side to be cool, open shirt, gold chain, smelling like lamb."[11]

Cultural historians like David R. Roediger and Noel Ignatiev argue that Irish American immigrants performed black face minstrelsy in large numbers because denigrating African Americans was a way to win status as white Americans during a period when many considered them to be neither white nor American.[12] Robert Nowatzki adds that the new immigrants were well suited to this role not only because of a history of cultural sharing between Irish Americans and free African Americans, but also because the Irish themselves had been the subject of minstrel shows performed by native-born Americans during earlier waves of immigration.[13] By the 1920s, Michael Rogin reports, Irish and Jewish performers adapted these performances to cinema screens in order to deliver a sense of African American culture to audiences while removing the threats that actual black performers implied.[14] To have been the subject of racist humor in the past offered entree to the field, suggesting that the most successful racist humor comes from those who are or have recently been the subject of it. Of course, by 2001, different ethnic groups were vying for wider acceptance into American culture, but the tendency for performers from vulnerable groups to attack even more vulnerable people remained.

Mencia's routine reflects many of the same strategies as minstrelsy from earlier periods. At the same time, his acknowledgment that this was somehow dangerous comedy places it in the twenty-first century. The comic's promise to "make fun of everybody" also functions as a justification since it guarantees some level of equity in his attacks on different races and ethnicities. To some extent, Mencia lives up to this promise, as he regularly mocked whites, blacks, Indians, and others on his show. Like many comics during this period, he used 9/11 as ground upon which to show off his willingness to engage in edgy and racially insensitive humor in the relatively safe manner of attacking the newly perceived threat. More significantly, it functions as rhetoric to rehabilitate African and Latinx Americans as more fully American. While the seemingly indefensible argument that 9/11 was good may shock some viewers, Mencia redirects these implications to buoy certain minorities at the expense of others.

Continuing the routine's use of comic metaphor, Mencia moves from the "giant game of tag" to comparing the United States to a fraternity. "In order to join our country," he argues,

> you must get hazed. And guess what? It's Greek week. . . . Every-
> body went through it. That's what I don't understand. I'm not
> afraid of people calling me a racist. Go ahead and call me a racist.
> Go ahead and do it. [adopting an Arabic accent] "Hey that's not
> fair; you're only checking me. Why don't you check the women?"
> [returning to his voice] Well, because women in this country,
> Achmed, were treated like crap for about 150 years when they
> couldn't vote. So unless you don't want to vote for that long and
> possibly give me head, I suggest you [agree to increased airport
> security].

Mencia attempts to short-circuit possible dismissals of his routine as racist by accepting all such criticism before again arguing for solidarity among all non–Middle Eastern, non-Muslim historically oppressed groups.

The rhetoric in this routine relies on a contradictory ideology of racial and gender equality and racist exceptionalism. While to some extent admitting the injustice of racial profiling, Mencia places the contemporary wave of xenophobia in relation to historical injustices to argue that such hardships are necessary for gaining acceptance into the dominant racial power bloc. Of course, European Americans are largely absent from this argument, but Mencia ingratiates himself to various historically oppressed categories of Americans by adopting a logic where past suffering is a patriotic virtue. African and Latinx Americans as well as women of all backgrounds earn the right to current liberties by virtue of past violations. While Mencia selectively subscribes to the classically liberal ideology of individual equality, it is a zero-sum game by which one group's equality comes at the expense of another's. Mencia's routine explicitly argues for a definition of American identity formed in opposition to the Other. If African and Latinx Americans were less fully American than were whites before 9/11, the trauma created an opportunity to form a coalition based on Islamophobia. Other comics used the image of Middle Eastern people to create a sense of greater cohesiveness among certain communities of Americans, though they were typically less overt in explaining the implications of this strategy.

JEFF DUNHAM AND ACHMED THE DEAD TERRORIST

Although Mencia hosted his own television show, his success paled in comparison to ventriloquist Jeff Dunham, whose Islamophobic comedy was more simply about humorously attacking a representative of terrorism. His dummy, Achmed the Dead Terrorist, followed the pattern of most popular culture during this period of articulating terrorism together with Islamic and Middle Eastern identity. By comically abusing this representative of the new American Other, Jeff Dunham constituted a sense of American identity that appealed to his largely white, conservative audience.

Though performing in relative obscurity since the early 1990s, Jeff Dunham's self-conscious attempts to appeal to a conservative, rural, Christian audience enabled him to become one of the most financially successful stand-up comics of the decade following 9/11.[15] In a telling interview, Dunham confessed to mocking everything equally with the exception of "basic Christian-values stuff."[16] More generally, he revealed that while often working blue and trying to attract a large audience, he intends his humor for a particular type: "the conservative 'country crowd.'"[17] And even though a *New York Times Magazine* piece intends kindness to both Dunham and his fans, even the writer could not help but poke fun as she describes the "not thin" audience.[18] While offering different views of his fans, both the comic and the interviewer depict a particular taste culture. In his Comedy Central specials and short-lived weekly show, Dunham codes his routines to speak to culturally conservative audiences, often classified in news articles as "red state" crowds.[19]

In this way, Dunham mirrors what Andy Medhurst sees as the appeal of comedian Roy "Chubby" Brown, a northern English comedian, to working-class audiences in his own country.[20] Similarly offensive though far more profane than Dunham, Brown also rails against immigrants and ethnic minorities. To Medhurst, this is an expression of anti-globalization that appeals to his working-class audience's sense of job insecurity in postindustrial Britain. A similar economic logic might have driven Dunham to produce the puppet named José Jalapeño on a Stick, but it is less clear that Achmed represents a reaction against immigrant labor driving down wages. Instead, the dead terrorist symbolizes the perceived danger of ethnic and religious diversity brought to the United States by globalization and symbolized for many, including presumably Dunham's fans, by 9/11. However, it is a danger pleasurably neutered by Achmed's incompetence and Jeff Dunham's mastery over him.

Dunham justifies the inherent racism in his routines by performing with a range of stereotyped dummies, including a redneck, black hustler, and elderly man. In one interview, Dunham responded to charges of racism by arguing, "I've skewered whites, blacks, Christians, Jews, Muslims, gays, straights, rednecks, the elderly, and my wife. As a stand-up comic, it is my job to make the majority of people laugh, and I believe that comedy is the last true form of free speech."[21] However, Dunham's fans do not appear to be as evenhanded in their preferences as the ventriloquist was in providing options for comedic scorn. By many indicators—from on-screen audience reactions to internet video views to journalist estimations—Achmed the Dead Terrorist, a skeletal puppet primarily used to poke fun at Muslim terrorists, proves repeatedly to be the comic's signature and most popular character. *Time* points out, "The explosion [of popularity] came, appropriately enough, with Achmed the Dead Terrorist, a character Dunham debuted in late 2007 on his [Comedy Central special and] DVD *Spark of Insanity*."[22]

Blatantly satirical and parodic, Achmed functions as a symbolic straw man. Having only managed to kill himself (and, in one routine, his son) with his suicide bombing, he operates as a pathetic figure at which the audience laughs. In this way, he serves as the target of imagined physical violence and more immediate verbal violence. Upon introducing the puppet in this special, Dunham plays it straight. "As we all know, there's a big mess going on in the Middle East right now, and when it comes to the terrorists," he explains, "most of us don't understand their extremist views and beliefs. And I got to thinking the other day, *How would it be just to sit down and talk to one of those guys?*" Adopting the language of cross-cultural curiosity and ecumenism performs a number of tasks. Most crucially, it sets up the ventriloquist as the reasonable counterpoint against which his puppet would contrast. But at another level, it critiques the ideology that underpins such attempts to understand the Other. As quickly becomes clear, there is little thinking necessary to "get" Achmed; he is single-mindedly violent. There is no point in trying to "understand their extremist views" and no point in adopting any stance toward the Middle East's "big mess" other than one of laughing derision.

While all of Dunham's dummies are about the same size, the obvious intercultural conflict and Achmed's role as an object of scorn make the contrast in appearance between puppet and master notable. Dunham, representing a culturally conservative idea of a typical American, stands far taller than Achmed, whose exaggeratedly large head and eyes, small body, and sitting posture suggest that of a toddler. This infantilization colors Achmed's emotions such that his and all other terrorists' anger is more associated with childish temper tantrums than legitimate political or religious frustration. Introducing himself as "a terrifying terrorist," Achmed repeatedly tries to frighten Dunham. Each time, the ventriloquist refuses to be scared, defeating the true point and threat of terrorism. This is a play on emotional nonconformity directed more against terrorism than the media discourses that enable it. Frustrated, Achmed mutters, "God dammit. Ooh! I mean, uh, Allah dammit!" simultaneously admitting defeat and profaning the religion that he supposedly serves.

Considering ventriloquism's roots in the type of verbal play associated with "Who's on First"–type vaudeville routines, which Susan Douglas calls "linguistic slapstick," Achmed the Dead Terrorist represents an exceptionally physical form of slapstick among ventriloquism acts generally and Dunham's routines in particular.[23] The fundamental joke of Achmed's being that he was a terrorist too incompetent to kill anyone but himself and perhaps his son.[24] While more often described than shown, Achmed's stories of botched attacks paint a picture of self-inflicted physical trauma that distinguishes him from Dunham's other puppets, whose humor relies more on wordplay. "If you must know, I am a horrible suicide bomber," he explains in his first appearance. "I had a premature detonation. . . . I was getting gas and I answered my cell phone." "What was the last thing that went through your mind?" asks Dunham. "My ass," replies Achmed. Considering Achmed's role as a ritual object—an already-burned effigy—this physicality makes sense. The symbolic shaming of verbal insults and humiliation as well as these comic celebrations of physical trauma against him demonstrate Achmed's role as a target for abuse. He represents all other terrorists, and perhaps Muslims and Middle Easterners, to an audience

Achmed suffers from a lack of ligaments on Jeff Dunham's Very Special Christmas Special.

that desires symbolic retribution for 9/11 and attacks on American soldiers abroad. In this and other stand-up specials, Achmed's physical humor goes beyond mere description. While all ventriloquist dummies rely on physicality to some extent, most stop at exaggerated facial expressions and head movement. In his first appearance, Achmed's skeletal feet fall upside down, leading him to exclaim, "I need some ligaments!" This same gag repeats in a 2009 Christmas special except that in addition to his foot problems, Achmed loses an arm. A victim of his own violence, Achmed shrinks from a threatening figure to a pathetically fragile, albeit comic, one.

Because its filmed format allowed for more complex staging, Dunham's sketch comedy show, in which his puppets leave Dunham's side to interact with people off the stage, provided an ideal place for Achmed to perform his self-destructive slapstick more physically. On more than one occasion, the show features Achmed trying to learn how to be a more effective perpetrator of violence only to be comically stymied. Most notably, he attempts in one sketch to become a United States Marine. Justified as an attempt to become a citizen so that he could attack the United States "from the inside," this bit is more about creating humorous contrast between the highly competent soldiers and Achmed, whose incompetence both highlights his harmlessness and offers an excuse for slapstick at his expense.[25] At the same time, Achmed fails spectacularly in his attempts to become American. This appeals to humor's superiority function by showing how bad he is at being American. The fact that he wants to be a marine only exaggerates the humor of these failed attempts. The show appeals to associations between nationalism and militarism by presenting marines as particularly strong examples of Americanism, heightening the contrast between the hyper-American soldiers and anti-American puppet. It also provides some comfort to see this terrorist as no match for the United States military.

Achmed continually fails at his training. As punishment for his incompetence, a drill sergeant repeatedly orders Achmed to do push-ups that he cannot perform, underscoring his physical weakness. Although he eventually performs a lone push-up, Achmed's arms fall off in an exaggerated display of fragility. The dummy reinforces this point in bits where he attempts to fire weapons. When using a rifle, the recoil violently drives him back. And when Achmed throws a grenade, his entire arm goes with it, again showing how easily he falls apart. However, because he is stupid in addition to weak, Achmed runs after his arm, stepping on the grenade just as it explodes to reenact his initial "death."

As one might imagine, these sorts of anti-terrorist abuse gags played out across multiple comedies in the years following 9/11 on shows like *Family Guy* and *South Park*. For these types of shows, however, anti–bin Laden, anti–al-Qaeda, and more general Islamophobia were less significant, serving as brief examples of these shows' general playfulness with regard to sensitive topics. For comics like Mencia and Dunham, however, Islamophobia and attacks on representative figures acted more clearly as a branding strategy. Mencia began the first episode of his show by celebrating xenophobia, while Dunham created a cottage industry of Achmed ringtones and T-shirts. September 11 created a particular demand for this type of humor, and comics easily played into discourses of national identity as they mockingly distinguished the implied "them" from the implied "us." Nevertheless, like television and culture more generally, there was also a countervailing discourse that reacted against the invigorated xenophobia of the 2000s.

THE SIMPSONS, MEDIA REFLEXIVITY, AND LIBERAL PLURALIST TOLERANCE

While Islamophobia dominated in certain segments of the television market, it was not the only comic discourse on Muslims and Middle Eastern Americans. In the narrowcasted world of 2000s television, comedy also staked out negotiated and opposing positions as well. While comics like Dunham and Mencia defined Americanism against this convenient Other, shows like *The Simpsons* and *The Daily Show* argued for a more inclusive sense of national identity that included Americans of Middle Eastern descent. Sitcoms frequently demonstrated a liberal pluralist approach to difference by having a character assume the worst about a new Muslim family only to learn a valuable lesson in tolerance. This became a common plot device after 9/11 on shows like *American Dad*, *30 Rock*, and *The Simpsons*.[26] It was common enough, in fact, that *South Park* reflexively subverted it as a cliché in 2007.[27] Even as late as 2018, the character Roseanne Conner grew suspicious of her Muslim neighbors for buying fertilizer before realizing her mistake and coming to their defense against less enlightened people.[28] While there are a bevy of examples from which to choose, *The Simpsons* is usefully representative but also proves unique in its criticism of other media texts' reinforcement of post-9/11 Islamophobia.

Islam was not the first form of difference encountered by Homer Simpson. Over the years, he has first overreacted and eventually learned to accept or at least tolerate Lisa's vegetarianism, John Waters's sexuality, and Apu's immigration status, among other affronts.[29] Aware of this tendency, *The Simpsons* satirizes its own use of this stock plot device as the Simpsons hang a banner reading "Pardon my intolerance." Homer looks at the dingy, tattered sign and reminisces, "That banner really paid for itself over the years." This episode's self-critique fits into its larger tendency toward criticizing television in general. However, while *The Simpsons* mocks itself for uncreative plot structure, it also takes other media to task for fomenting Islamophobia. Jonathan Gray argues that among its many parodic targets, *The Simpsons'* most pervasive and perhaps most important are other television genres.[30] His book, *Watching with the Simpsons*, concentrates on the series' relationship to sitcoms, news, and advertising, but this episode aims primarily at the dramatic political intrigue of the show *24*. In particular, and as Gray suggests with relation to both news and advertising, this episode of *The Simpsons* critiques television's ability to construct political reality to an unsuspecting and naive spectator.

In this episode, Bart befriends a young Jordanian immigrant named Bashir and his parents. Homer's media-inspired fearfulness is funny because his expectations and suspicions contrast sharply with Bashir's model immigrant family. The Simpson family is at first collectively tolerant, though others are not so generous. When Bashir professes himself to be a Muslim, a young bully makes explicit the 9/11 connection, complaining, "You're the reason I can't carry toothpaste on an airplane." However, Bashir manages to charm Homer for a time. Homer's friend Moe quickly changes Homer's opinion, arguing, "Bashir . . . is Muslim and therefore up to something." "I can't believe that until I see a fictional TV program espousing your point of view," responds Homer. Conveniently, a parody of the show *24* appears on a nearby television to do just that.[31] Just in case the parodic target is still unclear, Moe instructs Homer to "Jack Bauer them," meaning that he should use whatever means necessary to extract a terrorist confession. Besides the use of common mise-en-scène and references to *24*'s hero, *The Simpsons* adds to the intertextuality by using Shoreh Aghdashloo, a significant actor in what was arguably *24*'s most Islamophobic season, to voice Bahsir's mother, Mina. This parody of *24* calls upon its notably controversial representations of terrorism, torture, and other related issues. As *24* was characterized in public debate as a conservative program that rhetorized against civil liberty protections, this *Simpsons* episode positions itself as parodic counter-rhetoric.[32] Attacking *24* and its attendant discourses is not only a media critique but also an argument against the Islamophobia that the drama supports.

In the 1902 comedy film *Uncle Josh at the Moving Picture Show*, a country rube mistakes the movies for reality, attempting to romance an on-screen woman before fleeing from the projection of a locomotive.[33] Eventually, Uncle Josh tears down the screen, ruining the show. This was but an early precedent, expressing the anxiety that naive audiences could take media images too seriously and ruin it for the rest of us. In this *Simpsons* episode, Homer plays Uncle Josh for a television age, taking *24* to be accurate and thus going overboard. Despite the protests of his more levelheaded family members, Homer takes a cue from *24* and invites Bashir and his family to dinner in order to entrap them. Despite Homer's best efforts, Bashir and his parents remain model immigrants and polite despite mistreatment. Later, Homer eavesdrops on the family, leading to a dramatic irony in which he hears evidence of a terrorist plot while the audience discovers that Bashir's father, in fact, "love[s] blowing up buildings—safely and legally in order to make room for new buildings." Through a series of mishaps, Homer foils a planned demolition and instead destroys a bridge, demonstrating in exaggerated terms that only laughably irresponsible idiots practice unchecked Islamophobia.

While television inspires Homer's initial plans to entrap the Jordanian family, after a first failed attempt, Marge talks him out of further suspicion. However, Homer's unconscious produces another, more fantastic parody shown as a dream sequence. After drifting off to sleep, Homer imagines himself riding a magic carpet while a sound-alike version of "A Whole New World" from Disney's *Aladdin* plays in the background. Finding an oil lamp on the carpet, Homer rubs it to produce a parody of that film's genie. The genie tells Homer that he will "destroy [his] decadent Western

Stylistic parody highlights The Simpsons' *critique of 24.*

society." Confirming Homer's worst fears, the genie embarks on a series of decreasingly threatening transformations. He starts by turning the local church into a mosque and ends by replacing all the music at the local record store with Cat Stevens, a.k.a. Yusuf Islam, CDs. Most obviously, this is a companionate parody to the episode's more overarching critique of *24*'s ability to construct an inaccurate political reality through its realist mockumentary style. The dream sequence critiques Disneyfied Orientalism, arguing that although *Aladdin* and its ilk may not enter directly into political discourse the way more serious fictional fare might, it holds the ability to color understandings of Middle Eastern peoples and cultures. If perhaps not in the most obvious ways, texts like these at least subtly impact our understanding of the world, as represented by Homer's dream. As he awakes in a terror, Homer verbalizes that even the most fantastic media can affect one's understanding of the sphere of politics and culture, gasping, "The power of dreaming has convinced me the threat is real!"

The Simpsons' critique of media representations here attacks both an imagined gullible audience and the irresponsible media that feeds it. While the audience understands Homer's views to be idiotic from the start, he only realizes his mistake at the end, unfurling the "pardon my intolerance" banner. This episode stakes out a position in the culture wars of the 2000s, attacking what it proposes are irresponsible representations of the Other. More generally, it argues, using token model immigrants, that Muslims and Americans of Middle Eastern descent not only are good people but in fact put up with a lot of unjust abuse. More generally, then, it fits into the larger form of sitcoms arguing for the integration of the Other. Narrative form makes *The Simpsons'* rhetoric comparably subtle. Nevertheless, it counters the anti-immigrant rhetoric present in other comedies by showing a Jordanian Muslim family as model immigrants and attacking fictional texts that foment Islamophobia. News parody—an increasingly robust genre in the post-9/11 period—provides even clearer rhetoric on these points.

THE DAILY SHOW AND "THE REAL"

The work to humanize Middle Easterners at home and abroad was not limited to fictional narratives. While *The Daily Show* focused much of its satiric efforts in the years immediately following 9/11 on international issues, there were some attempts to engage with racial and religious profiling inside the United States. These episodes echo the anti-xenophobic rhetoric of sitcoms like *The Simpsons*. However, most *Daily Show* bits, especially before the introduction of Muslim American correspondent Aasif Mandvi in 2006, lacked the model immigrant figures of these sitcoms. Instead, the show tended to focus on xenophobic policies more than the victims of such policies. However, in doing so, it engaged more directly with the tangible politics of post-9/11 Islamophobia in ways that shows like *The Simpsons*, whose critique was more of fictional media representations, did not.

Writing about *The Daily Show*, Amber Day argues that the show holds the mimetic and the real in tension with one another in politically productive ways. "It is this blend of satire and political nonfiction," she writes, "that enables and articulates an incisive critique of the inadequacies of contemporary political discourse."[34] While much of the celebratory discourse surrounding *The Daily Show*, at least in its Jon Stewart–hosted incarnation, seemed in part based on the questionable assumption that television satire is most significant when engaging with "the real" in this way, Day nevertheless highlights the manner in which this show stood separate from other parodic and satiric television of this era. In addressing Islamophobia in the decade following 9/11, *The Daily Show* engaged "on the ground" individuals from President Bush to apartment building door attendants to outspoken xenophobes. Tracking these discourses over time shows how this lauded show not only developed its satire into more critical forms after the relative lull in critique that followed 9/11, but made real for viewers aspects of Islamophobia that might have otherwise escaped their notice.

In December 2001, the program used fictional suggestions of government profiling to satirize Islamophobic paranoia.[35] The "real" in this case was a photo op that allowed the president to perform his liberal tolerance for the cameras. In a gesture of goodwill toward Muslims, President Bush had invited a group of children to the White House in order to read them a book. In the news clip, he reads, "Allah loves children who care for others, who do deeds of kindness to sisters and brothers." Cutting back to Jon Stewart, the host jokes, "Bush then added, 'Now that being said, if anyone has any information that can be useful, please approach me after the meeting.'" This poke at the event's staginess and its unease with more general Islamophobic sentiment hints at the deeper anxieties of the moment that might have caused overreactions and unwarranted suspicion. It is not a full-on attack against Islamophobia, but it suggests the extent to which efforts by the administration to reconcile with American Islamic communities were hypocritical. Inasmuch as there was activism in this moment, it pointed to future attacks on Islamophobic policy by *The Daily Show*.

After a bit more time had passed, in July 2002, *The Daily Show* showcased a bit regarding FBI-suggested racial profiling by landlords in New York City.[36] Correspondent Steve Carell strolls toward the camera, eating an apple and invoking the pro–New York tourism language that had become more prominent since the attacks:

> The big apple: a melting pot where you live and work with people from all over the world. A place where you may be living next to the elderly Greek woman who makes a heck of a baklava. Or two adolescent Latinas listening to their salsa tunes . . . but more likely you're living next to a terrorist who wants to destroy your building and all buildings within an eight-block radius. So you can forget all about your precious baklava. Putting city dwellers on alert, the FBI has warned that a terrorist could be moving on up to your deluxe apartment in the sky-ay-ay. But there's no reason to panic. The new guidelines show landlords and realtors how to identify and prevent renting to terrorists.

Playing on contrasts between friendly pro-tourist and frightening anti-terrorist language as well as between news and sitcoms, this bit introduces the idea that New York, and by extension the United States, is a welcoming melting pot for some, but not all, in the new post-9/11 world.

Carell then goes "undercover as an apartment-hunting terrorist," posing essentially as his *Daily Show* persona—an overly precise-speaking, suit-wearing, white professional—who acts suspicious by owning no furniture and laughing awkwardly. While absurd in its execution and performance, the fact that his lack of furniture raises no suspicions suggests that such guidelines were cover for more nefarious purposes. Driving the point further, Carell continues, "Many people are claiming that these new guidelines for landlords are nothing more than a complicated form of racial profiling. Well that's just not true. They're in fact a simple and very easy-to-learn form of racial profiling." Carell talks through a series of graphics explaining that Caucasians and Canadians are good and that while Japanese people used to be bad, they are now good. This last point in particular subtly references World War II–era internment camps, reminding viewers of a shameful period of American xenophobia in response to a national trauma.

Eventually, Carell tests the door attendants of New York City on their anti-terrorist acumen. Against a backdrop of the Hagia Sophia and Arabic writing, Carell claims to have done "extensive research on Middle Eastern culture and [gone] even deeper undercover as a potential terrorist." His research leads to a satirical sight gag of extreme Orientalism that again mocks the apparent simplicity of the FBI guidelines. Carell walks the streets of Manhattan dressed like a cheap version of Disney's Aladdin in harem pants, gold lamé vest, and ridiculous hat. After a series of maladroit attempts to get past door attendants using obviously phony excuses, Carell concludes the piece by praising their vigilance in keeping New York safe. According to this routine, only in a world where identity is performed with the subtlety of a cheap Halloween costume does simplistic profiling address the threat posed by terrorism.

In this example, *The Daily Show* demonstrates a common tactic with regard to its satirical targets in that it plays a parodic devil's advocate, adopting an extreme version of the position it means to criticize in order to highlight its flaws. Performances of paranoia and unsubtle racism are a means to uncover their possible role in the creation and application of anti-terrorist measures. But while the wars in Iraq and Afghanistan gave reason to engage with Islam and Middle Easterners, *The Daily Show* only rarely engaged with the issues surrounding American Muslims' and Middle

Carrell goes undercover for The Daily Show.

Easterners' civil liberties at home for many years. The so-called Ground Zero Mosque controversy in 2010 was an ideal story with which *The Daily Show* would form a consistent ethical position. While different formats and performers within the program's repertoire performed different tasks, Jon Stewart's anchoring accomplished the lion's share of negotiation. In one of these segments, the show argues that the supposed enemies of Islam, whether Christianity, America, or Fox News, are more similar to their apparent foe than conservative pundits would care to admit. In the years after 9/11, comedies arguing for some measure of tolerance frequently compared Americans to those in the Middle East. When the children of *South Park* encounter the Other in Afghanistan, it is in the form of children that look uncannily similar to the boys from Colorado.[37] When *American Dad*'s Stan Smith moves to Saudi Arabia, he finds common cause with theocratic misogyny and repression, prompting him to "go native."[38] As the controversy over building Islamic centers and mosques was in its early phases of the news cycle, *The Daily Show* set up a series of jokes similarly arguing that "we" are more like "them" than it may seem. After showing a couple of talking heads warning that part of Islam's teachings were to proselytize on its behalf, Stewart sarcastically responds, "What!? One of the tenets of Islam is to spread Islam? That would be like if Christians went places and built churches to, quote, 'go and make disciples of all nations.'"[39] By this point the anchor had pulled out a Bible and was reading passages, eventually reading five in total, demonstrating Christianity's similar charge to its adherents. Continuing the bit, a number of clips show pundits arguing that Muslims were planning to overthrow the American legal system, culminating in one Fox News pundit claiming, "No other religious system makes rules for people who are outside the religion, but Islamic law does." Stewart again responds sarcastically: "What?! So I guess in your town I can go buy booze on a Sunday to bring to Adam and Steve's wedding reception?"[40]

The Daily Show commonly edits together clips in order to show pundits making contradictory statements with regard to different issues. In a sense, this technique puts different moments of time in dialogue with one another to humorously demonstrate hypocrisy. In this case, the technique contrasts certain pundits' fears regarding Islamic law with their belief that religion forms the basis of American law. Stewart continues, "If the new principle is that no one should have to live by the rules of someone else's religion, I know some people who are going to be very disappointed." A montage then demonstrates various conservative pundits and politicians arguing that American law is primarily Judeo-Christian in origin, to which Stewart responds, "Wait a minute. Now I know why you don't want mosques popping up all over the place: competition."

The Ground Zero Mosque controversy was one of the most sustained American public-sphere engagements with overt Islamophobia in the decade following 9/11, and in its dialogue with straight news and opinion programs, *The Daily Show* maintained a consistent defense of the right to build the community center over the course of July, August, and into September 2010. In so doing, it argued for religious tolerance in the face of Islamophobia in line with a liberal pluralist notion that accepts supposed Others into the imagined community of the United States. Many of these routines relied on the same techniques as those above, offering edited juxtapositions to demonstrate the hypocrisy of public figures like Glenn Beck or jokingly highlighting that the supposed "hallowed ground" upon which the center was to be built had housed a Burlington Coat Factory up to that point.[41]

Muslim American correspondent Aasif Mandvi stood out in particular during this period. In contrast to the example from *The Simpsons*, in which Arab Americans remain peripheral to a more central character's narrative of transformation, Mandvi's performances as a Muslim American on *The Daily Show* more often than not act as the audience's primary surrogate and his pieces' authorial voice. Introducing him for the first time in 2006, Jon Stewart announces, "We're lucky enough to be joined by an expert in Middle Eastern affairs—an experienced journalist from the region who can bring us a unique perspective for less than half the price of an American reporter."[42] This kind of parodic essentialism is a common joke on *The Daily Show*, with titles such as "senior black correspondent" and "senior women's issues commentator" serving similar roles. In most cases like these, recurring guests appear only occasionally to dialogue with Stewart over some issue relating to their identity. While Mandvi sometimes acted in this role, he was a more regular contributor than most. This granted him the ability to engage more deeply and serially as the "senior Middle East correspondent" and as the de facto Muslim representative on the show. Additionally, while it maintained a sense of essentialism, it also normalized Mandvi's presence on *The Daily Show*.

For instance, in a bit referencing fans of the *Twilight* fantasy series, Mandvi is called upon to debate other members of the staff as a member of "Team Mohammed."[43] Mandvi also used his religion as a way to perform a spin on *The Daily Show*'s common strategy of playing devil's advocate when doing correspondent pieces. In reporting on the opposition to a new mosque in Tennessee during the summer of 2010, Mandvi interviews the leader of the anti-mosque organization, whose views are akin to those of a paranoid conspiracy theorist.[44] After a montage shows the woman offering erroneous information about Islam and acting frightened of its benign aspects, like the proscription against eating pork, she claims that there are thirty-five training camps for Islamic terrorists in the United States. Acting startled, Mandvi excuses himself and turns his head as if to hide the conversation from his mark. Speaking to an imagined man named Achmed at the other end of the conversation, he excoriates, "She knows about the training camps, you idiot!"

Continuing his mock anger, Mandvi travels to the local Islamic center to discover why its members have been in the area for more than thirty years without having performed any jihadist violence. "You're not a sleeper cell," he scolds. "You're a comatose cell!" As a public figure assumed to have an established rapport with the audience, Mandvi sets up a contrast between the worst fears of Islamophobes and reality by demonstrating what he would be like as a threatening figure. To put this into sharper contrast, he interviews Cammie, a self-described spokesperson and mom. Mandvi again plays devil's advocate, allowing her to defend her position against his absurd insistences that they become violent. However, the bit ultimately devolves into wordplay in which Mandvi cannot decipher whether she was "a mom" or an "Imam." While silly, this routine also functions to blunt the threatening stance Mandvi parodically repudiates. Intercut with footage of the Three Stooges acting confused, the vaudevillian routine at once marks the pair as nonthreatening and the faux-threatening Mandvi as a harmless buffoon whose efforts to radicalize his fellow Muslims could be derailed by punnage. In a way, this echoes the role played by Jeff Dunham's puppet in making terrorism appear harmless for laughs, but the audience's familiarity with Mandvi and the clear irony of his performance make fearing Muslims seem silly. Unlike the dummy, who is an Other to be ritually abused, *The Daily Show* incorporated Muslim Americans into the collective American community—or, at least the part of that community who thinks the Islamophobic conspiracy theorist is an idiot.

THE AXIS OF EVIL COMEDY TOUR: MIDDLE EASTERN AMERICAN COMICS NEGOTIATE POST-9/11 IDENTITY

Compared to the previous chapter's study of African American comedy's response to the Los Angeles riots, Muslim and Middle Eastern Americans were frequently left out of television comedy conversations regarding their Americanness after 9/11, Aasif Mandvi's presence on *The Daily Show* notwithstanding. However, as Rebecca Krefting notes, politically charged comedy from Arab-, Persian-, and other Middle Eastern–descended American comics flowered in the years following 9/11.[45] While limited in reach compared to the other examples noted in this chapter, television specials and DVD releases provided a significant place for humorists to negotiate their own position to American identity.[46] In specials like *The Axis of Evil Comedy Tour*, joking provided a place to reject, negotiate, and even reinforce the sense of otherness attached to Middle Eastern descent in post-9/11 America.

Although I focus on the one-off television special of the same name to conclude this chapter, *The Axis of Evil Comedy Tour* began as a live show featuring four American comics of Middle Eastern descent. Dean Obeidallah and Aron Kader are Palestinian American while Ahmed Ahmed and Maz Jobrani are Egyptian American and Iranian American, respectively. In this television special, which presents a live performance, the four comics frequently joke about being victims of Islamophobia while also calling for more unity across religious and ethnic identities. They also perform Americanness by othering and mocking those whom they would prefer to not be identified with, from relatives living in the Middle East to Muslim-identified terrorists. In these ways, they borrow from the strategies of comics across the political spectrum noted above even as they appear to speak to an audience more sympathetic to an anti-Islamophobic message. At the same time, such humor operates to on-screen and larger audiences that share religious and/or ethnic ties as in-group community building.

Examples from black and Jewish comics' responses to oppression in chapter 4, as well as the sense that Jeff Dunham's humor speaks to a sense of white conservative victimhood, demonstrate how comedy frequently gives voice to grievances. As Mandvi's jokes on *The Daily Show* highlighted, this acted as a frequent theme for comics with Muslim and/or Middle Eastern identities in the years following 9/11. "Do you know what it's like being of Arab heritage with a Muslim last name living in America?" asked Dean Obeidallah near the start of the special. "I could use a hug." Obeidallah and other comics would riff on this theme in various ways throughout *The Axis of Evil* special, joking about insensitive friends, racial profiling, mental health issues, and so forth. In service of this theme, the comics frequently riffed on true facts, often citing their sources, which necessarily promised different meanings for various members of their audience. For example, Ahmed Ahmed cited a news story to set up his joke:

> I gotta say it's a bad time to be from the Middle East. In fact, I read a statistic on CBS.com that said right after 9/11 hate crimes against Arabs and Middle Eastern people and Muslims went up over a thousand percent. Yeah. Which apparently put us in fourth place behind blacks, gays, and Jews. You guys know this? We're still in fourth place. So what do we have to do? I mean, we can't even win in hatred. I want to be number one in something.

The ironic reversal on display in this joke, in which Ahmed wants to suffer the most, performs an emotionally nonconforming toughness that the audience can enjoy through identification. In another example, Aron Kader expresses frustration at people who do not know what it means to be Palestinian. "Pakastilian? What the hell? Pakastilia, that sounds made up. So where's Pakastilia?" As himself, Kader replies, "There's no such country as Pakastilia. I guess there's no Palestine either," in a semi-mournful tone. On-screen audience laughter to such jokes suggests that this humor salves the pain of similar experiences for oppressed groups. For those outside of the oppressed community, however, the joking communicates an often overlooked or misunderstood element of post-9/11 reality. In doing so, it also expresses a desire for justice, certainly for those identifying as Muslim and Middle Eastern, but arguably for all the other victims of hate crimes as well.

As was the case in *The Simpsons*, media representations were also a frequent target for complaints. Dean Obeidallah and Maz Jobrani both included bits about how news tended to focus on negative events when portraying Middle Eastern people. Jobrani in particular relayed,

> The thing that frustrates me is when I see us [Iranians] on TV
> nowadays, who do they always show? They always show the crazy
> dude burning the American flag, going, "Death to America!"
> Always that guy. Just once I wish they would show us doing some-
> thing good, man. Right? Just once . . . show us doing something
> good . . . like baking a cookie. Because I've been to Iran. We have
> cookies. Just once I want to see CNN be like, "Now we're going to
> go to Muhammad in Iran." They go to some guy, he's like, "Hello,
> I'm Muhammad and I'm just baking a cookie. I swear to God. No
> bombs, no flags, no nothing."

Similarly, Ahmed Ahmed criticizes media portrayals from a more insider
perspective, discussing how when he auditions for acting roles, he must
perform stereotypically, with directors encouraging him to "use that hidden
Middle Eastern anger that your people possess." Shamefully, but with a
sense of humor, he admits that he took one such part because it paid well.
Examples like these again bring the victims of such stereotyping together
through humor but also serve a didactic function in addressing crowds that
might be less familiar with these challenges.

As Ahmed's joke suggests, the focus on oppression also slipped easily
into calls for unity among different groups. In that particular case, he
drew symbolic connections between Americans of Muslim and Middle
Eastern descent and other victims of hate crimes. All of the comics in this
special made some overture toward reconciling the relationship between
the identities represented on stage and others in the United States. At
the broadest level, Dean Obeidallah appealed to a sense of common civil
rights and citizenship.

> To keep us safe we've got a thing called the Patriot Act. . . .
> Remember we had a thing called freedoms at one point? Now we
> have the Patriot Act. . . . As someone of Middle Eastern heritage,
> it's really important we catch terrorists as Americans, and also it
> makes our lives obviously so much more difficult if someone's Mid-
> dle Eastern does something. But did you guys know that under the
> Patriot Act, any book you take out of any library, the government
> can find out the name of that book? Do you actually think guys in
> al-Qaeda are going to public libraries and taking books out?

This sets up a routine that riffs on the idea that international terrorists
would use a public library because they are thirty dollars short and need
imagined books like *Chicken Soup for the Terrorist Soul* and *I'm al-Qaeda,*

You're al-Qaeda. Before getting to the punchlines, however, Obeidallah appeals to a common idea of lost American freedom that speaks directly to the discourses of freedom and unity going on at the time (especially notable in George W. Bush's assertions that terrorists "hate freedom").[47] Additionally, the comic appeals to the notion that he and his largely Middle Eastern American audience are American before anything else. In a similarly patriotic vein that echoes ideas about Western liberal democracies as superior to other forms of government, Maz Jobrani celebrates the United States as compared to Iran, arguing that the abilities to debate and criticize the government are "the beauty of this country." This theme of singular unity—that these comics are members of a unified American identity—are rare but significant within the larger themes of identity, belonging, and alienation at play in this special.

Like Jeff Dunham, these comics also make fun of terrorists and other apparently threatening Middle Eastern figures. Compared to a white Christian comic, their jokes take on different meanings in that by laughing at terrorists, these comics of Muslim and Middle Eastern descent do not Other their ethnicity from Americanness. Instead, these jokes draw distinctions between Americans of Middle Eastern descent and terrorists. In his discussion of the Patriot Act, Obeidallah imagines terrorists who are, like Achmed the Dead Terrorist, bad at their job in that they need to borrow terror-related books from the library. Maz Jobrani also mocks Osama bin Laden, first infantilizing the terrorist leader by comparing his behavior to a game of hide and seek, then ridiculing his publishing of *Jihad* magazine. "What kind of articles are in that?" he joked. "Fifty ways to lose weight. Number one: blow yourself up. Mustafa lost 200 pounds in one second." He continued in a similar vein by making fun of Iranian politicians for "talking shit" to the United States. Jobrani explains, "I'll tell you why Iran is talking shit. There's a lot of opium usage in Iran. Yes, the politicians are high. You have to be high to talk shit to America." With this, the comic demeans political and military leaders as stoners while also participating in discourses that celebrate American military power. Though these jokes take on a distinct set of meanings when Arab American and Persian American comics perform them, they nevertheless recreate many of the same comic strategies displayed by Jeff Dunham and others like him.

For the most part, appeals to a singular American identity happened in more earnest moments of the special, as opposed to in punchlines. However, more comic approaches characterized strategies that aligned Middle Eastern Americans and other subnational identities specifically. In other words, the work that reconciled relationships between Arab and

African, white, and/or Jewish Americans was more directly humorous. Mentioned toward the beginning of this chapter, Obeidallah riffs on the idea that "Arab is the new black" not in the zero-sum rhetoric of Carlos Mencia, but in the hopes that his culture would be considered cool enough to warrant cultural appropriation. In a subtle double move, this joke not only expresses similarity to African Americans, but also invites "white kids in the suburbs" to participate in his culture and identity. While this is less sincere than some of Obeidallah's commentary above, it also destabilizes some of the ways in which discourse distinguishes between ethnicities.

Obeidallah also uses humor to destabilize the boundaries that distinguish white Americans from Arab Americans. "Before 9/11 I'm just a white guy living like a typical white guy life. All my friends had names like Monica and Chandler and Joey and Ross. I go to bed September 10 white. I wake up September 11—I'm Arab." Even though he might look white, he argues that the privilege of avoiding blame when one member of the group does something wrong is what actually defines whiteness. "Honestly, white people, let's be honest. You've done your share of bad things. Corporate scandals, presidential assassinations, NASCAR, Paris Hilton, country music. That is audio terrorism to me." By making meanings of "terrorism" slippery, Obeidallah rhetorically marks as absurd the ways in which that term had been almost exclusively applied to Muslims.

Though expressed with varying degrees of irony as opposed to Mencia's more sincere and troubling assertions regarding the "giant game of [racial] tag," the humor in this special sometimes engaged similar strategies—putting down another group of people to win higher status. In a more clearly ironic example, Maz Jobrani distinguishes between Persians and Arabs so that he can be considered more legitimately white. "We're similar, you know; we're all getting shot at," he explains. "That's one thing, but you know Iranians are ethnically . . . Aryan. We're white! We're white, so stop shooting." The implication, of course, is that shooting at Arabs may continue. There is also some play with anti-Semitism, justified by various strategies including noting their relationships with actual Jews, the use of positive stereotypes, and/or self-deprecation. Ahmed Ahmed states that he has many Jewish friends, which confuses people. They are actually fairly similar, he argues, because Arabs and Jews have similar dietary restrictions and language. "The only difference between Muslims and Jews," he jokes, "is that Jews never like to spend any money and Muslims never have any money to spend." While the form and storytelling methods the comics use demonstrate that they are friendly with the group they mock, these strategies nevertheless reinforce certain forms of otherness in part as a strategy to justify their inclusion in the dominant power bloc. Obeidallah comes closest to recreating Mencia's historicizing of racism and attempt to shift blame when he jokes, "Sadly, Arabs, Muslims, Middle Eastern people, we are the new enemy in America. . . . We've replaced the Soviet Union, and we are stuck here until somebody replaces us. That's why I'm begging all of you to help me taunt North Korea as much as possible. . . . We tell Bush Kim Jong-Il has tons of oil—in his hair." Whether couched in stories of friendship, respect, or more blatant hostility, all of these bits build connections between subnational groups while simultaneously othering an identity to which the comic does not belong.

More ambiguous is the presence of somewhat self-deprecating humor, in which these comics mock those with whom they share religious and ethnic ties, but not necessarily citizenship or political ideology. Once again, this humor resembles Jeff Dunham's even though the comics' respective ethnic and religious identities alter the jokes' meanings. A number of scholars discuss the role of self-deprecating humor as a strategy with which marginalized comics negotiate between their specific identities and larger cultural formations.[48] As they note, this kind of humor can have various effects, from simply reinforcing oppressive discourses to demonstrating that the joker's community has a superior sense of humor. Self-deprecating humor in this context necessarily recreates elements of post-9/11 Islamophobic and xenophobic discourse, albeit in ways that build relationships with audiences that reinforce in-group identity while also appealing to larger understandings of American identity. In a simple example, Ahmed Ahmed makes fun of Arabic accents and diction, proving his ability to speak more proper English. Additionally, he riffs on the idea that Muslims will criticize him for joking about Islam as they drink alcohol. In fact, he notes that many of his Muslim friends drink, gamble, and have sex, even though they arbitrarily maintain the restriction against pork. Aron Kader makes similar jokes, mocking relatives still living in the Middle East who curse the United States in English because God only understands Arabic.

> You son of a bitch bastard United States. Think you're so big and strong and powerful. This is bullshit. United States. You are a paper tiger. You will fall. You'll see. You hungry? You want something to eat? You hungry? We got Burger King, McDonald's, Pizza Hut, Applebee's. There's a new place called T.A.I.F. Friday's [sic] that looks good. You don't want? You look tired. You want coffee? We got Starbuckus [sic]. You like Starbuckus? StarBUCKs, ah. I

like that place. They got a frappuccino, I like, that's a good, have you had? Oh you've had a—you've had that in the United States. Son of a bitch. United States think they own everything. Bullshit! Which hotel you going to? Sheraton? Hilton? Marriot?

These relatives have a love/hate relationship with the United States. While they curse America's interventionism and militarism, they cannot resist its consumer culture. As with many of the other jokes that appear comparable to Dunham's, Mencia's, or others', these necessarily take on different meanings in that they function at least partly as self-deprecating jokes. To an audience of Middle Eastern Americans, this kind of inwardly directed humor likely helps to build a sense of community among shared experiences dealing with relatives overseas or perceived hypocrisies at home. Nevertheless, they still exist within the larger discourses of Islamophobia and xenophobia and serve as lessons in how to distinguish between "good" and "bad" Others.

As *The Axis of Evil Comedy Tour* demonstrates, the discourses surrounding American national traumas frequently concern race. While earlier chapters in this book focused more on undifferentiated ideas of Americanism, the existence of subnational communities like African and Middle Eastern Americans means that culture must mediate between the senses of part and whole. The similar tension between television's narrowcasting strategies and national reach make it a particularly telling place where this work occurs. This is the most notable and significant aspect by which these events act as points for understanding the nation as a collection of people. In the case of the Rodney King beating and subsequent Los Angeles riots, the trauma symbolically belonged to a subgroup of Americans. Comedies reflected this by negotiating who did and did not deserve to claim connection to those events from the perspective of black characters and creative talent. In the case of Islamophobia after 9/11, while comedians of Middle Eastern descent had a say in the larger discourse, a wider range of comedies participated in negotiating the role of Middle Eastern and Muslim Americans in relation to national identity. In both cases, comedy television frequently concerned itself with the boundaries of in-group/out-group identity. While comedy separates out certain members from the larger understanding of nation or subnational group, these efforts are always counterintuitively tied to the understanding of the nation. The next chapter continues on this theme but examines the role of comedy and political affiliation, as opposed to ethnic or religious identity, in creating collective trauma for a subset of Americans.

COMEDY AND TRUMP AS TRAUMA IN NARROWCAST AMERICA

In early 2017, the sitcom *Black-ish* aired a very special episode responding to a national trauma.[1] In one scene, people nervously crowd around a television to watch the bad news unfold. In another, the main character, Dre, expresses the sense that everything had changed by noting, "The idea of business as usual had become anything but usual." Other characters also respond in familiar ways to the trauma. Countering the sense of powerlessness, one woman collects tchotchkes demonstrating that she had donated to causes that will aid in the recovery. Another dives deeply into conspiracy theory culture, questioning everything from the JFK assassination to the United States Constitution. With a similar logic, a group pores over the minute details of recent events in order to understand what went wrong, while others make sense of the present in relation to longer histories. This last point in particular slips into a melodramatic documentary mode, cutting between archival video and slow zooms onto still photographs of historical trauma while mournful music plays in the background. Although this has elements in common with the way both news and comedy television responded to events like 9/11, the Los Angeles riots, Hurricane Katrina, school shootings, and so on, it was actually about the 2016 United States presidential election. Although this episode appears to speak almost exclusively to a left-leaning view of the election as a trauma, it nevertheless gestured to a sense of unity over division. "Maybe we can get past all that racial BS that's held us up for so long and work with each other," hopes Dre, "to make sure that whatever happens next in this country, we do together. . . . It's time we stop calling each other names and we start trying to have . . . conversations. If we don't, we'll end up being in a country that's even more divided for a long time."

This chapter examines the role of comedy in responding to the 2016 election and subsequent political initiatives of President Donald Trump. Up to this point the book has mostly operated on a model that posits a linear temporality where news and documentary foster a sense of trauma, followed by engagement of that trauma by more entertainment-oriented genres including comedy. Factors including the development of narrowcasting and increasingly testy political culture in recent American history have informed the entirety of these chapters, but the Trump era brings certain of these tendencies into sharp focus and even forces me to adapt the temporality of this model to present circumstances. A significant portion of Americans and media texts view not just the election but also the administration's association with sexual assault and policies like family separation as traumas. At the same time, mainstream journalism struggles to balance competing drives to appear neutral, appeal to audiences, and normalize official government action. Television continues to play a role in expressing and even defining national traumas, but in the present moment, this role is less significant in news, falling instead to the more rhetorically and expressively free genre of comedy.

JOURNALISTIC NEUTRALITY AND PARTISAN COMEDY

Serious journalists on the major networks and cable news channels were emotionally staid on election night 2016. In keeping with generic conventions, television journalism focused on the horse race, counting electoral votes, discussing campaign strategies, and interviewing pollsters about what they had missed. While emotions were part of the coverage, it followed a common election-night balance. Clinton's supporters shed tears at her campaign headquarters. Jubilation characterized Trump's. In this coverage, there was very little sense of Trump's election as a national trauma. Even at self-identified left-leaning MSNBC, where Brian Williams and Rachel Maddow anchored the night's coverage, their voices remained steady as they called the race for Trump over swirling fanfare music that connoted celebration far more than trauma.[2] Fox News coverage was largely the same in tone, except for anchor Bret Baier commenting—in what might have been construed as negative editorializing on another network—that Trump had won "the most unreal, surreal election we have ever seen."[3] However, to watch Stephen Colbert's election night special on Showtime, the first *Saturday Night Live* after the election, later feminist comedies that drew metaphorical comparisons between sexual assault and the election, or masculine comedians shedding tears over children is to note the ways that comedy frequently presents the election and its aftermath as a national trauma.

As this book makes clear, although television has never spoken to its viewers as an undifferentiated mass, the increasingly fractious nature of television in the post-network, narrowcasted environment of the last forty-plus years drives television to speak to ever more specific audiences. News coverage of major traumas, especially but not limited to 9/11, is exceptional in the way it causes television to temporarily suspend its demographic targeting. Even in that privileged example, Americans managed to interpret those events in different ways. Those on the political fringes viewed it as the deserved punishment for American colonialism or Godlessness. Others, like a student of mine whose family had only recently immigrated to the United States in early 2001, simply did not feel connected to the destruction in Lower Manhattan, which was being articulated as a national event to a nation of which she did not yet feel a part. If Peter Griffin represented a type of nonconformity in his emotional detachment from the trauma, he was not entirely alone.

To speak of "national trauma" in one sense, then, is to describe a tacit agreement between a media construct and a significant portion of audience members to understand a particular event as both traumatic and national. To some, as has become abundantly clear, the election of Donald Trump is therefore a trauma. To others, the most significant national trauma of 2016 was that several high-ranking Democrats were involved in a child sex ring centered on a pizzeria in Washington, DC, which was a fabricated story.[4] While certain types of events in the 2010s, like mass shootings, tended to draw similar coverage in the trauma frame, the amount of coverage offered such events indicates how traumatic media producers expected an event to be.

As the example of election-night coverage indicates, other events that may be traumatic to some do not easily fit into journalism's trauma frame. Mainstream journalists largely do not treat the 2016 election or later actions by the Trump administration, including the nomination of Supreme Court Justice Brett Kavanaugh and the child separation policies at the southern border, as traumas. Even in cases of seemingly unconscionable actions like family separation, coverage largely operates in the emotionally neutral tone of everyday journalism. For instance, in reporting on allegations of sexual assault in a child detainment facility, *CBS This Morning* anchor Gail King read the news in a flat monotone. Although the piece used the trauma convention of slowly zooming in on pictures of detainees in overcrowded rooms, it lacked musical accompaniment and presented quotations from officials arguing that they treated those in their facility with "dignity and respect," relying on the "get both sides" approach that characterizes everyday journalism.[5] The good/evil binaries of trauma narratives do not allow a space in which to consider a legitimate other side.

Discussing the limits of neutrality's value in coverage of Trump's tweets encouraging four Congresswomen of color to "go back [to where] they came,"[6] Margaret Sullivan questioned the tendency to avoid critical language in reporting presidential misconduct:

> In general, the network news shows, with their efforts to appeal to everyone, regardless of political affiliation, like to be particularly careful not to offend. So they used what CNN's Brian Stelter accurately called, in his media newsletter, a "crutch"—for example, on NBC, Kate Snow noted that "many were decrying [the tweet] as racist." . . . It makes good sense for media organizations to be careful and noninflammatory in their news coverage. That kind of caution continues to be a virtue. But a crucial part of being careful is being accurate, clear and direct. When confronted with racism and lying, we can't run and hide in the name of neutrality and impartiality. To do that is a dereliction of duty.[7]

If news is at times in "dereliction of duty," as Sullivan claims, when it avoids emotionally evocative techniques in both audiovisual and verbal language, comedy has played a role in filling this gap. In many ways, this is merely a continuation of a role that some comedies have played in regard to other, more agreed-upon traumas. But while in earlier examples comedy reinforced and/or undercut the trauma frame established by news, more contemporary comedy plays a larger role in framing certain events as traumatic since journalism is not as clearly performing that role.

The reasons for this new relationship around the events of the Trump era speak to the larger themes of this book. Journalism, especially television journalism, attempts to maintain a sense of neutrality, in part, to appeal to a sense of a unified American audience in ways that continue to reflect journalistic neutrality's deeper roots, appealing to Americans across geography and ideology in the fractious era leading up to the Civil War.[8] Comedy seems more willing to question the discourses of neutrality and undifferentiated Americanism by speaking to the views of subnational cultures, which frequently double as demographic targets. This book has, in both its historical and theoretical understanding, tended to treat national trauma and television comedy as separate phenomena. However, this chapter examines more recent history to complicate this view at least somewhat. News appears less willing to forgo its standard unaffected tone, but comedy's more affective nature makes it more able to represent and speak to the emotional intensities surrounding contemporary politics. Though news is less willing to slip into the melodramatic mode that defines good and evil, comedy's expressive freedom allows it to dabble in this approach. Comedy is, in the era of Trump, more actively implicated in the creation of national trauma as a media discourse.

ESTABLISHING TRAUMA WITH HUMOR: ELECTION WEEK COMEDY IN LATE NIGHT

The day after the 2016 election, the *Atlantic*'s pop culture writer David Sims described Stephen Colbert's 2016 election night special on Showtime:

> In times of national strife and confusion, comedy has long served as a vital release valve, a therapeutic outlet for viewers confronting difficult moments. But Tuesday night, as Stephen Colbert aired a live special on Showtime during the most crucial hour of the election, catharsis seemed a million miles away. The election of Donald Trump as president was obviously a positive outcome for his many supporters. But for Colbert's crowd, news of Trump picking up more and more states across the map prompted loud groans, and a bewildered performance by a host who clearly found less and less relief in humor.[9]

Within this paragraph, Sims hyperlinked to another of his articles about how comedians were responding to the Paris terror attacks of a year before, explicitly linking Trump's election to traumas involving political violence on a large scale.[10] This article and the television comedy special to which it refers speak to many of the larger issues discussed in this book, especially the emotional juxtaposition of frivolity and mournfulness inherent to comedy's negotiation and management of national trauma. "It was a bizarre 90 minutes of television, a strange side dish to a similarly unpredictable night of broadcast TV," noted Sims.[11] "Perhaps it says something about the vast polarization of America that the country's divisions extend to the world of pop culture and to late-night television," the critic mused in relation to narrowcasting.[12] This passage highlights another significant aspect of nationalism in relation to the election: the way in which the election of Trump was traumatic for what seemed a slight majority of the country.

Colbert's special, which the *Hollywood Reporter* characterized as "a wake," also speaks to the strange sense of being a comedian responding in real time to what those on the show consider an unfolding trauma.[13] "Whoever wins, it's going to be a challenging time for America—good,

good line for a comedy show, eh?," asks Colbert's guest, journalist Mark Halperin.[14] "I'm not sure it's a comedy show at this point," replies the host, nodding meaningfully to his audience's uncomfortable laughter before continuing, "I think we're in the middle of a documentary right now." Halperin presses Colbert to do something memorable so that he can be part of a documentary the journalist was working on. "If Trump wins," replies Colbert, "how about bursting into tears and screaming 'fuck' for the next forty-five minutes?" After Trump had taken Florida and Colbert admitted that he was not sure that he could put a "happy face" on despite it being his job, Halperin reaches further back than Sims did for historical comparison. "Outside of the Civil War, World War II, and including 9/11, this may be the most cataclysmic event the country's ever seen."

In my definition, a particular style of framing by media discourse transforms an event or series of events into a national trauma. These become "sacred" in their appeal to nationalistic and emotional narratives of collective suffering and grief. Television journalism did not clearly respond to the election of Donald Trump in that way. This reflects the strategic neutrality of American journalism in the last century such that in 2016, even self-consciously partisan-leaning news sources were largely unable to reflect their viewers' likely response to the election for fear of appearing biased. Certainly, the election of a new president is a nationalistic ritual, but the sense that this spelled hardship for the nation or was a cause for mourning was left to the freer rhetorical environment of Colbert's election night special and other comedies.

The tonal gulf between Colbert's election night special and journalistic coverage of the same event indicates a notable role played by television comedy in recent history. Television culture in general reflects the siloing of subnational American cultures. Of course, American culture has always reflected a mishmash of various intersecting cultures and identities, but cultural commentators now identify this tendency as more pronounced and virulent than in times past.[15] As the most significant nationalizing media for at least the last century, radio and television have played a role in defining American culture and Americanism more generally. Television's tendency toward increasingly narrowcasted markets has both reflected and helped drive the move toward cultural divisiveness. These characteristics increasingly bubbled to the surface in the politics of the Obama years and boiled over with the election of Donald Trump.

Colbert's trauma coverage of the election happened on Tuesday, November 8. Other late night hosts responded the following night with emotion fitting a trauma. Although mostly joking and attempting to set

Kate McKinnon strikes a somber tone as Hillary Clinton on SNL.

a hopeful tone, Seth Meyers fought tears as he discussed the possibility that his mother might not survive long enough to see a female president.[16] Jimmy Kimmel was less emotive in his discussion of the previous night but spoke to the sense of grief among some: "A lot of voters woke up this morning happy Donald Trump won the election. The other half of them, especially in California, were very upset. Shocked. Despondent. Some were even crying."[17] This led to a series of jokes discussing responses to the election as the five stages of grief. By November 12, it was time for *Saturday Night Live* to weigh in. While the weekday late night hosts mostly practiced gallows humor around what they defined as a trauma, *SNL* was more ambiguous. In keeping with the more dialogic form of sketch comedy as opposed to a talk show unified by a singular stable personality, *SNL* presented a variety of moods and opinions in relation to the election, from somber to cautiously optimistic.

Like Halperin on Colbert, *SNL* appears to draw comparisons between Trump's election and 9/11. The first episode of *SNL* following 9/11 opens with New York City mayor Rudolph Giuliani onstage to earnestly praise first responders before he introduces Paul Simon. The singer solemnly performs his song "The Boxer" while police, firefighters, and others stand silent vigil in the background. Following this, show producer Lorne Michaels asks the mayor whether the show could be funny. "Why start now?" quips Giuliani.[18] In a strange echo of that episode, the first *SNL* following the 2016 election features performer Kate McKinnon dressed as Hillary Clinton singing "Hallelujah," a tune written by the recently deceased Leonard

Cohen.[19] It was at best vaguely funny to see Hillary Clinton, and the *SNL* performer destined for the coveted role of presidential impersonator, so openly mourning the election, but it mostly appeared to not be attempting humor. The post-9/11 cold opening punctuates the tense atmosphere with a pithy joke, but there is little relief before the credits on the November 12, 2016, show. Instead, McKinnon turns to the camera and speaks, her voice shaking with emotion, "I'm not giving up and neither should you. And live from New York, it's Saturday night!"

Humor eventually infiltrates this episode more fully, as host Dave Chappelle's monologue and various sketches show. Chappelle performs emotional nonconformity against the expectations for a black man as he presents a number of responses to the election, from rioting to threatening to leave the country, as overreactions. "All my black friends who have money said the same thing when Trump got elected: 'That's it, bro, I'm out. I'm leaving the country, you coming with us?' Nah, I'm good, dog. I'm going to stay here and get this tax break, see how it works out." Finally, he earnestly reaches across the aisle: "I'm wishing Donald Trump luck. And I'm going to give him a chance, and we, the historically disenfranchised, demand that he give us one too."

The next sketch continues on this same theme, putting the apparent catastrophe of the election in perspective using humor, albeit without the optimistic stinger. In this sketch, Chappelle plays a black man at an election party full of overconfident white liberals. As returns come in, the whites grow increasingly despondent as Chappelle and guest Chris Rock riff on their naivety at thinking Hillary was a lock. "Oh my God. I think America is racist," says one of the white people as the Electoral College slips away. "Oh my God," responds Chappelle sarcastically, "you know I remember my great-grandfather told me something like that. But he was like a slave or something." At the conclusion, a white character claims that the election of Donald Trump is "the most shameful thing America has ever done." After exchanging a knowing look to one another, Chappelle and Rock burst into laughter.

In dialogue with one another, these three bits reflect a range of comic responses to national traumas. The first, in its allusion to *SNL*'s notable first post-9/11 episode, illustrates the ways that *SNL* and other late night comic institutions often reflect somber moods by dialing down or altogether forgoing humor. In the others, Chappelle's sardonic optimism and cynical resignation demonstrate emotional nonconformity as well as the tendency of comedy to normalize such events and guide media discourse "back to normal." In other ways, this microcosm of television comedy also negotiated between national and subnational identities. Obviously, in discussing federal politics, the show engaged the national. On a more subtle level, however, by only representing the response of those who opposed Trump's election, and especially in the mournful cold opening song, *SNL* helped constitute the sense of national trauma.[20] Comedy has increasingly taken on this role following the election.

This volume notes the ways in which comedy can imitate the tone of news media in its discussion of national traumas (as did late night hosts following 9/11) or rebel against it (as the chapter on emotional nonconformity notes most specifically). In the Trump era, however, comedy appears to be more active in registering the sense of national trauma. Colbert was instructive in the sense that he provided breaking coverage of this emotional event and explicitly connected the sense of national trauma to the documentary/news genre. However, comedy continued to develop the sense of trauma around Trump in the months and years that followed, as examples below demonstrate. To support my argument, I load the discussion about comedy fostering a sense of trauma with examples that speak most directly to this model. But as Dave Chappelle demonstrates, and a fuller description of the November 9 responses by Seth Meyers and Jimmy Kimmel also suggest, comedies made some effort to reframe the election as less than traumatic. For instance, Seth Meyers jokes optimistically,

> I've been wrong about [Trump] at every turn. When he first came down the escalator at Trump Tower and announced, I boldly said on this show it was a stunt and he would never really run. I then said he would never win the GOP nomination, and I certainly didn't think he would be our next president. But the good news is, based on this pattern of being wrong in every one of my Donald Trump predictions, he's probably going to be a great [bleep] president.

Although the examples I have discussed so far treat Trump and/or events within his presidency as traumatic, they are not monolithic in their approach. Late night hosts, especially Colbert, Kimmel, and Meyers, continually mock Trump as a buffoon, which diminishes his symbolic power and the sense that he is a threat. Moreover, comedians' tendency to speak in multivocal "dialogic" styles holds the power to create a self-correcting discourse that, in a reflection of journalism's performance of neutrality, can normalize Trump. However, the remainder of this chapter focuses on examples where comedy expressed the emotional registers associated with national trauma. In doing so, it closely examines the politics of gender and emotional performance to note the ways in which comedy takes on particularly political meaning in these contexts.

THE PERSONAL (TRAUMA) IS POLITICAL (COMEDY): SEXUAL ASSAULT, *FULL FRONTAL*, AND *BROAD CITY*

As time passed after the 2016 election, a number of comedies continued to recreate the argument that the election itself was a trauma. This pushed back against the kind of normalizing work that goes on in the wake of such events. Among the starkest examples of this come from feminist comedies that develop a metaphor equating the election to sexual assault into larger comic and political pieces. *Full Frontal with Samantha Bee* and *Broad City* focus on the troubled gender politics of the Trump presidency using specific examples like Brett Kavanaugh's and Donald Trump's alleged sexual assaults, but also metaphorically connect the personal trauma of sexual assault to the larger sense that the Trump presidency is a national trauma. The affiliations between the Trump administration and sexual assault are plain to see, considering the infamous *Access Hollywood* tape on which Trump brags about groping women along with the numerous other accusations against him. Moreover, the nomination of Supreme Court Justice Brett Kavanaugh uncovered allegations that he had sexually assaulted multiple women in his high school and college years.[21] Trump also supported and/or maintained close relationships with other powerful men accused of sexual misconduct, including Republican Senate candidate Roy Moore and Fox News figures Roger Ailes and Bill O'Reilly, among others.[22]

Beginning in 2016, but especially picking up in 2018, popular critics registered the sense that angry women were becoming more prominent on television.[23] As the timeline suggests, while some of these articles make brief mention of electoral politics, they more often relate this tendency to the #MeToo movement, which developed significant momentum in the final months of 2017. While not exclusively focused on dramas, these pieces tend to give the bulk of their attention to serious genres and/or the dramatic acting that occurs in dramedies. A notable exception to this tendency occurs in a 2016 *Los Angeles Times* article. Though it, too, primarily focuses on actors like Sarah Paulson in *The People Versus O. J. Simpson* and Lena Headey in *Game of Thrones*, commentator Lorraine Ali concludes her piece using *Full Frontal with Samantha Bee* as the ultimate example of an angry woman on television.

No one is more determined to tear down the angry-equals-mad-equals-crazy stereotype than Samantha Bee. In a late night talk show landscape dominated by men, the host of TBS' *Full Frontal* regularly chooses "tone it up" over "tone it down."

Following the mass shooting at a gay nightclub in Orlando, Fla., Bee rejected the traditional role of a calming influence.

"After a massacre," she said matter of factly on her show, "the standard operating procedure is that you stand on stage and deliver some well-meaning words about how we will get through this together. How love wins, how love conquers hate.

And that is great, that is beautiful. But you know what? I am too angry for that. . . . Is it OK if instead of making jokes I just scream for seven minutes?"

As the endless retweets and commentary proved, it was more than OK. It was a scream that spoke for millions.[24]

As this commentary shows, Bee's performance of anger peaks around moments of trauma. Her scream on behalf of millions grew newly resonant around issues of sexual assault and Trump.

Speaking in the summer of 2019 after journalist and advice columnist E. Jean Carroll became the twenty-second woman to publicly accuse Trump of sexual assault, Samantha Bee notes how such stories were not garnering the same attention by journalists that they once had. "I'm sorry that the media is tired of talking about how the president did sexual assault a bunch," she bemoans,

but imagine how tired women are of having a sexual assaulter for president. Of course it's impossible to hear accusation after accusation without getting accustomed to it. That's no one's fault and I'm not singling anyone out, but when you let him off with softball questions about where he's going to build his library without mentioning his many accusers, you are dropping the ball, [NBC journalist] Chuck Todd.[25]

Joanne Gilbert notes the significance of anger for comedy in general, but also its particular importance for performances of social critique.[26] Bee's performances match this analysis, even rising and falling in relation to the severity of the injustices in question. Here, Bee also echoes the desire by gun-control advocates to remain angry in defiance of normalization,

Samantha Bee's frustration boils over on Full Frontal.

connecting activist concerns and strategies for framing events as traumas in news coverage.

A few months after arguing that Trump's alleged assaults should remain in the news, Bee joked that because it was fall, "the air is getting crisper, I am preparing to eat a dump truck full of apple cider donuts, and Brett Kavanaugh is in the news for allegedly putting his penis in a place it wasn't invited." This was about a year after Kavanaugh's Supreme Court confirmation hearing, in which Christine Blasey Ford had testified that the nominee had sexually assaulted her in high school. The discussion of Brett Kavanaugh in this case focused on additional information uncovered in new reports but also served the function of keeping the issue of his assaults in the cultural forum of television despite the news cycle's tendency to move past such issues. At the same time, the discussion of Kavanaugh and sexual assault metaphorically spoke to the tendency of sexual assault to cause clinical trauma as well as the larger political ramifications of anti-feminist politicians.

The Trump administration and the Kavanaugh appointment bring into the foreground the slippery relationship between discussions of national trauma as I describe them in this book and the way culture makes sense of individual, clinical trauma in and through mass media. The extent to which media can clinically traumatize audiences remains unresolved in the field, and it is a metaphor that deserves caution, lest PTSD become confused with general distress to the point where survivors' resources dry up.[27] Describing the broader impacts of sexual assault in her life during the Kavanaugh hearing, Christine Blasey Ford listed "anxiety, phobia, and PTSD-like symptoms . . . more specifically claustrophobia, panic, and that type of thing" before also describing the negative impacts Kavanaugh's actions had on her personal relationships and academic studies.[28] In the wake of this testimony, television, print, and online journalism produced a number of articles describing the effect Blasey Ford's story was having on other sexual assault survivors. For instance, NBC News' website quoted a physician named Eve Rittenberg: "A patient with a history of sexual abuse said she had been suffering flashbacks. 'She held out her left arm to me, where for the first time since her adolescence, she had started cutting herself,' Rittenberg wrote. 'Many of my patients named the Kavanaugh hearings as a source of dread,' she added." *Time* magazine more explicitly drew comparisons between the many individual cases of clinical trauma and the more metaphorical sense of collective trauma by quoting another expert: "'When there's a national disaster, there's a period of aftermath,' says Dr. Jennifer Freyd, a psychology professor at the University of Oregon who specializes in studying trauma among survivors of sexual violence. 'I think it's going to be like that. I think we're talking about a big national health crisis.'"[29]

Media scholars, too, make note of the potentially complex ways in which symbolic representation and medical symptoms can lead into and/or be confused for one another. This is a problem usefully taken up by E. Ann Kaplan in her book *Trauma Culture*, which is in large part devoted to sorting out the contradictory impulses to collectivize the experience of trauma in media theory while understanding its personal and idiosyncratic nature. "It is hard to separate individual and collective trauma," she writes, yet "how one reacts to a traumatic event depends on one's individual psychic history, on memories inevitably mixed with fantasies of prior catastrophes, and on the particular cultural and political context within which a catastrophe takes place, especially how it is 'managed' by institutional forces."[30] Although I tend to err on the side of considering individual and collective trauma to be more a differentiated phenomenon than does Kaplan, her study proves instructive for the ways these concepts slip into one another. For instance, she mobilizes the concept of vicarious trauma—a phenomenon in which professionals working with sufferers of PTSD develop symptoms of the disorder themselves—to entertain the notion that mediated and clinical trauma may in fact be causally connected.

Comedies can do a similar kind of work, considering the question of whether the differences between mass and individual trauma are of scale or type. In a clever criticism of taking metaphors of trauma too literally, the cartoon comedy *Duckman* had its main character spend an episode suffering from PTSD from his time in Vietnam.[31] This prompted a number of flashbacks that functioned as movie parodies of scenes from films like *Apocalypse Now* and *The Deer Hunter*. However, mere pastiche did not entirely explain why his flashbacks took the form of well-known movies. Duckman had developed "PSAWFTS: Post-traumatic Southeast Asian War Film Trauma Syndrome. . . . He was never in the war. He was flashing back to scenes from the sixty-odd films he's seen on the subject." Laughable in the context of this narrative, the idea that mediated communication can cause clinical trauma is nevertheless taken more seriously by media theorists, psychologists, and even other comedies.

Despite reservations in academic and popular discourse over the possibility for literal relationships between clinical and collective trauma, the transposition of the two concepts proves rhetorically powerful. In fact, this power may at times explain the temptation to exploit their connection. For comedies operating in the "just kidding" mode, expressive freedom allows for experimentation without fully arguing for or against a causal relationship between media and clinical trauma. In the wake of Trump's election and the particular importance of the *Access Hollywood* tapes, in which the future president brags about "grab[bing women] by the pussy," numerous comedies made the tragicomic metaphor that Trump had also assaulted the United States. More extended pieces explored this in greater detail, often using themes of clinical trauma to express political themes.

In a 2017 episode of *Broad City*, the character Ilana, played by Ilana Glazer, discusses a problem with her therapist.[32] As part of her treatment for low libido, she speaks to her vulva while looking at it through a mirror. "You've been stubborn lately," she begins. With growing intensity and anger, she continues, "Like, withholding. You're so full of shit. You can't even focus enough to relax. You're not even a butthole or vagina. You're just a butthole that happens to bleed! I [bleep] hate you, bitch! [Bleep] you!" The therapist helps her dig deeper through her anger. Ilana responds emotionally, "I—I know it's not you. It's me. I increased my dosage of antidepressants. And I've also just been more anxious and depressed this whole disgusting, gross year. And now I have dead pussy." The words "dead pussy" repeat a few more times as a crossfade reveals a calendar turning back to November and focusing in on Election Day 2016. Donald Trump's voice takes over saying "dead pussy" as a montage of clips from the 2016 election flies by, with a particular focus on the "grab 'em by the pussy" audio. Snapping back from her internal journey, Ilana exclaims, "Oh, my God! Game show president [bleep] in chief! I haven't come since the election! And come is a lot of who I am. I'm a come queen." The therapist comforts her. "You're not alone. Orgasms have been down 140 percent since [bleep] was elected."

Perhaps the most foundational work in feminist comedy studies, Kathleen Rowe's *The Unruly Woman* discusses the significance of gender nonconformity to women's comic personas.[33] Samantha Bee's occupation of a critical place in the public sphere and especially her ability to attack the most powerful members of society using jokes defines her "unruliness." However, *Broad City*'s Ilana Glazer more fully embodies the concept of the unruly woman, most especially with regard to her confident and largely unrestrained sexuality. For those familiar with the show, her being a "come queen" would have been no surprise. Though funny in delivery, the loss of her sexuality is especially tragic and traumatic for Ilana. In the larger sense in which Trump and his politics represent an attack on women's bodies and sexualities—on issues ranging from reproductive rights to male criminal sexuality—this episode provides a useful confluence of ideas through which to articulate trauma, profane comedy, and significant political issues.

In light of this book's larger themes, this episode is notable for reasons beyond its expression of anger. *Broad City* garnered headlines for bleeping the word "Trump"—while words like "bitch" and "pussy" and phrases like "fat titties" and "hairy taints" remain audible—and releasing an internet browser extension that replaced instances of the president's name online with "Tr**p."[34] In keeping with the discussion in chapter 2 of the ways in which *South Park* weaponized censorship, this provides an additional example. By censoring his name, *Broad City* profanes Trump in classically carnivalesque play. At the same time, Ilana's bawdy body humor re-inverts the comic power inversions of Bakhtin's model. Instead of using the profane sphere of sexuality, excrement, and blood to symbolically erode the sacredness of the presidency, this episode presents a scenario wherein the sacred sphere of American politics has come to ruin the carnival of Ilana's sexuality. Of course, to the laughing audience, it remains more traditionally carnivalesque in its use of raunchy sexuality to profane Trump's presidency.

Like more serious discussions about the impact of reporting on Trump and Kavanaugh, this episode of *Broad City* erodes the distinctions between personal and collective trauma as Ilana suffers from PTSD-like symptoms because of the election. Moreover, the portrayal of Ilana's sexual dysfunction uses expressive formal techniques that fall outside of the show's governing style, creating stylistic parallels to the way otherwise dry journalism slips into melodramatic techniques in covering traumas. In fact, *Broad City* outsourced the creation of this segment to an experimental comedic video editor named Vic Berger, who had gained notoriety over the course of the 2016 election cycle for videos that exaggerated and heightened the weirdness of its debates and political speeches. In separate interviews, both of *Broad City*'s creators and stars made clear that they hired Berger because of his ability to evoke emotional responses with his found-footage art. "His work is incredible," explained co-creator Glazer. "He does all of these political videos and animations that just heighten the way we're feeling right now."[35] The other half of this duo, Abby Jacobson, explained that the key to the segment's power lies in its expressive exaggeration. "He takes it to this heightened state. . . . It zooms into his mouth. There's fire. He takes it to extremes."[36] As with news, then, formal appeals to heightened emotion characterized these events as traumas. Indeed, following the video montage, her therapist explains that Ilana is "traumatized by the fact that a sexual-assault-bragging steak salesman has become our president."

Feminist comedies in the Trump era perform significant work that news struggles with due to the business and ethics of journalistic neutrality. For a figure like Samantha Bee, comedy provides cover to express anger in a way that expectations of gender performance prevent in the serious and "rational" discourse of political news and debate. This echoes the way in which *Def Comedy Jam* provided a similar venue for black comics in the wake of the 1992 Los Angeles riots. For other shows, like *Broad City*, comedy's artistic and expressive freedom opens a space for explorations of and rhetoric using the relationship between clinical and collective trauma. Still other comedies perform the emotions that constitute national traumas in longer and more sustained ways, performing national trauma's compulsion to repeat.

MALE EMOTION AND CHILDREN'S TRAUMA: JIM JEFFERIES
AND JIMMY KIMMEL

Responding on his show to the Kavanaugh confirmation and linking the judge's alleged sexual assault to Trump's, Jim Jefferies plays a clip of the Supreme Court justice angrily characterizing those opposed to his nomination as illegitimate.[37] "This whole two-week effort has been a calculated and orchestrated political hit," Kavanaugh begins, "fueled with apparent pent-up anger about President Trump, revenge on behalf of the Clintons, and millions of dollars in money from outside left-wing opposition groups." Commenting on the clip, Jefferies asks, "Despite getting everything he ever wanted, is Brett Kavanaugh the real victim here?" This launches into a larger routine in which Jefferies runs through a number of unsympathetic figures claiming victimhood, from "Unite the Right" organizer

The Jim Jefferies Show *plays* Who's the Real Victim?

Jason Kessler to BP in response to its own oil spill. "In a way," Jefferies jokes in relation to another trauma, "the 9/11 hijackers were victims of a plane crash." Eventually, this segues into a parody game show called *Who's the Real Victim?* When contestants realize that "the real victim is always you," they win. The grand prize? "An all-expenses paid trip to a children's migrant detention center." As jaunty game show music plays, the host explains, "You're gonna get to spend three days and two nights in beautiful Brownsville, Texas, teaching a captive immigrant child what real struggle is really like." *The Jim Jefferies Show* uses the child in a cage as a running gag to put other issues in perspective. For instance, discussing online anger in relation to seemingly trivial issues, Jefferies complains, "Sometimes it feels like we move from outrage to outrage so quickly that we forget about the things we should actually be paying attention to. Isn't that right, kid still being held in a cage in a border detention facility who will never see his parents again?"[38] The same child in the same cage appears on-screen, ironically complaining about *Green Book* winning the Oscar for best picture.

This recurring bit pushes back against the tendency to accept traumas in the Trump era as ordinary due to familiarity and the desire to move on. Like Samantha Bee's explicit discussion of normalizing Trump's sexual assault, this runs counter to Chappelle's work on *SNL* as well as the general tendency discussed in chapter 3 for comedy to help television and culture more generally "get back to normal" after a national trauma. Like Bee, Jefferies keeps the sense of trauma around family separation present in discourse. Unlike on *Full Frontal*, however, the use of the caged child as a running gag more closely matches the compulsion in both clinical and mediated trauma to repeat. No matter the issue, it seems family separation should be present in our minds and discussions.

Jefferies also links the politics of emotion to family separation in segments more exclusively about the border crisis. In one, titled "Oh God, This Is Sad, Is There Anything Here We Can Even Joke About? F**k It, Let's Have a Go," Jefferies's analysis appeals to particularly emotionally intense trauma by comparing this policy to the Holocaust. Responding to reports that parents were separated from children under the guise of giving the children baths, Jefferies asks, "You're actually saying you're taking them to bathe? Like—to the showers? You really don't see the parallels? 'Oh, okay not the showers. I mean I'm taking you kids on a choo choo train. [Bleep]! No! I'm—um—I'm taking you kids to a eugenics lab. [Bleep]! I'm really bad at not being a Nazi!'" While most of the bit contains jokes, Jefferies, like comics frequently do in response to national trauma, turns mostly serious at the end.

> Answer me this: if you have children, or grandchildren, or a niece, or a nephew and they ask you why these kids are being locked up in cages, can you honestly look them in the eye and say it's a good thing? And if you can say that, you're a [bleep]ing [bleep]. [Audience applauds.] Some people might argue when it comes to politics, you're not supposed to let your emotions get in the way. But if there's ever a time we should let our emotions get in the way, it's now.

In discussing that episode on his podcast, Jefferies shares that his performance of emotion was genuine.[39] "It fucking shook me to my core to know what's going on in these things. And as I read the statement I actually did tear up. Now I didn't cry like Jimmy Kimmel does. He loves a good cry on TV." As the conversation continues between Jefferies and his head writer, they compare writing about this story to both the Charlottesville white power riot and the Holocaust, discussing the struggle to write jokes about something that made them so angry and sad. The podcast's conversation helps bring into focus the relationship between comedy, gender, and the performance of emotion. In many ways, emotions, especially those associated with vulnerability like concern, do not fit the wise-ass, boozy masculinity of Jefferies's comic personas. Despite his own admission of human emotion, Jefferies nevertheless mocks his fellow comedy host Jimmy Kimmel for expressing comparable feelings on air. But if political events and comedy give cover for performers like Samantha Bee and Ilana Glazer to express outrage in regard to sexual assault, then threats to children in forms like family separation, lack of health care, and gun violence offer cover to male comics to perform a subtle gender nonconformity as well. These examples are notable for their breaking of expected gender performance, but in doing so, they also aid in constituting these events as traumas.

Jimmy Kimmel has developed an everyman comic persona over many years. After a few years in radio and as a game show host, he became a significant player in television when he co-created *The Man Show* for Comedy Central. On this program, the comedian performed a brand of toxic masculinity for laughs. For instance, each episode of this program opened with the "Juggies," a group of mostly silent, buxom, female dancers and concluded with footage of "girls jumping on trampolines." Starting in 2003, *Jimmy Kimmel Live* toned down the overt sexism of *The Man Show* but continued to showcase its host's masculine performance in sticking to themes like heavy drinking and sports. However, around the middle of the 2010s, Kimmel had begun, as Jefferies points out, to let his sensitive side show on television. Though Kimmel had displayed tears on television earlier, the Trump era saw the host reacting emotionally to political issues such as health care and gun violence.[40] According to Rowe, the ability to speak of and frankly express sexuality defines the gender nonconformity of female comic personas, but displays of emotion that do not easily fit a masculine persona are less universal among male comics. This explains in part why Jimmy Kimmel's displays of vulnerability garner comment by those like Jefferies. In 2017, Kimmel relayed on-air the story of his son, who had been born with a congenital heart defect and needed immediate surgery.[41] While he jokes throughout the story, he also chokes back tears at numerous points. Segueing into a call for unity in the face of threats to children, Kimmel then mentions his opposition to Trump's proposed spending cuts to the National Institute of Health and his support for Obamacare. "I think if your baby is going to die and it doesn't have to," he argues as his voice tightens with emotion,

> it shouldn't matter how much money you make. I think that whether you're a Republican or a Democrat or something else, we all agree on that, right? . . . This isn't football. There are no teams. We are the team. It's the *United* States. Don't let their partisan squabbles divide us on something every decent person wants. We

need to take care of each other. I saw a lot of families [at the hospital], and no parent should ever have to decide if they can afford to save their child's life.

This moment made headlines in the debate over whether to repeal the Affordable Care Act.[42] However, it is also notable for connecting potential Congressional action to the themes of national unity and public emotion that are intertwined with the discursive articulations of national trauma.

Shortly after he spoke out against the Trump effort to repeal Obamacare in terms that drew on the rhetoric of trauma, he performed similarly in relation to a public health crisis more easily characterized as a national trauma. As the introduction discussed, the February 2018 shooting at Marjory Stoneman Douglas High School followed many of the common scripts of a national trauma, including emotional performance, nationalizing discourses, and comment by federal officials. While national traumas like natural disasters and terror attacks frequently trigger discourses of American unity, mass shootings are more complex, if not entirely exceptional. That said, Columbine did not produce the same level of political fractiousness outside of the odd Michael Moore and Rush Limbaugh types. Over the course of the Obama and Trump presidencies, however, these events have triggered debate alongside the kind of flag-waving calls to unity that characterize other traumas. Nevertheless, expectations regarding the performance of unity have become an element of debates over gun violence. There has been some attempt, mostly on the part of conservative politicians, to create moratoria on political debate around these issues, as Kimmel demonstrated on this episode by showing a montage of Republicans arguing that it was too soon after the shooting to begin discussing policy before criticizing that tactic as cynical.

Though critical of how others utilized these techniques, Kimmel joined in the discourses of national trauma as emotionally intense and unifying. On the evening following the shooting in Parkland, Florida, he once again fought back tears as he spoke about endangered children. After introducing the issue, he plays a clip of Trump activating collectivist understanding of national trauma. "We are all joined together," speaks the president, "as one American family and your suffering is our burden also. No child, no teacher should ever be in danger in an American school."[43] "Agreed," responds Kimmel,

and here's what you do to fix that: tell your buddies in Congress, tell . . . all the family men who care so much about their communities that what we need are laws—real laws—that do everything possible to keep assault rifles out of the hands of people who are going to shoot our kids. . . . Force these allegedly Christian men and women who stuff their pockets with money from the NRA year after year to do something now. Not later. Now. And don't you dare let anyone say it's too soon to be talking about it because you said it after Vegas. You said it after Sandy Hook. You say that after every one of these *eight now* fatal school shootings we've had in this country this year. Children are being murdered!

Once again, Kimmel weighs in using overtly emotional performance on a national trauma rife with implications for national identity and unity. Unlike the cases noted above—the election, the nomination and confirmation of Brett Kavanaugh, and Republican efforts to repeal the Affordable Care Act—the Parkland shooting did not need comedies to help define it as a national trauma. However, Kimmel's inveighing against politicians and national organizations like the NRA represents a shift from an earlier period. Though it was famously shocking for Kanye West to accuse George W. Bush of racism in the immediate wake of Hurricane Katrina, Kimmel felt empowered to inveigh against politicians more immediately following a national trauma by 2018.[44]

There has always been a tension in television, not to mention in nationalizing discourses more generally, between the part and the whole. America's current political climate, along with its media structures and other factors, appear to be tipping the balance of such discourses away from unity in favor of increased factionalism. While stalwart institutions like mainstream news maintain a sense of nonpartisanship that speaks to older models of broadcasting and journalistic neutrality, their significance in determining a shared sense of reality, much less the rules of political discourse, appear to be lessening. Within this environment, other modes of discourse, like comedy, play an increasingly prominent role. Moreover, because comedy as a genre is allowed a wider range of expressive and representational strategies, it plays a role in determining a political reality for its audience, even defining national traumas in the absence of a journalistic culture willing to do so. The conclusion continues on this theme to explore what the historical trajectory and present moment say about the future of national trauma and television comedy.

CONCLUSION

As I write the conclusion to this book in February 2020, the United States Senate has just voted not to remove President Donald Trump from office following his impeachment by the House of Representatives on charges of abuse of power and obstruction of Congress. Although the sides agreed on little else, both Democrats and Republicans characterized the proceedings as highly partisan. Republicans accused Democrats of political grandstanding, while Democrats argued that Republicans undermined justice by, for instance, voting not to have witnesses testify in the Senate trial. Except for one Republican defector, Trump's acquittal followed a party line vote. In the immediate wake of the trial, the emboldened president began to purge the government of perceived enemies by firing witnesses who testified against him in the House impeachment hearings, as well as a witness's brother who had nothing to do with the impeachment. Nearly concurrently, the Justice Department requested a lighter sentence than prosecutors had initially requested for Trump ally Roger Stone. These events triggered outrage among commentators like Ali Velshi on MSNBC, who historicized them by comparing them to Richard Nixon's "Saturday Night Massacre."[1] Right-leaning pundits like Fox News' Tucker Carlson argued that the left was abusing justice by seeking overly harsh penalties against political opponents like Stone, using a similar frame of American democracy in crisis from strongarm tactics.[2] While neither of these examples of commentary quite rose to the level of the trauma frame that uses formal techniques to mark the events as particularly exceptional and emotional, both speakers relied on a now familiar tone of anger at the other side. As expected from the last chapter's discussion of political comedy in the Trump era, some comics have used similar language in discussing these events, albeit with the freedom to use more extreme language and hyperbolize through comic metaphor. Samantha Bee earnestly described Trump's acquittal as a "devastating precedent," while Stephen Colbert joked, "Trump has gone full strongman. He's making a list of enemies and he's changed the name of his resort to Mar-a-Gulago."[3]

These examples continue to demonstrate many of this book's larger themes. MSNBC and Fox News illustrate the narrowcasting described in chapter 1 that allows for both the heightened partisanship described in detail in the last chapter, but also the kind of humor—especially the potentially offensive and politically charged variety—that characterizes most of the comedy in this book as a whole. In line with the place of politics and comedy within television's industrial logic, partisan television shows like *The Late Show with Stephen Colbert* and *Full Frontal with Samantha Bee* have taken sides supporting Velshi's understanding. While the serious MSNBC commentator historicized Trump's actions with regard to a clear crisis in American history in order to declare this a contemporary crisis, Bee's description of Trump's actions as a "devastating precedent" look to future implications, effectively historicizing the present from the imagined perspective of the future. Meanwhile, Colbert draws connections to historical traumas of another nation by comparing Trump's actions to Stalin's Gulag agency, which oversaw the extrajudicial forced labor camps synonymous with the punishment of political dissidents in the Soviet Union.

In the broadest sense of American culture, politics, and mass media, the structures that create the conditions for political polarization and related comedy appear to be growing stronger. As cable hosts more channels, the appeals presented by news and entertainment will continue to grow more specific. Besides traditional broadcasting and cable, additional venues for programming, including streaming services like Netflix and Hulu, will add even more specific ways to address demographic and political subsets. Moreover, the culture of on-demand programming offered by such services as well as digital cable and DVR services weaken the old model of what Raymond Williams once described as television's "flow."[4] Where once viewers were at least somewhat more likely to encounter programming that was not exactly what they wanted to see because it came on after their favorite program, or simply because they could only watch whatever was on at a given time, that experience is decreasingly common. While other factors like demographic and economic changes will certainly play a role in determining the future of American politics, trends in media show little sign of turning back the tendency of Americans to sort themselves into ideologically homogenous communities.[5]

For comedy, this means that the tendencies and trends noted in this book will continue for the foreseeable future as well. There may be exceptional events like 9/11 that temporarily create a sense of national unity across these divisions, but comedy's tendency to perform emotional nonconformity will help the culture "get back to normal." At the same time, there will continue to be periodic "smaller" traumas like mass shootings and racialized violence that may or may not be treated as traumas in different venues. Nonetheless, there will also be events that create common topics of interest across racial, political, and other divisions, even if groups understand them through different media and with varying frames of understanding. Regardless of how collective the experience is, comedy will play a role in negotiating identity. This is true in the broad sense in which this book examined the way comedy negotiates the intersection between American identity as a whole and subnational identities including African American, Muslim and Middle Eastern Americans, and political factions. However, it also has something to say about the complexities in which these many overlapping and intersectional identity categories speak to one another. On these and other grounds, comedies will also continue testing the limits of acceptable speech as they navigate cultural and ideological contradictions.

Parallel to the directly political developments of the Trump impeachment, in late January 2020 former NBA basketball player Kobe Bryant died in a helicopter crash that also took the lives of his daughter and seven others. Coverage of his death more clearly took the form of a trauma. While certainly smaller in scope than that of 9/11 or the death of John F. Kennedy, news coverage interrupted regularly scheduled programming to cover the crash and Bryant's death. These programs featured many of the hallmarks of trauma coverage. For instance, CNN's breaking coverage featured emotionally evocative language, still photograph montages set to mournful music, and long-take video shots of both the accident scene and mourners who had gathered nearby.[6] On this same broadcast, CNN contributor Christine Brennan brought up the allegations that Bryant had sexually assaulted a woman in 2003, although she gave it a positive spin as a learning experience for Bryant that allowed him to become a better person in the end. "It seems difficult to mention at this moment of his death that we're talking about the sexual allegations, the trial. That was a terrible moment that was not good, obviously. I'm not going to sugarcoat that at all," the journalist sugarcoated, "but within those mistakes there was also learning and there was also a sense from him . . . [of] this new world for women and opportunities for women and girls."

In the days following Bryant's death, commentators highlighted the apparent tensions going on between various communities in how they made sense of the NBA star. Sports journalists and fans, African Americans, rape survivor advocates, and those who praised his efforts to support women's athletics found themselves in a larger conversation about Bryant's legacy. Notably, ABC News journalist Gayle King came under fire for an interview with Bryant's friend Lisa Leslie in which she asked, "It's been said that his legacy is complicated because of a sexual assault charge. . . . Is it complicated for you as a woman? As a WNBA player?" Leslie replied that Bryant's legacy was uncomplicated because she did not believe that her friend had used forced on the night in question. As Leona Allen notes in an op-ed, a number of celebrities including Snoop Dogg, 50 Cent, and Bill Cosby attacked King, some including vague threats. For her part, Allen defends King's line of questioning, noting that Oprah Winfrey also agreed. At the same time, the piece notes the fraught position occupied by the journalist:

> The reason this case still strikes a nerve with folks is that we live in a society that still doesn't believe rape victims. It's horrific that so many guys get away with these crimes.
>
> We also live in a world that can vilify black men. I read the evidence in this case. There were questions, absolutely. But all we know for sure is that this case was dismissed in criminal court and settled in civil court. All of the parties appear to have moved on. Why haven't we?
>
> It's also a fact that King is expected by many to represent black folks. As one of the few black people leading a news program, she is expected to bear the responsibility of representing and supporting a full race of people. Of course, she should bring her unique perspective to the table and shout loud for fairness and authenticity. That's why we fight so hard for a seat at the table. But man oh man, is it fair to ask this of a black journalist and not of journalists of any other persuasion? The weight of it gets mighty heavy.[7]

As the races and genders of King's critics and defenders indicate, there can be tension in how identity positions appeal to different ideologies. This is not to say that identity is destiny in terms of one's opinions, but it can create contradictions in the tense discursive environment of a national trauma. Just as the Los Angeles riots revealed fault lines between African Americans of different classes, Kobe Bryant's death revealed fault lines between gendered positions and discourses of feminist activism among some African Americans in the public sphere.

Although played out in the starkest terms, similar contradictions emerged in the way white comics responded to Kobe Bryant's death. Television comics mostly responded with messages of condolence, with perhaps small acknowledgments of the issues that King confronted more directly. In keeping with its penchant for sentimentalism, *Jimmy Kimmel Live!* devoted an entire episode to Bryant, with the host explaining, "Tonight's show is going to be different from our usual show. We don't have a studio audience here tonight because going forward with a comedy show didn't feel right considering what happened yesterday."[8] Kimmel goes on to praise Bryant as a father and champion of worthy causes, frequently choking back tears. He also notes,

> Yes, I know he was not a perfect person. I understand that. My intention is not to canonize him or make judgments about things I don't know anything about, but I will say he loved his family, he worked very hard, and he brought a lot of joy to a lot of people in [Los Angeles]. And we're going to miss him.

The episode that followed presented a series of interviews that Kimmel had done with Bryant over the years. As has become common, the distinct lack of humor on this comedy show echoed the larger coverage going on, marking the event as traumatic. Moreover, in keeping with the kind of discursive shifts that happened when John F. Kennedy and his son died, the way Kimmel spoke of Bryant focused on his public virtues and not the possibility of shameful private behavior. In the sense that Kimmel's earnest approach to Bryant's death minimized, even while not entirely ignoring, that troubling aspect of the athlete's history, it set a tone for how to remember and emotionally engage with him. On the other hand, some comics took a more provocative tone.

On the day of Bryant's death, comic Ari Shaffir took to Twitter to perform emotional nonconformity. "Kobe Bryant died 23 years too late today. He got away with rape because all the Hollywood liberals who attack comedy enjoy rooting for the Lakers more than they dislike rape. Big ups to the hero who forgot to gas up his chopper. I hate the Lakers. What a great day! #Fuckthelakers."[9] Pushback was severe as comedy clubs canceled Shaffir's performances and his talent agency dropped him from its roster.[10] While this comic was not currently a television fixture, he had a history of provocative humor on the medium, most notably as host of Comedy Central's *This Is Not Happening*. Although not directly exemplary of the kind of censorship explored in chapter 2, losing gigs and an agent certainly created roadblocks for Shaffir's television career, even if his notoriety might have gained him attention. Explaining his provocative comic strategy, Shaffir posted a mea culpa to Instagram:

> Every time a famous person dies I post some horrible shit about them. I've been doing it for years now. I like destroying gods. And

right when a famous person dies they're at their most worshipped. So as a response to all the outpouring of sympathy on social media, I post something vile. It's just a joke. I don't really hate any of the people.[11]

Nevertheless, Shaffir faced backlash even from fellow comedians, perhaps most forcefully from Godfrey, a veteran African American comic. In an Instagram video, Godfrey registers the sense of Kobe's death as a trauma: "This week has been really tough for everybody. . . . My heart sank this week. . . . It makes you really look at life and sit back and really appreciate things."[12] He then chastises Shaffir, arguing that there is nothing funny about those events and that he had crossed a line. "Kobe was an icon," Godfrey explains, "especially when you're talking about the African American community, a guy like himself who was a role model to young African American men and women." With growing intensity, the comic also highlights Bryant's work supporting women's basketball and other prosocial endeavors without discussing the sexual assault charges. "And you decided to mock that shit, see? So everything you're getting, you're deserving, Ari Shaffir. You get what you motherfucking deserve. . . . You fucked up, see? Because he meant a lot to a lot of people." Godfrey's video demonstrates how the conversations happening in and around comedy mirrored discourses in more serious genres like news. As Kobe Bryant's legacy was being constructed and negotiated as history, Shaffir used comedy to profane it. In so doing, he exposed some of the contradictions inherent in an uncomplicated lionizing of a celebrity like Bryant in the era of #MeToo and faced backlash similar to that faced by journalists at times.

As these examples indicate, the relevance of comedy to both construct and negotiate the issues of national trauma will remain a significant and relevant element of American national culture for the foreseeable future. Such humor continues to create opportunities for comedy to engage with the most notable moments of our national history and popular memory. When comedies speak to these issues, they might draw from a sense of shared experience and speak to an ideal, however illusory, of unity, or they might perform the complex labor of speaking to identity positions in conversation, contrast, and/or conflict with other identities, including American identity itself. And when they do so, comedy will continue to test the limits of what is sayable in moments where new dictates of speech are being figured out. This will happen on television, with direct and indirect censorship, but it will also occur in other media and in the interaction between forms—as when a comic offends to the point of having his or her access to television screens limited. When comedy in this form occurs, it will continue to play a role in characterizing our emotional relationship to collective traumas, and it will even help define political reality by supporting and attacking different understandings of history and/or defining what counts as a national trauma. Comedy will continue to speak to smaller and smaller segments of the population, flattering the imagined viewpoint of their target demo. As always, but increasingly so, comedians will not speak in any singular voice, nor will they define any singular American identity. However, they will continue to uniquely demonstrate the complexities of how American culture expresses and understands its communicative possibilities, popular memory, and collective identities.

AFTERWORD

Soon after I finished this book's conclusion in February 2020, the novel coronavirus COVID-19 grew from a localized crisis in one Chinese province to a global pandemic. Nevertheless, American media outlets have thus far concentrated on the national impacts of the disease in the United States, such as known cases and deaths, as well as American federal and state responses. That is to say, despite its global scale and impact, television and other media have treated it largely as a national event. This work includes the typical markers of national trauma, including melodramatic montages of medical workers suffering for the greater good and advertisements promising that corporations are suffering alongside all Americans. As chapter 7 noted, comedy has become increasingly involved in marking events as traumatic in recent years. This is true of comedy during the coronavirus outbreak, but the relationships between comedy and trauma have taken on new inflections during this period.

While this book demonstrates how national traumas continually impact television comedy, the effects of COVID-19 are in some ways more immediately recognizable than in most crises it discusses. After 9/11, late night comedies shut down for a week or two before returning to broadcast from their usual studio locations with heartfelt messages of hope and resilience. In early to mid-March 2020, late night shows also paused production before returning a week or two later. However, these breaks primarily served to allow the late night shows to hastily move production to the homes of their respective hosts. Since guests could not visit, celebrity interviews occurred over video chat. The new at-home production aesthetic not only indicates the practical necessities of making television under such circumstances, but also reflects and helps normalize a larger shift in labor for white- and gray-collar workers who increasingly labor from home using video chat technology such as Zoom. Although they look more like contemporary YouTube celebrity videos, *The Tonight Show* and *The Late Show* of 2020 also speak to older television traditions: shows like *The George Burns and Gracie Allen Show* (1950–1958) and *A Tour of the White House with Mrs. John F. Kennedy* (1962) were sold in part on the promise of mediated intimacy as viewers virtually entered the homes of famous people. Television comedy during social distancing is simultaneously high tech and amateurish in style, reflexively addressing the challenges of staying at home for long periods and the creeping demand for productive labor in less-than-ideal circumstances. For example, Stephen Colbert shot a special episode while sitting in a bubble bath dressed in a full suit, while Seth Meyers consistently jokes about the wasp infestation plaguing the attic in which he performs.[1]

Like comedies in earlier periods of national trauma, these and other shows play around with performances of national unity. The introduction to this book laid out some of the subtle ways in which television's technologies and discourses foster senses of togetherness around collective traumas. Social distancing measures, along with the perceived amateurishness associated with live at-home video, have drawn greater attention to the technological bases of such appeals. For example, the broadcast networks and a number of cable channels carried a special titled *Graduate Together: America Honors the High School Class of 2020*, which edits together messages from celebrities and politicians, typically shot from home, with additional amateur-produced content from students.[2] Perhaps the most telling moment of the show's performance of technology-facilitated national unity comes when a group of graduating seniors sing the national anthem together through a series of individual recordings, represented as separate video screens on a single virtual stage. In this case as in many others, multiscreen mise-en-scène, editing, and other formal techniques combine with discourses of national unity to deliver a message of togetherness despite the particular need for physical isolation in response to the disease.

Comedies have also played into this sense of togetherness through technology. *Parks and Recreation*, which ended its run in 2015, aired a reunion special to raise money for charity.[3] In it, Leslie Knope, the resourceful and community-minded heart of the show, keeps all of her old friends and coworkers socially connected through video chat despite their geographic spread and the social distancing measures in place due to coronavirus. This is in keeping with *Parks and Recreation*'s overarching sense of moderate-leftist community-mindedness, but it obviously takes on a different inflection in its use of amateur video technology and as a special in response to COVID-19. Comedies like the late night talk shows and *Parks and Recreation* celebrate implicitly or explicitly the ability of amateur digital video technology to help users remain productive and unified. At the same time, they also frequently satirize these discourses, as when the schlemiel and schlimazel of *Parks and Recreation*, Garry, struggles with the filters on his digital camera. This joke reaches a carnivalesque peak as Garry

Graduate Together: America Honors the High School Class of 2020 *presents national unity through technology as graduating seniors sing the national anthem.*

grows emotional over coronavirus with a filter on that makes his head look like a turd, complete with stink lines and buzzing flies.

Other comedies take sharper aim at the expectations of work-from-home orders. For example, one of *Saturday Night Live*'s shot-from-home coronavirus episodes features a couple of office workers, played by Aidy Bryant and Kate McKinnon, who struggle with digital technology.[4] It begins with these two technically incompetent characters having difficulty with issues like appropriate webcam framing during a virtual meeting. Eventually, the mishaps snowball toward absurdity as they frantically try to participate while, for instance, broadcasting themselves using the bathroom. With each new mishap, the pair grows ever more distraught, until they weep openly out of fear and frustration; ultimately, their boss admits that their presence in such meetings is unnecessary. In moments such as this, television mocks the dystopic proposition that workplace surveillance has entered the home and forced employees to remain productive even during an ongoing national trauma. Despite their pervasiveness, such anxieties might not be as easily identifiable as those related to contracting the virus. Nevertheless, humor offers some relief for these more everyday fears.

Television comedy during this time also highlights key issues about the temporality of comedy and national trauma discussed in this book. As has been typical at least since the 2016 election, there is no clear latency period between trauma and television comedy's engagement with it. Late night shows have been joking about the pandemic and its impacts since they became common topics in American media. Hosts take moments to express sincere sadness and gratitude, but the kind of handwringing over humor's overall acceptability after earlier traumas is not much on display. Although the political and media landscapes certainly play a role in this, the contrast is also due in part to the different temporal nature of COVID-19 compared to other traumas. Unlike most of the events examined in this book, in which there was an inciting disaster that lasted between a few minutes and a few days, the pandemic's beginning is less clear, and it continues into the moment of my writing this afterword in late May 2020. Never mind asking how soon after a catastrophe one can joke—comedy has been a part of the media landscape the entire time this trauma has been unfolding.

While the types of jokes discussed above have mostly focused on the foibles and challenges of dealing with technology and working from home, comedy television remains committed to the kind of politically critical comedy that undercuts certain unity discourses. Colbert opened his April 15, 2020, monologue with a joke suggesting the language of uniting behind a president in a time of crisis. "Folks," he begins, "if you watch the show, you know I criticize Donald Trump a lot, but with this coronavirus gripping the nation, it's made me realize I don't do it enough."[5] This kind of bait-and-switch joke is significant not only for mocking the president but also for invoking the idea that comedians should stop being funny during moments like this. Such irreverent stances became especially pronounced after Trump suggested that doctors investigate the treatment option of injecting disinfectants into the body. Essentially every comedy dealing with topical news focused on this moment. For instance, *The Daily Show*, whose coverage of the conservative response to the coronavirus it had dubbed "The Pandumbic," introduced the story with Trevor Noah stating, "President Trump created shockwaves of stupidity with his latest and probably greatest unlicensed medical opinion yet."[6] Discussing reports that people were calling health departments to inquire about the safety of such measures, Noah quips, "Even the people who are dumb enough to drink bleach are still smart enough not to trust something that Donald Trump says." In this case, even Jimmy Fallon, who typically avoids directly political humor more than his counterparts, made a relatively subtle joke about Trump's medical advisors being embarrassed of him at the press conference where he made the comments.[7]

In terms of the nation's imagined community and public sphere, to watch television comedy is, with few exceptions, to see that the sense of unity fostered by media discourses in response to COVID-19 includes a united opposition to the Trump administration and conservative politicians more generally.[8] However, the general political landscape is more fractious than comedy television suggests. While Trump might be the main target of these attacks, comedies also mock Trump supporters and other conservatives, especially protestors arguing for an early end to stay-at-home orders. This reflects a more recent trend in post-2016 America, as well as in television's increasingly narrowcast landscape, to maintain a sense of political fractiousness despite moments of national trauma. As these examples indicate, television comedy's response to the coronavirus pandemic continues to reveal and investigate the complex ways in which Americans understand themselves and the nation. It does so while testing and flaunting the limits of acceptable speech and working through the contradictory impulses to both divide and come together in the face of a national trauma.

Introduction. Broadcast Nationalism, National Trauma, and Television Comedy

1. Frank DiGiacomo, "Front Page 6," *New York Observer*, October 8, 2001, http://observer.com/2001/10/front-page-6/.

2. *The Aristocrats*, directed by Paul Provenza (2005; New York: Thinkfilm, 2006), DVD; *Comedy Central Presents: The New York Friars Club Roast of Hugh Hefner*, directed by John Smith, written by Jeffrey Gurian, aired November 4, 2001, on Comedy Central.

3. Michael Hirschorn, "Irony, the End of: Why Graydon Carter Wasn't Entirely Wrong," *New York Magazine*, August 27, 2011, http://nymag.com/news /9-11/10th-anniversary/irony/; Michiko Kakutani, "Critic's Notebook: The Age of Irony Isn't Over after All; Assertions of Cynicism's Demise Belie History," *New York Times*, October 9, 2001, http://www.nytimes.com/2001/10/09/arts/critic -s-notebook-age-irony-isn-t-over-after-all-assertions-cynicism-s-demise.html?ref= michikokakutani; Marc Peyser, "Worst Predictions #6: Graydon Carter Proclaims the End of Irony," *Newsweek*, accessed February 2, 2020, http://2010.newsweek .com/top-10/worst-predictions/graydon-carter.html; Eric Randall, "The 'Death of Irony,' and Its Many Reincarnations," *Atlantic Wire*, September 9, 2011, http://www .theatlanticwire.com/national/2011/09/death-irony-and-its-many-reincarnations /42298/#; Roger Rosenblatt, "The Age of Irony Comes to an End," *Time*, September 24, 2001, http://content.time.com/time/magazine/article/0,9171,1000893 ,00.html. Roger Rosenblatt and Graydon Carter both appear to have used this phrase. Rosenblatt made his prediction in *Time*, but *Vanity Fair* editor Graydon Carter's quotation is a bit more tricky. While the original article appears to have disappeared from record, numerous sources attribute the initial use of the phrase to a quote given by Carter to a now-defunct website called Inside.com on or about September 17, 2001. While widely criticized for these predictions, it should be noted that neither explicitly declared an end to comedy, sick humor, or political satire—the kinds of texts these critics normally point to as proof that their declaration was wrong. Michael Hirschorn suggests that the kind of cynical disconnect denoted by certain uses of the phrase never did appear to make a full comeback after 9/11, as even the most notable ironists like Stephen Colbert demonstrate a commitment to certain political ideals.

4. Jon Macks, *Monologue: What Makes America Laugh before Bed* (New York: Penguin, 2015).

5. See Benedict Anderson, *Imagined Communities: Reflections on the Origin and Spread of Nationalism*, new ed. (New York: Verso, 2006); Ernest Gellner, *Nations and Nationalism*, 2nd ed. (Malden, MA: Blackwell Publishing, 2013); Eric J. Hobsbawm, *Nations and Nationalism since 1780: Programme, Myth, Reality*, 2nd ed. (Cambridge: Cambridge University Press, 2017).

6. Anderson, *Imagined Communities*, 35.

7. Kevin M. Lerner, "Magazines as Sites of Satire, Parody, and Political Resistance," in *The Handbook of Magazine Studies*, ed. Miglena Sternadori (Hoboken, NJ: John Wiley & Sons, 2020), 345–357. Lerner articulates the significance of humorists

like Jonathan Swift and Alexander Pope to early magazine culture, highlighting an early example of comedy's role in nationalistic media.

8. Jürgen Habermas, *The Structural Transformation of the Public Sphere: An Inquiry into a Category of Bourgeois Society*, trans. Thomas Burger and Frederick Lawrence (Cambridge, MA: MIT Press, 1989).

9. Mary Ann Doane, "Information, Crisis, Catastrophe," in *Logics of Television: Essays in Cultural Criticism*, ed. Patricia Mellencamp (Bloomington: Indiana University Press, 1990), 222–239; Jane Feuer, "The Concept of Live Television: Ontology as Ideology," in *Regarding Television: Critical Approaches—an Anthology*, ed. E. Ann Kaplan (Frederick, MD: University Publications of America, 1983), 12–22; Robert Vianello, "The Power Politics of 'Live' Television," *Journal of Film and Video* 37, no. 3 (Summer 1985): 26–40.

10. Daniel Dayan and Elihu Katz, *Media Events: The Live Broadcasting of History* (Cambridge, MA: Harvard University Press, 1992).

11. Federal Communications Commission, *Public Service Responsibility of Broadcast Licensees* (Washington, DC: Government Printing Office, 1946); Kevin Hawley, "Diversity, Localism, and the Public Interest: The Politics of Assessing Media Performance," *International Journal of Media and Cultural Politics* 1, no. 1 (2005): 103–106.

12. Arthur Frank Wertheim, "The Rise and Fall of Milton Berle," in *American History/American Television*, ed. John E. O'Connor (New York: Ungar, 1983), 55–77; David Marc, *Comic Visions: Television Comedy and American Culture* (Malden, MA: Wiley-Blackwell, 1998), 84–120.

13. Allen J. Scott, *On Hollywood: The Place, The Industry* (Princeton, NJ: Princeton University Press, 2005), 30, 128.

14. Christopher B. Daly, *Covering America: A Narrative History of a Nation's Journalism* (Amherst: University of Massachusetts Press, 2012), 75–85; Kevin Williams, *Read All about It: A History of the British Newspaper* (New York: Routledge, 2010), 6–7. The United Kingdom was perhaps the most notable exception in that London served as the centralized source of news prior to broadcasting.

15. Dayan and Katz, *Media Events*.

16. Elihu Katz and Tamar Liebes, "'No More Peace!': How Disaster, Terror, and War Have Upstaged Media Events," *International Journal of Communication* 1 (2007): 157–166.

17. *Late Show with David Letterman*, "Episode no. 1676," directed by Jerry Foley, aired September 24, 2001, on CBS.

18. Matt Roush, "A Nation Rallies," *TV Guide*, December 22, 2001, Chicago metropolitan ed., 10.

19. Ibid.

20. Ibid., 10–11.

21. Karl Marx and Frederic Engels, *The German Ideology* (Amherst, NY: Prometheus, 1998).

22. Jeffrey C. Alexander, "Toward a Theory of Cultural Trauma," in *Cultural Trauma and Collective Identity* (Berkeley: University of California Press, 2004), 8.

23. Stuart Hall, "The Problem of Ideology: Marxism without Guarantees," in *Stuart Hall: Critical Dialogues in Cultural Studies*, ed. David Morley and Kuan-Hsing Chen (New York: Routledge, 1996), 25–45.

24. Nick Couldry, *Media Rituals: A Critical Approach* (New York: Routledge, 2003).

25. For more on overt appeals to nationalism, see Anna McCarthy, *The Citizen Machine: Governing by Television in 1950s America* (New York: New York University Press, 2010).

26. Michael Billig, *Banal Nationalism* (London: Sage, 1995).

27. Emile Durkheim, *The Elementary Forms of Religious Life*, trans. Joseph Ward Swain (London: George Allen & Unwin, 1915).

28. Sara Ahmed, *The Cultural Politics of Emotion* (New York: Routledge, 2004), 13.

29. *South Park*, "Imaginationland Episode I," written and directed by Trey Parker, aired October 17, 2007, on Comedy Central; *South Park*, "Imaginationland Episode II," written and directed by Trey Parker, aired October 24, 2007, on Comedy Central; *South Park*, "Imaginationland Episode III," written and directed by Trey Parker, aired October 31, 2007, on Comedy Central.

30. Jean Baudrillard, "The Spirit of Terrorism," in *The Spirit of Terrorism and Requiem for the Twin Towers*, trans. Chris Turner (London: Verso, 2002), 1–26; Slavoj Zizek, "Welcome to the Desert of the Real!," in *Cultures of Fear: A Critical Reader*, ed. Uli Linke and Danielle Taana Smith (New York: Pluto Press, 2009), 70–77.

31. Baudrillard, "Spirit of Terrorism," 28.

32. Michel Foucault, *The Archaeology of Knowledge and the Discourse on Language*, trans. A. M. Sheridan Smith (New York: Pantheon Books, 2010).

33. Daniel J. Boorstin, *The Image: A Guide to Pseudo-Events in America*, 25th anniversary ed. (New York: Vintage, 1987), 11.

34. *News at Noon*, "February 14, 2018," aired February 14, 2018, on KTVU.

35. Gellner, *Nations and Nationalism*, 1. Ernest Gellner defines nationalism as "primarily a principle which holds that the political and national unit should be congruent." In this sense, a federal response to a mediated catastrophe is a textbook example of nationalist discourse.

36. *Jimmy Kimmel Live!*, "Natalie Portman/Kyrie Irving," directed by Maureen Baroocha, aired February 15, 2018, on ABC; *The Tonight Show Starring Jimmy Fallon*, "John Lithgow, Kelly Clarkson, Kacey Musgraves," directed by Dave Diomedi, aired February 26, 2018, on NBC.

37. Stacy Takacs, *Terrorism TV: Popular Entertainment in Post-9/11 America* (Lawrence: University Press of Kansas, 2012), 30–58.

38. Peter Brooks, *The Melodramatic Imagination* (New Haven, CT: Yale University Press, 1976), 11–12.

39. Lynne Joyrich, *Re-viewing Reception: Television, Gender, and Postmodern Culture* (Bloomington: Indiana University Press, 1996), 49.

40. *Massacre in Theater 9*, aired July 21, 2012, on CNN.

41. *America under Attack*, aired September 11, 2001, on CNN; *Attack on America*, aired September 11, 2001, on NBC.

42. "Attack on America—Cheers, Tears Fill Yankee Stadium—Thousands Gather to Honor Victims in 'Prayer for America,'" *Yakima Herald-Republic*, September 24, 2001, A9.

43. Sigmund Freud, *Beyond the Pleasure Principle*, trans. James Strachey (New York: Liveright, 1950); Patricia Mellencamp, "TV Time and Catastrophe, or Beyond the Pleasure Principle of Television," in *Logics of Television: Essays in Cultural Criticism*, ed. Patricia Mellencamp (Bloomington: Indiana University Press, 1990), 240–266.

44. Susannah Radstone, "Trauma and Screen Studies: Opening the Debate," *Screen* 42, no. 2 (Summer 2001): 188–193; Susannah Radstone, "Trauma Theory: Contexts, Politics, Ethics," *Paragraph* 30, no. 1 (March 2007): 9–29.

45. The presence of nonfiction comedy shows like *Full Frontal with Samantha Bee* and *Last Week Tonight with John Oliver* as well as more stylized news and documentary programs like HBO's *Vice* add dimensions to the comparison I sketch here, but they do not negate the reality that television news is increasingly and primarily understood through a left versus right political spectrum model.

46. Lynn Spigel, "Entertainment Wars: Television Culture after 9/11," *American Quarterly* 56, no. 2 (June 2004): 235–270; Takacs, *Terrorism TV*.

47. Matt Sienkiewicz, "Speaking Too Soon: SNL, 9/11, and the Remaking of American Irony," in *Saturday Night Live and American TV*, ed. Nick Marx, Matt Sienkiewicz, and Ron Becker (Bloomington: Indiana University Press, 2013), 93–111.

48. Mary Douglas, "Jokes," in *Rethinking Popular Culture: Contemporary Perspectives in Cultural Studies*, ed. Chandra Mukerji and Michael Schudson (Berkeley: University of California Press, 1991), 301.

49. Henri Bergson, *Laughter: An Essay on the Meaning of the Comic*, trans. Cloudesley Brereton and Fred Rothwell (Rockville, MD: Arc Manor, 2008), 64; Sigmund Freud, *Jokes and Their Relation to the Unconscious*, ed. and trans. James Strachey (New York: Norton, 1963), 151.

50. Ted Cohen, *Jokes: Philosophical Thoughts on Joking Matters* (Chicago: University of Chicago Press, 1999), 12–32.

51. Lawrence E. Mintz, "American Humor as Unifying and Divisive," *Humor* 12, no. 3 (1999): 237.

52. John Limon, *Stand-up Comedy in Theory, or, Abjection in America* (Durham, NC: Duke University Press, 2000), 3.

53. Geoffrey Baym and Jeffrey P. Jones, "News Parody in Global Perspective: Politics, Power, and Resistance," *Popular Communication*, no. 1–2 (February 10, 2013): 2–13; Amber Day, *Satire and Dissent: Interventions in Contemporary Political Debate* (Bloomington: University of Indiana Press, 2011).

54. Alice Bardan, "'The Tattler's Tattle': Fake News, Linguistic National Intimacy and New Media in Romania," *Popular Communication* 10, no. 1–2 (February 2012): 145–157; Brett Mills and Erica Horton, *Creativity in the British Television Comedy Industry* (Abingdon, Oxfordshire: Routledge, 2017).

55. Mikhail Bakhtin, *Rabelais and His World*, trans. Hélène Iswolsky, 1st Midland book ed. (Bloomington: Indiana University Press, 1984).

56. For more on this, see Philip Scepanski, "Sacred Catastrophe, Profane Laughter: *Family Guy*'s Comedy in the Ritual of National Trauma," in *The Comedy Studies Reader*, ed. Nick Marx and Matt Sienkiewicz (Austin: University of Texas Press, 2018), 33–44.

57. Marita Sturken, *Tourists of History: Memory, Kitsch, and Consumerism from Oklahoma City to Ground Zero* (Durham, NC: Duke University Press, 2007).

58. *Family Guy*, "Baby Not on Board," directed by Julius Wu, written by Mark Hentemann, aired November 2, 2008, on Fox.

59. *Family Guy*, "Trading Places," directed by Joseph Lee, written by Steve Callaghan, aired March 20, 2011, on Fox.

60. "Who Are the Trenchcoat Mafia?," BBC Online Network, April 21, 1999, http://news.bbc.co.uk/2/hi/americas/325054.stm.

61. This episode is not entirely negative in its engagement with this issue, for instance criticizing racism in the justice system.

62. Lauren Berlant and Sianne Ngai, "Comedy Has Issues," *Critical Inquiry* 43, no. 2 (Winter 2017): 233–249.

63. Umberto Eco, "The Frames of Comic 'Freedom,'" in *Carnival!*, ed. Thomas A. Sebeok (Berlin: Mouton, 1984), 1–9; Linda Hutcheon, *Irony's Edge: The Theory and Politics of Irony* (London: Routledge, 1995).

64. Anderson, *Imagined Communities*, 26.

65. Herman Gray, *Watching Race: Television and the Struggle for "Blackness"* (Minneapolis: University of Minnesota Press, 1995).

66. Spigel, "Entertainment Wars."

67. See Bergson, *Laughter*; Freud, *Jokes and Their Relation to the Unconscious*; Mintz, "American Humor."

Chapter 1. The Kennedy Assassination and the Growth of Sick Humor on American Television

1. *Family Guy*, "Road to the Multiverse," directed by Marc Vulcano, written by Anthony Valsucci and Mike Desilets, aired September 27, 2009, on Fox.

2. For a discussion of this phrase's various iterations, see note 3 in the introduction. Especially Randall, "'Death of Irony.'"

3. Associated Press, "Humor Muted on Late-Night Shows," *USA Today*, September 17, 2001, http://usatoday30.usatoday.com/life/enter/tv/2001-09-17-late-night-humor.htm#more.

4. David Gurney, "Everything Changes Forever (Temporarily): Late-Night Television Comedy after 9/11," in *A Decade of Dark Humor: How Comedy, Irony, and Satire Shaped Post-9/11 America*, ed. Ted Gournelos and Viveca Greene (Jackson: University Press of Mississippi, 2011), 3–19. Shortly after 9/11, Maher agreed with his guest, conservative Dinesh D'Souza, in stating that terrorists were not cowards. Maher doubled down, stating that Americans "lobbing cruise missiles from two thousand miles away" were more cowardly.

5. *Team America: World Police*, directed by Trey Parker (Hollywood, CA: Paramount, 2004), DVD. With their movie, *Team America: World Police*, Parker and Stone took to criticizing jingoism generally but also viciously satirized celebrities who had spoken out against post-9/11 American military efforts.

6. Sienkiewicz, "Speaking Too Soon."

7. Christie D'Zurilla, "Gilbert Gottfried Fired by Aflac over Japan Tsunami Jokes [Poll]," *Los Angeles Times*, March 4, 2011, http://latimesblogs.latimes.com/gossip/2011/03/gilbert-gottfried-fired-aflac-tsunami-jokes.html. In 2011, Gottfried was fired as the voice of the Aflac duck after tweeting a number of jokes about the devastating Japanese tsunami.

8. Constance Penley, *NASA/Trek: Popular Science and Sex in America* (New York: Verso, 1997).

9. Mary Ann Watson, *The Expanding Vista: American Television in the Kennedy Years* (New York: Oxford University Press, 1990), 3–17.

10. Michael Curtin, *Redeeming the Wasteland: Television Documentary and Cold War Politics* (New Brunswick, NJ: Rutgers University Press, 1995).

11. Barbie Zelizer, *Covering the Body: The Kennedy Assassination, the Media, and the Shaping of Collective Memory* (Chicago: University of Chicago Press, 1992).

12. Aniko Bodroghkozy, "Black Weekend: A Reception History of Network Television News and the Assassination of John F. Kennedy," *Television and New Media* 14, no. 6 (September 4, 2012): 560–578.

13. Ibid., 571.

14. Aniko Bodroghkozy, *Groove Tube: Sixties Television and Youth Rebellion*

(Durham, NC: Duke University Press, 2001), 123–163; David Scott Diffrient, *M*A*S*H* (Detroit, MI: Wayne State University Press, 2008). For reasons discussed in the introduction, Vietnam does not fit the type of trauma I examine in this project. Nevertheless, it remains a possible exception to my timeline, seeing as how comedies like *The Smothers Brothers Comedy Hour* and *M*A*S*H* engaged with the war during and immediately following that conflict.

15. Dennis McLellan, "Obituaries; Vaughn Meader, 68; Comedian Known for Impersonating JFK," *Los Angeles Times*, October 30, 2004.

16. Joe Queenan, *Closing Time: A Memoir* (New York: Viking, 2009), 205; Tony Hendra, *Going Too Far: The Rise and Demise of Sick, Gross, Black, Sophomoric, Weirdo, Pinko, Anarchist, Underground, Anti-establishment Humor* (New York: Dolphin, 1987), 166. Sources vary on the exact wording of the joke. While many support this version, quoted here from Joe Queenan's memoir, Tony Hendra, for example, records the line as the cleaner, "Phew—Vaughn Meader!"

17. Elizabeth McCracken, "The Temporary Kennedy," *New York Times Magazine*, December 26, 2004, http://www.nytimes.com/2004/12/26/magazine/the-temporary-kennedy.html.

18. Ethan Thompson, "What, Me Subversive?: Television and Parody in Postwar America" (PhD diss., University of Southern California, 2004); Hendra, *Going Too Far*.

19. Thompson, "What, Me Subversive?," 31–92.

20. Ibid., 44.

21. Jacob Smith, *Spoken Word: Postwar American Phonograph Cultures* (Berkeley: University of California Press, 2010).

22. Ibid., 155–156.

23. "A Time for Tears," *National Lampoon*, February 1977.

24. "The Young Troubadours of Camelot," *National Lampoon*, February 1977, 54.

25. David Lamb, "A Long Way from Camelot: Vaughn Meader's JFK Impersonation Made Him a Star. Then an Assassin's Bullet Took Everything Away," *Los Angeles Times*, April 20, 1997; Paley Center for Media, "The Museum of Radio and Television Presents Two Five-Letter Words: Lenny Bruce," press release, October 1, 2004, http://www.paleycenter.org/pressrelease-2004-lenny-bruce; Alisha Berger, "Playing in the Neighborhood," *New York Times*, August 1, 1999.

26. Newton N. Minnow, "Television and Public Interest," last updated May 2, 2019, http://www.americanrhetoric.com/speeches/newtonminow.htm.

27. Tim Brooks and Earle Marsh, *The Complete Directory to Prime Time Network and Cable TV Shows*, 9th ed. (New York: Ballantine Books, 2007), 1684. Hogan's Heroes, which premiered in 1965, featured some story lines related to Nazi assassinations. As a general rule, though, killing Nazis is generally safer comedic fodder than killing American government officials.

28. The remote control meant that a bored but lazy viewer could change the channel without moving very much, while cable multiplied the number of channels, thus splitting the audience into smaller groups.

29. Hendra, *Going Too Far*, 173–174.

30. Hendra, *Going Too Far*, 166. The British satirical news program *That Was the Week That Was*, after having attacked him on numerous issues, offered, in Tony Hendra's words, "a bittersweet, sometimes sentimental tribute to Kennedy."

31. Todd Gitlin, *Inside Prime Time*, rev. ed. (Berkeley: University of California Press, 2000), 203–220.

32. David Marc, *Demographic Vistas: Television in American Culture*, rev. ed. (Philadelphia: University of Pennsylvania Press, 1996), *149*.

33. Bodroghkozy, *Groove Tube*, 123–163. "Success" is obviously a debatable descriptor, and though the Smothers Brothers garnered fairly good ratings, their well-known content struggles with the network prevented them from being as successful as *SNL*. Additionally, Tom and Dick Smothers' respective 1937 and 1939 birth dates mark them as technically outside of the baby boom, even if they appeared to speak as members of that demographic.

34. Hendra, *Going Too Far*.

35. Marc, *Demographic Vistas*, 151.

36. *Saturday Night Live*, "Bruce Dern/Leon Redbone," directed by Dave Wilson and Claude Kerven, aired March 12, 1983, on NBC.

37. "Oswald Shooting a First in Television History," *Broadcasting*, December 2, 1963, quoted in Zelizer, *Covering the Body*, 61.

38. Hutcheon, *Irony's Edge*.

39. Mark M. MacCarthy, "Broadcast Self-Regulation: The NAB Codes, Family Viewing Hour, and Television Violence," *Yeshiva University Cardozo Arts & Entertainment Law Journal* 13 (1995): 667–696.

40. Racquel Gates, "Bringing the Black: Eddie Murphy and African American Humor on *Saturday Night Live*," in *Saturday Night Live and American TV*, ed. Nick Marx, Matt Sienkiewicz, and Ron Becker (Bloomington: Indiana University Press, 2013), 155.

41. Bhoomi K. Thakore and Bilal Hussain, "'Indians on TV (and Netflix)': The Comedic Trajectory of Aziz Ansari," in *The Comedy Studies Reader*, ed. Nick Marx and Matt Sienkiewicz (Austin: University of Texas Press, 2018), 195–205.

42. Renee Loth, "Oliver Stone's 'JFK' Reopens Old Wounds: In a Society That Often Views Life through Pop Culture, Film May Force Reexamination," *Boston Globe*, December 22, 1991.

43. Ibid. This response likely arises in part from a hope among city officials that Dallas be known for things other than the assassination.

44. Associated Press, "'JFK' Director Condemned: Warren Commission Attorney Calls Stone Film 'a Big Lie,'" *Washington Post*, December 16, 1991.

45. *The Critic*, "Every Doris Has Her Day," directed by Alan Smart and Greg Vanzo, written by Steve Tompkins, aired June 1, 1994, on ABC. Besides *Seinfeld*, the television show *The Critic* mocked the film. Like *Seinfeld*, the parody's focus was more on Stone's style than on the events the film references.

46. *Seinfeld*, "The Boyfriend (1)," directed by Tom Cherones, written by Larry David and Larry Levin, aired February 12, 1992, on NBC; *Seinfeld*, "The Boyfriend (2)," directed by Tom Cherones, written by Larry David and Larry Levin, aired February 12, 1992, on NBC.

47. Frederic Jameson, *Postmodernism, or, The Cultural Logic of Late Capitalism* (Durham, NC: Duke University Press, 1991), 16–19.

48. *"Inside Look: 'The Boyfriend,'" Seinfeld*, season 3 (Culver City, CA: Columbia TriStar Home Entertainment, 2004), DVD.

49. Øyvind Vågnes, *Zaprudered: The Kennedy Assassination in Film and Visual Culture* (Austin: University of Texas Press, 2011), 79–90.

50. Ibid.

51. Brooks and Marsh, *Complete Directory, 1692–1695*.

52. Ibid., 1614.

53. "Television," *New York Times*, February 12, 1992.

54. *Family Guy*, "A Hero Sits Next Door," directed by Monte Young, written by Mike Barker and Matt Weitzman, aired May 2, 1999, on Fox.

55. *Family Guy*, "Road to the Multiverse."

56. Thanks to Jeffrey Sconce for letting me know when he saw the gag returned to an Adult Swim rerun.

57. *Family Guy: Cast and Creators Live at the Paley Center*, directed by the Paley Center for Media (2006; Paley Center for Media, 2010), DVD.

58. Though Kennedy's affairs were kept secret from the public for a time, it is still fair to assume that the aura granted in part by the assassination dampened some of the negative fallout from their eventual discovery.

59. *South Park*, "Hooked on Monkey Fonics," written and directed by Trey Parker, aired November 10, 1999, on Comedy Central.

60. *The Simpsons*, "Lisa's Rival," directed by Mark Kirkland, written by Mike Scully, aired October 9, 1994, on Fox.

Chapter 2. Censored Comedies and Comedies of Censorship

1. Maureen Muldauer, *Smothered: The Censorship Struggles of the Smothers Brothers Comedy Hour* (New Video Group, 2003), DVD.

2. Ibid.

3. Bodroghkozy, *Groove Tube*, 123–163.

4. Michael Schneider, "Michael Jackson Episode Removed from 'The Simpsons,'" *Variety*, March 7, 2019, https://variety.com/2019/tv/news/the-simpsons-michael -jackson-leaving-neverland-stark-raving-dad-1203158114/.

5. Jerry Adler, "'I Love Lucy' and the Cuba of America's Dreams," Yahoo! News, December 16, 2015, https://www.yahoo.com/news/i-love-lucy-and-the-cuba-of -americas-dreams-040653345.html.

6. Jacques Derrida, *Archive Fever: A Freudian Impression*, trans. Eric Prenowitz (Chicago: University of Chicago Press, 1998).

7. Habermas, *Structural Transformation*.

8. Newcomb and Hirsch, "Television as a Cultural Forum," in *Television: The Critical View*, ed. Horace Newcomb, 5th ed. (New York: Oxford University Press, 1994), 503–515.

9. Anderson, *Imagined Communities*.

10. For more on censorship in the writers' room, see Felicia D. Henderson, "The Culture behind Closed Doors: Issues of Gender and Race in the Writers' Room," *Cinema Journal* 50, no. 2 (Winter 2011): 145–152.

11. John Blanchard et al., *Kids in the Hall—The Complete Collection + Digital* (Minneapolis, MN: Mill Creek Entertainment, 2018), DVD; *The Complete Monty Python's Flying Circus*, directed by Ian McNaughton and John Howard Davies (New York: A&E Home Video, 2000), DVD. It was not until I purchased DVDs of *Monty Python's Flying Circus* and *Kids in the Hall* that I saw many of their episodes in their original form and length.

12. Joe Flint, "Cable TV Shows Are Sped Up to Squeeze in More Ads," *Wall Street Journal*, February 18, 2015, https://www.wsj.com/articles/cable-tv -shows-are-sped-up-to-squeeze-in-more-ads-1424301320?mod=WSJ_hpp _MIDDLENexttoWhatsNewsThird.

13. "A Guide to Censored MGM Cartoons," Golden Age Cartoons,

February 5, 2007, https://web.archive.org/web/20070205112019/http://looney.goldenagecartoons.com/ltcuts/mgmcuts.html.

14. *Family Guy*, "Road to Rhode Island," directed by Dan Povenmire, written by Gary Janetti; aired May 30, 2000, on Fox.

15. Neal Affleck et al., *Family Guy: The Freakin' Sweet Collection* (Beverly Hills, CA: 20th Century Fox Home Entertainment, 2004), DVD.

16. Thomas C. Blanton, "The President's Daily Brief," National Security Archive, April 8, 2004, https://nsarchive2.gwu.edu//NSAEBB/NSAEBB116/index.htm.

17. *The Simpsons*, "The City of New York vs. Homer Simpson," directed by Jim Reardon, written by Ian Maxtone-Graham, aired September 21, 1997, on Fox.

18. Bill Oakley, Josh Weinstein, and Jim Reardon, "Commentary, Episode 179," *The Simpsons Complete Ninth Season* (Beverly Hills, CA: 20th Century Fox Home Entertainment, 2006), DVD; Dan Snierson, "'Simpsons' Exec Producer Al Jean: 'I Completely Understand' If Reruns with Nuclear Jokes Are Pulled," *Entertainment Weekly*, March 27, 2011, https://ew.com/article/2011/03/27/simpsons-al-jean-nuclear-japan/.

19. Nancy K. Miller, "Reporting the Disaster," in *Trauma at Home: After 9/11*, ed. Judith Greenberg (Lincoln: University of Nebraska Press, 2003), 46.

20. Sturken, *Tourists of History*.

21. *Friends: The Complete Eighth Series* (Burbank, CA: Warner Home Video, 2004), DVD.

22. Rachel Hall, *The Transparent Traveler: The Performance and Culture of Airport Security* (Durham, NC: Duke University Press, 2015), 2.

23. Bakhtin, *Rabelais and His World*; Bergson, *Laughter*, 54.

24. *The Simpsons*, "Cape Feare," directed by Rich Moore, written by Jon Vitti, aired October 7, 1993, on Fox.

25. *Family Guy: The Freakin' Sweet Collection*.

26. Piya Sinha-Roy, "CBS Pulls 'Mike & Molly' Finale with Tornado Storyline from Air," Reuters, May 20, 2013, https://www.reuters.com/article/entertainment-us-mikeandmolly-tornado/cbs-pulls-mike-molly-finale-with-tornado-storyline-from-air-idUSBRE94K01B20130521.

27. Dave Itzkoff, "Fox Postpones Animated Comedies with Hurricane Story Line," *ArtsBeat* (blog), *New York Times*, April 29, 2011, https://artsbeat.blogs.nytimes.com/2011/04/29/fox-postpones-animated-comedies-with-hurricane-story-line/?partner=rss&emc=rss.

28. Associated Press, "Cartoon on MTV Blamed for Fire," *New York Times*, October 10, 1993, https://www.nytimes.com/1993/10/10/us/cartoon-on-mtv-blamed-for-fire.html.

29. Raymond K. K. Ho, "How Many Children Must We Bury?," *Chicago Tribune*, December 26, 1994, https://www.chicagotribune.com/news/ct-xpm-1994-12-26-9412260033-story.html.

30. Ibid.

31. *Sex and the City*, "Four Women and a Funeral," directed by Allen Coulter, written by Jenny Bicks, aired July 4, 1999, on HBO.

32. "'Sex and the City' Trivia," *Entertainment Weekly*, May 16, 2008, http://www.ew.com/ew/article/0,,20201140,00.html.

33. Isabel Jones, "Why Sarah Jessica Parker Called Dating John Kennedy Jr. 'The Kennedy Fiasco,'" *InStyle*, May 15, 2019, https://www.instyle.com/news/tbt-sarah-jessica-parker-john-f-kennedy-jr.

34. *In Memory Of*, aired July 23, 1999, on CNN.

35. *Talkback Live*, aired July 23, 1999, on CNN.

36. Michael Powell, "JFK Jr.: As Child and Man, America's Crown Prince," *Washington Post*, July 18, 1999; Katherine Q. Seelye, "John F. Kennedy, Jr.: Heir to a Formidable Dynasty," *New York Times*, July 19, 1999.

37. Daniel Jeffreys, "JFK's Trouble with George," *Independent*, March 24, 1997, http://www.independent.co.uk/news/media/jfks-trouble-with-george-1274767.html.

38. Jane Arthurs, "*Sex and the City* and Consumer Culture: Remediating Post-feminist Drama," *Feminist Media Studies* 3, no. 1 (2003): 83.

39. Ibid., 92.

40. Kathleen Rowe, *The Unruly Woman: Gender and the Genres of Laughter* (Austin: University of Texas Press, 1995).

41. Joyce Wadler, "The Sexiest Kennedy," *People*, September 12, 1988.

42. *Seinfeld*, "The Contest," directed by Tom Cherones, written by Larry David, aired November 18, 1992, on NBC.

43. With the possible exception of George, according to some episodes. See *Seinfeld*, "The Cartoon," directed by Andy Ackerman, written by Bruce Eric Kaplan, aired January 29, 1998, on NBC; *Seinfeld*, "The Note," directed by Tom Cherones, written by Larry David, aired September 18, 1991, on NBC.

44. "TV's Top 100 Episodes of All Time," *TV Guide*, June 15, 2009.

45. "Smothers Brothers Comedy Hour, The: Smothered Sketches (The Glaser Foundation First Amendment Collection) (TV)," Paley Center for Media, accessed April 21, 2019, https://www.paleycenter.org/collection/item/?q=Smothers+Brothers+Comedy+Hour&p=1&item=T:22125.

46. *South Park*, "200," written and directed by Trey Parker, aired April 14, 2010, on Comedy Central; *South Park*, "201," written and directed by Trey Parker, aired April 21, 2010, on Comedy Central.

47. Josh Grossberg, "Did Scientology Go Gunning for South Park Guys?," E! Online, October 24, 2011, http://www.eonline.com/news/271142/did-scientology-go-gunning-for-south-park-guys.

48. *South Park*, "Super Best Friends," written and directed by Trey Parker, aired July 4, 2001, on Comedy Central.

49. Dave Itzkoff, "'South Park' Episode Is Altered after Muslim Group's Warning," *ArtsBeat* (blog), *New York Times*, April 22, 2010, http://artsbeat.blogs.nytimes.com/2010/04/22/south-park-episode-is-altered-after-muslim-groups-warning/?_r=0.

50. See "200," South Park Studios, April 14, 2010, http://southpark.cc.com/full-episodes/s14e05-200; Itzkoff, "'South Park' Episode."

51. See "Super Best Friends," South Park Studios, July 4, 2001, http://southpark.cc.com/full-episodes/s05e04-super-best-friends.

52. Sean O'Neal, "An Uncensored Version of South Park's Controversial Muhammad Episode Has Surfaced," AV Club, January 31, 2014, http://www.avclub.com/article/the-uncensored-version-of-south-parks-controversia-107422.

53. In reference to still other episodes, people with red hair and freckles represent another hostile party. Suffice it to say, their significance is less obviously in dialogue with any off-screen controversies faced by *South Park* and thus have less significance to this chapter. Plus, the narrative summary is complicated enough without having to account for them.

54. Animated Anon, "South Park Family Guy Muhammad," Vimeo video, posted January 11, 2015, https://vimeo.com/116475218.

Chapter 3. Emotional Nonconformity in Comedy

1. Bakhtin, *Rabelais*, 91.

2. Noël Carroll, "Horror and Humor," *Journal of Aesthetics and Art Criticism* 57, no. 2 (Spring 1999): 145–160.

3. For more on comedy's play of illogic, see Jerry Palmer, *The Logic of the Absurd: On Film and Television Comedy* (London: BFI, 1987).

4. Sigmund Freud, "Humour," in *Collected Papers: Authorized Translation under the Supervision of Joan Riviere*, ed. James Strachey, trans. Joan Riviere, 1st American ed., vol. 5 (New York: Basic Books, 1959), 162.

5. Bergson, *Laughter*, 80.

6. Michel Foucault, and Cahiers du Cinema, "Film and Popular Memory: An Interview with Michel Foucault," *Radical Philosophy* 11 (Summer 1975): 24–29.

7. *Anthony Jeselnik: Fire in the Maternity Ward*, directed by Marcus Raboy, written by Anthony Jeselnik, streamed April 30, 2019, on Netflix.

8. I struggled to decide between calling this phenomenon "emotional non-conformity" or "emotional rebellion," but settled on *nonconformity* as a more general term that allows for performers to give the impression of inadvert and/or negotiated emotional reactions. Emotional rebellion is a subset of emotional nonconformity that describes a more conscious and purposeful performance of emotion against expectation.

9. D'Zurilla, "Gilbert Gottfried Fired"; Gurney, "Everything Changes."

10. Jared Champion, "'This Kindergarten Country of Ours': Daniel Tosh's Postmodern Social Politics," *Journal of Popular Culture* 51, no. 3 (2018): 597.

11. *Tosh.0*, "Zakar Twins," directed by John Elerick, written by Sam Jarvis and T. K. Kelly, aired September 19, 2017, on Comedy Central.

12. Hutcheon, *Irony's Edge*; Linda Hutcheon, *A Theory of Parody: The Teachings of Twentieth-Century Art Forms*, 1st Illinois paperback ed. (Urbana: University of Illinois Press, 2000).

13. Elissa Bassist, "Why Daniel Tosh's 'Rape Joke' at the Laugh Factory Wasn't Funny," Daily Beast, July 11, 2012, https://www.thedailybeast.com/why-daniel-toshs-rape-joke-at-the-laugh-factory-wasnt-funny.

14. *Family Guy*, "Padre de Familia," directed by Pete Michels, written by Kirker Butler, aired November 18, 2007, on Fox.

15. *Family Guy*, "Padre de Familia"; Orrin E. Klapp, *Heroes, Villains, and Fools: The Changing American Character* (Englewood Cliffs, NJ: Prentice-Hall, 1962); David Wolfsdorf, "The Irony of Socrates," *Journal of Aesthetics and Art Criticism* 65, no. 2 (2007): 175–187.

16. *Family Guy*, "The Father, the Son, and the Holy Fonz," directed by James Purdum, written by Danny Smith, aired December 8, 2005, on Fox. *Family Guy* often makes use of this dynamic between virtuality and reality, with characters in this show's narrative universe often crossing into and interacting with the diegeses of other fictional texts in a way that more often than not has little or no bearing on events in the central narrative. Other times, characters take fictional texts too seriously—as when Peter started a religion dedicated to worshiping Fonzie from *Happy Days*. The woman pilot gag relies on a similar joke structure but reverses it by denying the realness of 9/11.

17. Amanda Holpuch, "Daniel Tosh Apologises for Rape Joke as Fellow Comedians Defend Topic," *Guardian*, July 11, 2012, https://www.theguardian.com/culture/us-news-blog/2012/jul/11/daniel-tosh-apologises-rape-joke; Jason Zinoman, "How to Get Away with Sociopathy," *New York Times*, May 1, 2019.

18. For more on Tosh as "post-PC," see Ethan Thompson, "Tosh.0, Convergence Comedy, and the 'Post-PC' TV Trickster," in *Taboo Comedy: Television and Controversial Humour*, ed. Chiara Bucaria and Luca Barra (London: Palgrave MacMillan, 2017), 155–171.

19. Jonah Lehrer, "The Forgetting Pill: How a New Drug Can Target Your Worst Memories—and Erase Them Forever," *Wired*, March 2012, 88.

20. Derrida, *Archive Fever*.

21. Cathy Caruth, "An Interview with Jean Laplanche," *Postmodern Culture* 11, no. 2 (2001), http://www.iath.virginia.edu/pmc/text-only/issue.101/11.2caruth.txt.

22. *Third Watch*, "In Their Own Words," directed by Christopher Chulack and Julie Hébert, written by Edward Allen Bernero, aired October 15, 2001, on NBC. For episodes that deal most explicitly with 9/11, see *Third Watch*, "September Tenth," directed by Guy Norman Bee, written by John Wells, aired October 22, 2001, on NBC; *Third Watch*, "After Time," directed by Félix Enríquez Alcalá, written by Edward Allen Bernero and John Wells, aired October 29, 2001, on NBC.

23. *13 Reasons Why*, "Bye," directed by Kyle Patrick Alvarez, written by Brian Yorkey, streamed May 18, 2018, on Netflix; *Glee*, "Shooting Star," directed by Bradley Buecker, written by Matthew Hodgson, aired April 11, 2013, on Fox; *Madam Secretary*, "Family Separation: Part 1," directed by Rob Greenlea, written by Barbara Hall and David Grae, aired December 23, 2018, on CBS; *Madam Secretary*, "Family Separation: Part 2," directed by Martha Mitchell, written by Barbara Hall and David Grae, aired January 6, 2019, on CBS.

24. Freud, *Beyond the Pleasure Principle*. This tendency indicates a common drive with Freud's clinical trauma sufferers in that he theorized the compulsion to repeat as an attempt to both master the past and build up an emotional callous in preparation for future shocks.

25. Robert Turnock, *Interpreting Diana: Television Audiences and the Death of a Princess* (London: BFI, 2000), 32–54.

26. For more on how television returned to normal after 9/11, see Spigel, "Entertainment Wars."

27. *The Opposition with Jordan Klepper*, "Andrew Marantz," directed by Chuck O'Neil, aired March 15, 2018, on Comedy Central.

28. *Full Frontal with Samantha Bee*, "Super Lobbyist," directed by Paul Pennolino, aired September 19, 2016, on TBS.

29. *South Park*, "Two Days before the Day after Tomorrow," written and directed by Trey Parker, aired October 19, 2005, on Comedy Central.

30. *The Sarah Silverman Program*, "The Patriot Tact," directed by Dan Sterling, written by Harris Wittels, aired October 23, 2008, on Comedy Central.

31. Peter Sloterdijk, *Critique of Cynical Reason*, trans. Michael Eldred (Minneapolis: University of Minnesota Press, 1987).

32. Sturken, *Tourists of History*.

33. Susan Sontag, *Against Interpretation and Other Essays* (New York: Delta, 1961), 288.

34. Jonathan Gray, *Watching with the Simpsons: Television, Parody, and Intertextuality* (New York: Routledge, 2006).

35. Sasha Torres, "Televising Guantánamo: Transmission of Feeling during the Bush Years," in *Political Emotions: New Agendas in Communication*, ed. Janet Staiger, Ann Cvetkovich, and Ann Reynolds (New York: Routledge, 2010), 45.

36. Nick Gass, "Obama Decries Latest Mass Shooting: 'We've Become Numb to This,'" Politico, October 1, 2015, https://www.politico.com/story/2015/10/obama-oregon-shootings-214352.

Chapter 4. Conspiracy Theories and Comedy

1. Jane Coaston, "ABC Canceled Roseanne's Show over a Racist Tweet. Her Feed's Been Full of Racism and Conspiracy Theories for a Decade," Vox, May 29, 2018, https://www.vox.com/2018/5/29/17406014/roseanne-racism-abc-trump-twitter.

2. Comedy Central, "This Can't Wait: 'Roseanne' Gets Canceled—The Opposition w/ Jordan Klepper—Uncensored," YouTube video, posted May 29, 2018, https://www.youtube.com/watch?v=QY28g6IBWdE.

3. Patrick Leman, "The Born Conspiracy: When an Unforgettable Event Rocks Our World, Why Do We So Often Mistrust the Official Explanation? Psychologist Patrick Leman Has a Theory," *New Scientist*, July 14, 2007, http://www.lexisnexis.com.turing.library.northwestern.edu/hottopics/lnacademic/?verb=sr&csi=158275.

4. Ibid.

5. Mark Fenster, *Conspiracy Theories: Secrecy and Power in American Culture*, rev. and updated ed. (Minneapolis: University of Minnesota Press, 2008).

6. Sloterdijk, *Critique of Cynical Reason*.

7. "Cynic" here refers to a group of Greek philosophers who believed in and lived severely ascetic lifestyles.

8. Gray, *Watching with the Simpsons*.

9. "The Third Campaign," *Time*, August 15, 1960, 42–49.

10. Edward Linn, "The Comic Who'll Never Be In," *Saturday Evening Post*, September 19, 1964, 28–29.

11. More recent examples of this kind of engagement include Zach Galifianakis's hosting Barack Obama and Hillary Clinton on his web series *Between Two Ferns*. However, even in those instances Galifianakis maintained his belligerent and insulting tone toward the politicians whose programs and campaigns he ostensibly supported. Perhaps a closer comparison in terms of tone would be Sarah Silverman's sincere support of Bernie Sanders for the 2016 and 2020 elections. However, Silverman differs from Sahl in that her stage persona is often an ironic send-up of a kind of privileged white femininity.

12. "American Humor: Hardly a Laughing Matter," *Time*, March 4, 1966, 46–47; "The Campaign Jokes," *Time*, September 18, 1964.

13. Mort Sahl, *Heartland* (New York: Harcourt Brace Jovanovich, 1976).

14. Andrew Wantuck, "Mort Sahl," The Comedy & Magic Club, accessed July 11, 2014, http://comedyandmagicclub.com/page.cfm?id=1661; "Honors," Mort Sahl, accessed May 5, 2020, http://www.theofficialmortsahl.com/honors.html.

15. Vincent Canby, "Sahl (He's Not All Sunshine) Digressing at the Village Gate," *New York Times*, August 31, 1968; *American Masters*, "Mort Sahl: The Loyal Opposition," written and directed by Robert B. Weide, aired September 18, 1989, on PBS.

16. John Leonard, "Private Lives: Stand Up, Comedy," *New York Times*, January 18, 1978.

17. Gary Webb, *Dark Alliance: The CIA, the Contras, and the Crack Cocaine Explosion* (New York: Seven Stories Press, 1998).

18. Jeffrey A. Hall, "Aligning Darkness with Conspiracy Theory: The Discursive Effects of African American Interest in Gary Webb's 'Dark Alliance,'" *Howard Journal of Communication* 17, no. 3 (2006): 205–222; Fenster, *Conspiracy Theories*, 4–5.

19. Fenster, *Conspiracy Theories*, 4.

20. Don Wycliffe, "Dangers of Questioning Government Actions," *Chicago Tribune*, January 6, 2005; Nick Schou, "The Truth in 'Dark Alliance,'" *Los Angeles Times*, August 18, 2006; Hall, "Aligning Darkness," 206.

21. Michael Kazin, "The Nation; Conspiracy Theories: The Paranoid Streak in American History," *Los Angeles Times*, October 27, 1996.

22. Mel Watkins, *On the Real Side: A History of African American Comedy from Slavery to Chris Rock* (Chicago: Lawrence Hill Books, 1999); Bambi Haggins, *Laughing Mad: The Black Comic Persona in Post-Soul America* (New Brunswick, NJ: Rutgers University Press, 1997), 14–68.

23. Richard Greenier, "On the Trail of America's Paranoid Class: Oliver Stone's *JFK*," *National Interest*, Spring 1992, 84, quoted in Daniel Pipes, *Conspiracy: How the Paranoid Style Flourishes and Where It Comes From* (New York: The Free Press, 1997), 2. Pipes quotes Greenier in the epigraph to a section devoted to conspiracy theories within African American communities. While they are not his words precisely, they neatly sum up his attitude toward the phenomenon.

24. Johan Huizinga, *Homo Ludens: A Study of the Play-Element in Culture* (New York: J. & J. Harper Editions, 1970). Huizinga defines play in part as taking place within boundaries that mark it as having rules distinct from those of the larger culture. For example, a soccer game takes place within marked boundaries wherein players may, within a set of rules, violently tackle one another but may not touch the ball with their hands. Humor and comedy function similarly. Although the comic stage offers a physical analog, more symbolic discursive and generic boundaries separate this type of communication from other forms as more "playful" than earnest speech.

25. Peter Knight, *Conspiracy Culture: From the Kennedy Assassination to* The X-Files (London: Routledge, 2000), 46–51.

26. *The Boondocks*, "The Trial of Robert Kelly," directed by Anthony Bell, written by Rodney Barnes and Aaron McGruder, aired November 13, 2005, on Adult Swim, Cartoon Network.

27. *The Boondocks*, "The Real," directed by Anthony Bell and Lesean Thomas, written by Aaron McGruder, aired January 8, 2006, on Adult Swim, Cartoon Network.

28. *The Boondocks*, "Invasion of the Katrinians," directed by Dan Fausett, written by Aaron McGruder and Rodney Barnes, aired December 10, 2007, on Adult Swim, Cartoon Network.

29. See *Treme*, "Do You Know What It Means," directed by Agnieszka Holland, written by David Simon and Eric Ellis Overmyer, aired April 11, 2010, on HBO; *When the Levees Broke: A Requiem in Four Acts*, directed by Spike Lee (2006; New York: HBO Documentary Films, 2006), DVD.

30. Jeffrey Sconce, "What If? Charting Television's New Textual Boundaries," in *Television after TV: Essays on a Medium in Transition*, ed. Lynn Spigel and Jan Olsson (Durham, NC: Duke University Press, 2004), 93–112; *The Boondocks*, "It's

a Black President, Huey Freeman," directed by Sung-hoon Kim, written by Aaron McGruder, aired May 2, 2010, on Adult Swim, Cartoon Network; *The Boondocks*, "The Return of the King," directed by Kalvin Lee, written by Aaron McGruder, aired January 15, 2006, on Adult Swim, Cartoon Network.

31. *The Boondocks*, "Trial of Robert Kelly."

32. *Deep in the Heart of Texas: Dave Chappelle Live at Austin City Limits*, directed by Stan Lathan, written by Dave Chappelle, streamed March 21, 2017, on Netflix.

33. *Undercover Brother*, directed by Malcolm D. Lee (Universal City, CA: Universal Studios Home Entertainment, 2015), DVD.

34. *Chappelle's Show*, "Tyrone Biggums at School & Wrap It Up Box," written by Neal Brennan and Dave Chappelle, aired January 29, 2003, on Comedy Central.

35. *The Rush Limbaugh Show*, "July 19, 1995," aired July 19, 1995, on WABC.

36. Corky Siemaszko, "InfoWars' Alex Jones Is a 'Performance Artist,' His Lawyer Says in Divorce Hearing," NBC News, April 17, 2017, https://www.nbcnews.com /news/us-news/not-fake-news-infowars-alex-jones-performance-artist-n747491.

37. *King of the Hill*, "Dale to the Chief," directed by Anthony Lioi, written by Garland Testa, aired January 30, 2005, on Fox.

38. Obviously not literal camera movement, as this is cel animation.

39. John Fiske, *Media Matters: Race and Gender in U.S. Politics* (Minneapolis: University of Minnesota Press, 1996), 216. This is not to say that Fiske is entirely wrong, but his championing of conspiracy theories as necessarily resistant is overly simplistic. There are obvious cases—from Watergate to more everyday abuses of police and judicial power—in which a belief in conspiracy made or makes individuals sensitive to abuses of power. However, he too-readily dismisses as "conservative" the argument that a belief in an overly powerful government might make African Americans feel helpless when victimized and thus prevent them from addressing such concerns.

40. *South Park*, "The Mystery of the Urinal Deuce," directed by Trey Parker, written by Trey Parker and Susan Hurwitz Arneson, aired October 11, 2006, on Comedy Central.

41. Michel Foucault, *Discipline and Punish: The Birth of the Prison*, 2nd Vintage Books ed., trans. Alan Sheridan (New York: Vintage, 1977); Michel Foucault, *The History of Sexuality*, vol. 1, *An Introduction*, trans. Robert Hurley, Vintage Books ed. (New York: Vintage, 1990).

42. *Meet the Press*, "January 22, 2017," aired January 22, 2017, on NBC.

43. Fenster, *Conspiracy Theories*; Knight, *Conspiracy Culture*.

44. In terms of conspiracy theories, Trump's attacks on Barack Obama's citizenship status remain the most notorious example. However, he also dabbled in theorizing about national trauma in the 2016 election when he floated the idea that Ted Cruz's father was in on the Kennedy assassination.

45. Nellie Andreeva, "'The Opposition' to End as Comedy Central Orders New Jordan Klepper Weekly Series," Deadline Hollywood, June 15, 2018, https:// deadline.com/2018/06/the-opposition-canceled-end-comedy-central-orders-new -jordan-klepper-weekly-series-1202411168/.

46. *The Opposition with Jordan Klepper*, "Matt Taibbi," directed by Chuck O'Neil, aired October 23, 2017, on Comedy Central.

Chapter 5. African American Comedies and the 1992 Los Angeles Riots

1. Robert Reinhold, "Rebuilding Lags in Los Angeles a Year after Riots," *New York Times*, May 10, 1993; Associated Press, "Los Angeles Riot Toll Dropped to 51 after Review," *New York Times*, August 13, 1992, http://www.nytimes.com/1992/08/13/us/los-angeles-riot-toll-dropped-to-51-after-review.html.

2. Rebecca Krefting, *All Joking Aside: American Humor and Its Discontents* (Baltimore, MD: Johns Hopkins University Press, 2014).

3. *Live*, aired April 30, 1992, on KNBC.

4. Gray, *Watching Race*, 57–69.

5. Kristal Brent Zook, *Color by FOX: The FOX Network and the Revolution in Black Television* (New York: Oxford University Press, 1999), 2.

6. Newcomb and Hirsch, "Television as a Cultural Forum."

7. Haggins, *Laughing Mad*.

8. J. Fred MacDonald, *Blacks and White TV: African-Americans in Television Since 1948*, 2nd ed. (Chicago: Nelson-Hall, 1992); Beretta Smith-Shomade, *Shaded Lives: African-American Women and Television* (New Brunswick, NJ: Rutgers University Press, 2002).

9. Gray, *Watching Race*, 134, 146; Zook, *Color by FOX*, 16–24.

10. Stuart Hall, "What Is This 'Black' in Black Popular Culture," in *Stuart Hall: Critical Dialogues in Cultural Studies*, ed. David Morley and Kuan-Hsing Chen (New York: Routledge, 1996), 465–475; E. Patrick Johnson, *Appropriating Blackness: Performance and the Politics of Authenticity* (Durham, NC: Duke University Press, 2003).

11. Zook, *Color by FOX*, 20.

12. Gray, *Watching Race*, 52–53; Hall, "What Is This 'Black,'" 474.

13. Greg Braxton, "Has Black Comedy Been Beaten Blue?," *Los Angeles Times*, February 20, 1994.

14. Jonathan Hicks, "A Big Bet for the Godfather of Rap," *New York Times*, June 14, 1992, 90.

15. *Def Comedy Jam*, "Cedric the Entertainer, Andre Covington, Angela Means," directed by Jeff Ross, aired August 15, 1992, on HBO.

16. *Def Comedy Jam*, "Chris Tucker, Kevin Anthony, Alonzo Jones, Bernie Mac," directed by Jeff Ross, aired August 8, 1992, on HBO.

17. John Thornton Caldwell, *Televisuality: Style, Crisis, and Authority in American Television* (New Brunswick, NJ: Rutgers University Press, 1995), 317.

18. Johnson, *Appropriating Blackness*, 4.

19. Charles T. Banner-Haley, *The Fruits of Integration: Black Middle-Class Ideology and Culture, 1960–1990* (Jackson: University Press of Mississippi, 1994); Crystal M. Fleming and Lorraine E. Roses, "Black Cultural Capitalists: African-American Elites and the Organization of the Arts in Early Twentieth Century Boston," *Poetics* 35, no. 6 (2007): 368–387.

20. Mikhail Bakhtin, *The Dialogic Imagination: Four Essays*, ed. Michael Holquist, trans. Caryl Emerson and Michael Holmquist (Austin: University of Texas Press, 1981). I use the term "dialogic" to contrast the dialogue of these forms, but also to invoke the Bakhtinian sense that these characters use different linguistic and ideological positions within the same text to dialectic and/or Manichaean ends.

21. Zook, *Color by FOX*, 18.

22. *The Fresh Prince of Bel-Air*, "Will Gets Committed," directed by Shelley Jensen, written by Leslie Ray and David Steven Simon, aired September 21, 1992, on NBC.

23. Smith-Shomade, *Shaded Lives*.

24. Johnson, *Appropriating Blackness*, 2.

25. Andy Medhurst, *A National Joke: Popular Comedy and English Cultural Identities* (London: Routledge, 2011).

26. *A Different World*, "Honeymoon in L.A. (1)," directed by Debbie Allen, written by Susan Fales, aired September 24, 1992, on NBC; *A Different World*, "Honeymoon in L.A. (2)," directed by Debbie Allen, written by Glenn Berenbeim, aired October 1, 1992, on NBC.

27. Bergson, *Laughter*.

28. Jameson, *Postmodernism*, 16–19; David Foster Wallace, "E Unibus Pluram: Television and U.S. Fiction," *Review of Contemporary Fiction* 13, no. 2 (Summer 1993): 151–194.

29. Gray, *Watching Race*, 130.

30. Ibid., 135.

31. Ibid., 136.

32. Hall, "What Is This 'Black,'" 474.

33. *In Living Color*, "Rodney King and Reginald Denny Speak Out," directed by Terri McCoy, aired September 27, 1992, on Fox.

34. Sloterdijk, *Critique of Cynical Reason*.

35. Bob Sipchen, "Denny—Beaten but Unbowed," *Los Angeles Times*, December 24, 1992.

36. *In Living Color*, "Forever Silky," directed by Terri McCoy, aired February 7, 1993, on Fox.

37. *In Living Color*, "Stacey Koon's Police Academy," directed by Terri McCoy, aired April 25, 1993, on Fox.

38. Steven Herbert, "Fox's 'In Living Color' Plans Lampoon of Koon Television: Police Officer's Attorney Protests Parody as 'Sad Public Treatment of My Client,'" *Los Angeles Times*, April 24, 1993, 2.

Chapter 6. Television Comedy and Islamophobia after 9/11

1. *The Axis of Evil Comedy Tour*, directed by Michael Simon, aired March 10, 2007, on Comedy Central.

2. *Herr Meets Hare*, in *Looney Tunes Golden Oldies Volume 6*, directed by Friz Freling (1945; Burbank, CA: Warner Home Video, 2008), DVD; *Bugs Bunny Nips the Nips*, in *The Golden Age of Looney Tunes*, directed by Friz Freling (1944; Culver City, CA: MGM/UA, 1991), laserdisc.

3. *South Park*, "Osama bin Laden Has Farty Pants," written and directed by Trey Parker, aired November 7, 2001, on Comedy Central.

4. Hamid Naficy, "Mediating the Other: American Pop Culture Representations of Postrevolutionary Iran," in *The U.S. Media and the Middle East: Image and Perception*, ed. Yahya R. Kamalipour (Westport, CT: Greenwood, 1995), 73–90.

5. Geoffrey Hughes, *Political Correctness: A History of Semantics and Culture* (Malden, MA: Wiley-Blackwell, 2010), 1.

6. Doris Lessing, "Censorship," in *Time Bites: Views and Reviews* (London: Fourth Estate, 2004), 7–12, quoted in Hughes, *Political Correctness*, 13.

7. Bernard Saper, "Joking in the Context of Political Correctness," *Humor* 8,

no. 1 (1995): 65–76; Salvatore Attardo et al., "Debate: Humor and Political Correctness," *Humor* 10, no. 4 (1997): 453–513.

8. See *Seinfeld*, "The Outing," directed by Tom Cherones, written by Larry Charles, aired February 11, 1993, on NBC; *The Simpsons*, "Homer's Phobia," directed by Mikel B. Anderson, written by Ron Hauge, aired February 16, 1997, on Fox.

9. *Mind of Mencia*, season 1, episode 1, directed by Kelly D. Hommon, aired July 6, 2005, on Comedy Central.

10. Lanita Jacobs-Huey, "The Arab Is the New Nigger: African American Comics Confront the Irony and Tragedy of September 11," *Transforming Anthropology* 14, no. 1 (2006): 60–64.

11. *The Axis of Evil Comedy Tour*.

12. David R. Roediger, *The Wages of Whiteness: Race and the Making of the American Working Class*, rev. ed. (London: Verso, 2007), 115–163; Noel Ignatiev, *How the Irish Became White* (New York: Routledge, 1995).

13. Robert Nowatzki, "Paddy Jumps Jim Crow: Irish-Americans and Blackface Minstrelsy," *Éire-Ireland* 41, no. 3/4 (Fall/Winter 2006), 162–184.

14. Michael Rogin, *Blackface, White Noise: Jewish Immigrants in the Hollywood Melting Pot* (Berkeley: University of California Press, 1996).

15. Scott King, "Inside the Mind and Career of Ventriloquist Comedian Jeff Dunham," *Forbes*, October 31, 2018, https://www.forbes.com/sites/scottking/2018/10/31/inside-the-mind-and-career-of-ventriloquist-comedian-jeff-dunham/.

16. Jon Mooallem, "Comedy for Dummies," *New York Times Magazine*, November 1, 2009, 42.

17. Ibid., 41.

18. Ibid., 41.

19. Ibid., 42; Brian Lowry, "The Jeff Dunham Show," *Variety*, October 22, 2009; Neil Genzlinger, "No Puppet to Political Correctness," *New York Times*, December 4, 2009.

20. Medhurst, *A National Joke*, 187–203.

21. Joshua Rhett Miller, "Comedian Defends 'Achmed the Dead Terrorist' Puppet Routine against South African Ban," Fox News, October 2, 2008, https://www.foxnews.com/story/comedian-defends-achmed-the-dead-terrorist-puppet-routine-against-south-african-ban.

22. Belinda Luscombe, "The Puppet Master," *Time*, June 8, 2009, http://content.time.com/time/magazine/article/0,9171,1901490,00.html.

23. Susan Douglas, *Listening In: Radio and the American Imagination* (Minneapolis: University of Minnesota Press, 2004), 100–123.

24. *Jeff Dunham's Very Special Christmas Special*, directed by Michael Simon, written by Jeff Dunham, aired November 16, 2008, on Comedy Central.

25. *The Jeff Dunham Show*, episode 6, directed by Manny Rodriguez and Matthew McNeil, written by Ian Busch and Cece Pleasants, aired December 3, 2009, on Comedy Central.

26. *30 Rock*, "Somebody to Love," directed by Beth McCarthy, written by Kay Cannon and Tina Fey, aired November 15, 2007, on NBC; *American Dad*, "Homeland Insecurity," directed by Rodney Clouden and Ron Hughart, written by Neal Boushell and Sam O'Neal, aired June 19, 2005, on Fox; *The Simpsons*, "MyPods and Boomsticks," directed by Steven Dean Moore and Mike B. Anderson, written by Marc Wilmore, aired November 30, 2008, on Fox.

27. *South Park*, "The Snuke," written and directed by Trey Parker, aired March 28, 2007, on Comedy Central.

28. *Roseanne*, "Go Cubs," directed by Andrew W. Weyman, written by Dave Caplan, aired May 8, 2018, on ABC.

29. *The Simpsons*, "Homer's Phobia"; *The Simpsons*, "Lisa the Vegetarian," directed by Mark Kirkland, written by David S. Cohen, aired October 15, 1995, on Fox; *The Simpsons*, "Much Apu about Nothing," directed by Susie Dietter, written by David S. Cohen, aired May 5, 1996, on Fox.

30. Gray, *Watching with the Simpsons*.

31. The parody visually quotes a common mise-en-scène from the series as shown in the images on page 146. *24*, "Day 4: 4:00 p.m.–5:00 p.m.," directed by Brad Turner, written by Stephen Kronish and Peter M. Lenkov, aired February 21, 2005, on Fox.

32. Adam Green, "Normalizing Torture, One Rollicking Hour at a Time," *New York Times*, May 22, 2005; Alessandra Stanley, "Abu Ghraib and Its Multiple Failures," *New York Times*, February 22, 2007.

33. Edwin S. Porter, *Uncle Josh at the Moving Picture Show* (Edison Manufacturing Co., 1902), 35 mm film, from Library of Congress, MOV video, 1:57 at 16 fps, https://www.loc.gov/item/00694324.

34. Amber Day, "And Now . . . the News?: Mimesis and the Real in *The Daily Show*," in *Satire TV: Politics and Comedy in the Post-Network Era*, ed. Jonathan Gray, Jeffrey P. Jones, and Ethan Thompson (New York: New York University Press, 2009), 85–103.

35. *The Daily Show with Jon Stewart*, "December 18, 2001," directed by Chuck O'Neil, aired December 18, 2001, on Comedy Central.

36. *The Daily Show with Jon Stewart*, "July 8, 2002," directed by Chuck O'Neil, aired July 8, 2002, on Comedy Central.

37. *South Park*, "Osama bin Laden Has Farty Pants."

38. *American Dad*, "Stan of Arabia: Part 1," directed by Rodney Clouden and Ron Hughart, written by Nahnatchka Kahn, aired November 6, 2005, on Fox; *American Dad*, "Stan of Arabia: Part 2," directed by Anthony Lioi and Ron Hughart, written by Carter Bays and Craig Thomas, aired November 13, 2005, on Fox.

39. *The Daily Show with Jon Stewart*, "July 7, 2010," directed by Chuck O'Neil, aired July 7, 2010, on Comedy Central.

40. This was, of course, before gay marriage was fully legalized by the US Supreme Court in 2015.

41. *The Daily Show with Jon Stewart*, "August 10, 2010," directed by Chuck O'Neil, aired August 10, 2010, on Comedy Central; *The Daily Show with Jon Stewart*, "August 16, 2010," directed by Chuck O'Neil, aired August 16, 2010, on Comedy Central.

42. *The Daily Show with Jon Stewart*, "August 9, 2006," directed by Chuck O'Neil, aired August 9, 2006, on Comedy Central.

43. *The Daily Show with Jon Stewart*, "August 19, 2010," directed by Chuck O'Neil, aired August 19, 2010, on Comedy Central.

44. *The Daily Show with Jon Stewart*, "August 25, 2010," directed by Chuck O'Neil, aired August 25, 2010, on Comedy Central.

45. Krefting, *All Joking Aside*, 74–79.

46. Besides *The Axis of Evil Comedy Tour*, see, for example, *Allah Made Me Funny: Live in Concert*, directed by Andrea Kalin (Washington, DC: Unity Productions Foundation, 2008), DVD; *Bridging the Gap: A Middle East Comedy Conference*,

directed by Scott L. Montoya, aired September 16, 2010, on Showtime.

47. "Text: President Bush Addresses the Nation," *Washington Post*, September 20, 2001, https://www.washingtonpost.com/wp-srv/nation/specials/attacked/transcripts/bushaddress_092001.html.

48. For examples, see Regina Barreca, *They Used to Call Me Snow White . . . But I Drifted Women's Strategic Use of Humor* (Hanover, NH: University Press of New England, 2013), 23–26; Carl Hill, *The Soul of Wit: Joke Theory from Grimm to Freud* (Lincoln: University of Nebraska Press, 1993); Lawrence W. Levine, *Black Culture and Black Consciousness: Afro-American Folk Thought from Slavery to Freedom* (Oxford: Oxford University Press, 1977), 298–366; Nancy A. Walker, *A Very Serious Thing: Women's Humor and American Culture* (Minneapolis: University of Minnesota Press, 1988), 101–138.

Chapter 7. Comedy and Trump as Trauma in Narrowcast America

1. *Black-ish*, "Lemons," written and directed by Kenya Barris, aired January 11, 2017, on ABC.

2. *MSNBC Election Night 2016*, aired November 8, 2016, on MSNBC.

3. *Election Night 2016*, aired November 8, 2016, on Fox News.

4. Gregor Aisch, Jon Huang, and Cecelia Kang, "Dissecting the #PizzaGate Conspiracy Theories," *New York Times*, December 10, 2016, https://www.nytimes.com/interactive/2016/12/10/business/media/pizzagate.html.

5. *CBS This Morning*, "July 10, 2019," aired July 10, 2019, on CBS.

6. Donald J. Trump (@realDonaldTrump), Twitter, July 14, 2019, 8:27 a.m., https://twitter.com/realdonaldtrump/status/1150381394234941448?lang=en.

7. Margaret Sullivan, "Tiptoeing around Trump's Racism Is a Betrayal of Journalistic Truth-Telling: The Longtime Goal of Impartiality Should Never Translate into Euphemism—or Avoiding Reality," *Washington Post*, July 15, 2019.

8. Daly, *Covering America*, 56–85.

9. David Sims, "How Stephen Colbert Tried to Process Trump's Victory," *Atlantic*, November 9, 2016, https://theatlantic.com/entertainment/archive/2016/11/stephen-colbert-donald-trump-election-special/507110/.

10. David Sims, "Tragedy + Comedy = Catharsis," *Atlantic*, November 17, 2015, https://www.theatlantic.com/entertainment/archive/2015/11/john-oliver-stephen-colbert-paris-attacks/416352/.

11. Sims, "How Stephen Colbert Tried."

12. Ibid.

13. Frank Scheck, "Critic's Notebook: Stephen Colbert Turns Election Night Comedy Special into a Wake," *Hollywood Reporter*, November 8, 2016, https://www.hollywoodreporter.com/news/critics-notebook-election-night-945640.

14. *Stephen Colbert's Live Election Night Democracy's Series Finale: Who's Going to Clean Up This Sh*t?*, directed by Jim Hoskinson, aired November 8, 2016, on Showtime.

15. See James E. Campbell, *Polarized: Making Sense of a Divided America* (Princeton, NJ: Princeton University Press, 2016); Darrell M. West, *Divided Politics, Divided Nation: Hyperconflict in the Trump Era* (Washington, DC: Brookings Institute Press, 2019).

16. *Late Night with Seth Meyers*, "Wendy Williams, Chris Hayes, Lukas Graham, Keith Carlock," directed by Alex Vietmeier, aired November 9, 2016, on NBC.

17. *Jimmy Kimmel Live!*, "Robert DeNiro, Gigi Hadid, Willie Nelson," directed by Maureen Bharoocha and Jonathan Kimmel, aired November 9, 2016, on ABC.

18. *Saturday Night Live*, "Reese Witherspoon/Alicia Keys," directed by Beth McCarthy Miller, aired September 29, 2001, on NBC.

19. *Saturday Night Live*, "Dave Chappelle/A Tribe Called Quest," directed by Don Roy King, aired November 12, 2016, on NBC.

20. This, of course, did not represent the experience of many in the country, from Trump zealots to the merely apolitical.

21. Nicholas Fandos and Michael D. Shear, "Before Kavanaugh Hearing, New Accusations and Doubts Emerge," *New York Times*, September 26, 2018.

22. Meghan Keneally, "6 Men Trump Has Defended amid Accusations of Assault or Misconduct," ABC News, September 22, 2018, https://abcnews.go.com/US /men-trump-defended-amid-assault-accusations/story?id=53045851.

23. For examples, see Arielle Bernstein, "Mad Women: How Angry Sisterhood Is Taking Over the Small Screen," *Guardian*, March 7, 2018, https://www.theguardian .com/tv-and-radio/2018/mar/07/mad-women-angry-sisterhood-taking-over-tv; Sophie Gilbert, "Is Television Ready for Angry Women?," *Atlantic*, June 2018, https://www.theatlantic.com/magazine/archive/2018/06/marti-noxon/559115/; Lili Loofbourow, "All Hail the Angry Women of 2016," *Week*, December 28, 2016, https://theweek.com/articles/669346/all-hail-angry-women-2016.

24. Lorraine Ali, "Anger Is an Energy for a New Wave of Women in Pop Culture," *Los Angeles Times*, July 15, 2016, https://www.latimes.com/entertainment/tv /la-ca-anger-angry-women-20160707-snap-story.html.

25. *Full Frontal with Samantha Bee*, "June 26, 2019," directed by Paul Pennolino, aired June 26, 2019, on TBS.

26. Joanne R. Gilbert, *Performing Marginality: Humor, Gender, and Cultural Critique* (Detroit, MI: Wayne State University Press, 2004), 117, 140.

27. See Amit Pinchevski, "Screen Trauma: Visual Media and Post-Traumatic Stress Disorder," *Theory, Culture, and Society* 33, no. 4 (2016): 51–75; Radstone, "Trauma Theory"; Anne Rothe, *Popular Trauma Culture: Selling the Pain of Others in the Mass Media* (New Brunswick, NJ: Rutgers University Press, 2011).

28. PBS NewsHour, "Ford Says She's Coped with PTSD-like Symptoms after Incident with Kavanaugh," YouTube video, posted September 27, 2018, https:// www.youtube.com/watch?v=N58umMFF7xg.

29. Eliana Dockterman, "The Battle over Brett Kavanaugh Has Ended. But the Pain His Hearing Triggered Has Not," *Time*, October 11, 2018, https://time.com /5413109/brett-kavanaugh-supreme-court-survivors-trigger-ptsd/.

30. E. Ann Kaplan, *Trauma Culture: The Politics of Terror and Loss in Media and Literature* (New Brunswick, NJ: Rutgers University Press, 2005), 1.

31. *Duckman: Private Dick Family Man*, "In the Nam of the Father," directed by Norton Virgien, written by Jeff Astrof and Mike Sikowitz, aired May 24, 1995, on USA.

32. *Broad City*, "Witches," directed by Abby Jacobson, written by Gabe Liedman, aired October 25, 2017, on Comedy Central.

33. Rowe, *Unruly Woman*.

34. Rebecca Rubin, "'Broad City' Helps Bleep Trump's Name from the Internet," *Variety*, October 25, 2017, https://variety.com/2017/tv/news/broad-city-bleeps -trump-internet-1202599285/.

35. Jackie Strause, "'Broad City': How Trump Fueled the Show's Feminist Manifesto," *Hollywood Reporter*, October 25, 2017, https://www.hollywoodreporter.com /live-feed/broad-city-trump-orgasm-episode-abbi-jacobson-election-frustrations -season-5-1051916.

36. Ben Travers, "'Broad City': Ilana Glazer and Abbi Jacobson Break Down the Badass Feminist Statement of 'Witches,'" IndieWire, October 25, 2017, https://www.indiewire.com/2017/10/broad-city-season-4-ilana-glazer-abbi-jacobson-donald-trump-episode-1201888833/.

37. *The Jim Jefferies Show*, "The Exploitation of Victimhood," directed by Brian McAloon, aired October 9, 2018, on Comedy Central.

38. *The Jim Jefferies Show*, "The Rise of White Nationalism," directed by Brian McAloon, aired March 19, 2019, on Comedy Central.

39. "Detention Centers, Baguettes & the World Cup (with Eric Lampaert)," *The Jim Jefferies Show Podcast*, June 17, 2018, MP3 audio, 50:33, https://art19.com/shows/the-jim-jefferies-show-podcast/episodes/28b76694-dcfc-4e4a-ace2-74447f2ec41d.

40. *Jimmy Kimmel Live!*, "Armie Hammer, Natasha Leggero, Big Talk," directed by Sandra Restrepo and Zach Bornstein, aired July 28, 2015, on ABC.

41. *Jimmy Kimmel Live!*, "Dr. Mehmet Oz, Shaun White, Kings of Leon," directed by Jonathan Kimmel, aired May 1, 2017, on ABC.

42. Brandon Carter, "Jimmy Kimmel Makes Emotional ObamaCare Plea while Revealing Newborn Son's Heart Defect," *In the Know* (blog), The Hill, May 2, 2017, https://thehill.com/blogs/in-the-know/in-the-know/331500-jimmy-kimmel-makes-emotional-plea-for-obamacare; Matthew Herper, "Jimmy Kimmel Turns a Tearful Story about His Newborn into an Obamacare Defense," *Forbes*, May 2, 2017, https://www.forbes.com/sites/matthewherper/2017/05/02/jimmy-kimmel-tearfully-explains-how-surgeons-saved-his-newborn-and-why-that-means-obamacare-should-stay/#4649dfb35cb4; Matt Wilstein, "Jimmy Kimmel Delivers Tear-Filled Plea for Obamacare after Infant Son Nearly Dies," Daily Beast, May 2, 2017, https://www.thedailybeast.com/jimmy-kimmel-delivers-tear-filled-plea-for-obamacare-after-infant-son-nearly-dies.

43. *Jimmy Kimmel Live!*, "Natalie Portman / Kyrie Irving," directed by Maureen Baroocha, aired February 15, 2018, on ABC.

44. *A Concert for Hurricane Relief*, aired September 2, 2005, on NBC.

Conclusion

1. *The Last Word with Lawrence O'Donnell*, "February 7, 2020," aired February 7, 2020, on MSNBC.

2. *Tucker Carlson Tonight*, "February 14, 2020," aired February 14, 2020, on Fox News.

3. *Full Frontal with Samantha Bee*, "February 5, 2020," directed by Paul Pennolino, aired February 5, 2020, on TBS; *The Late Show with Stephen Colbert*, "John Oliver, Alex Ebert," directed by Jim Hoskinson, aired February 10, 2020, on CBS.

4. Raymond Williams, *Television: Technology and Cultural Form* (New York: Shocken, 1974), 77–120.

5. Paul Taylor, "The Demographic Trends Shaping American Politics in 2016 and Beyond," Pew Research Center, January 27, 2016, https://www.pewresearch.org/fact-tank/2016/01/27/the-demographic-trends-shaping-american-politics-in-2016-and-beyond/.

6. *CNN Newsroom with Fredricka Whitfield*, "January 26, 2020," aired January 26, 2020, on CNN.

7. Leona Allen, "Was Gayle King Wrong to Question Kobe Bryant's Legacy? It's Complicated," *Dallas Morning News*, February 14, 2020, https://www.dallasnews

.com/opinion/commentary/2020/02/16/was-gayle-king-wrong-to-question-kobe
-bryants-legacy-its-complicated/?utm_source=pushly//.

8. *Jimmy Kimmel Live!*, "Remembering Kobe Bryant," directed by Andy Fisher, aired January 27, 2020, on ABC.

9. Paul Farrell, "Ari Shaffir Says Twitter Account Was 'Hacked' after Kobe Tweet," Heavy, January 26, 2020, https://heavy.com/sports/2020/01/ari-shaffir-kobe-bryant/. Although the tweet was taken down shortly after its posting, it gained notoriety as screenshots spread across the internet and other media.

10. Nicole Behnam, "Talent Agency Drops Ari Shaffir in Light of Kobe Bryant Remarks," *Jewish Journal*, January 28, 2020, https://jewishjournal.com/culture/hollywood-schmooze/309984/talent-agency-drops-ari-shaffir-in-light-of-kobe-bryant-remarks/; "N.Y. Comedy Club Receives Threats after Comedian's Jokes about Kobe Bryant," *Hollywood Reporter*, January 29, 2020, https://www.hollywoodreporter.com/news/new-york-comedy-club-receives-threats-comedians-kobe-bryant-jokes-1274600.

11. Ari Shaffir (@arishaffir), "This is NOT an Apology," Instagram photo, January 28, 2020, https://www.instagram.com/p/B73EHlTFrBy/.

12. Godfrey (@ComedianGodfrey), "Mocking the death of Kobe Bryant was the wrong move dude!!," Instagram photo, January 29, 2020, https://www.instagram.com/p/B769QLIHzgI/.

Afterword

1. *The Late Show with Stephen Colbert*, directed by Jim Hoskinson, aired March 16, 2020, on CBS. See also *Late Night with Seth Meyers*, "Gov. Gavin Newsom, Retta," directed by Alex Vietmeier, aired April 30, 2020, on NBC; *Late Night with Seth Meyers*, "Tina Fey, C Pam Zhang," directed by Alex Vietmeier, aired May 11, 2020, on NBC.

2. *Graduate Together: America Honors the High School Class of 2020*, directed by Hamish Hamilton, aired May 16, 2020, on ABC, CBS, CNN, The CW, Fox, Fox News, Freeform, MSNBC, and NBC.

3. *A Parks and Recreation Special*, directed by Morgan Sackett, aired April 30, 2020, on NBC.

4. *Saturday Night Live at Home*, "Tom Hanks / Chris Martin," directed by Don Roy King, aired April 11, 2020, on NBC.

5. *The Late Show with Stephen Colbert*, "Shaquille O'Neal, Jessica Meir, Matt Berninger," aired April 15, 2020, on CBS.

6. *The Daily Show with Trevor Noah*, "Keisha Lance Bottoms," directed by David Paul Meyer, aired April 27, 2020, on Comedy Central.

7. *The Tonight Show with Jimmy Fallon*, "Kate Hudson, Alessia Cara," aired April 27, 2020, on NBC.

8. The most notable exception here is *The Greg Gutfeld Show*, which does topical comedy from a conservative perspective Saturday nights on Fox News.

BIBLIOGRAPHY

Adler, Jerry. "'I Love Lucy' and the Cuba of America's Dreams." *Yahoo! News*, December 16, 2015. https://www.yahoo.com/news/i-love-lucy-and-the -cuba-of-americas-dreams-040653345.html.

Affleck, Neal, Greg Colton, Gavin Dell, Michael DiMartino, and Jack Dyer III. *Family Guy: The Freakin' Sweet Collection*. DVD. Beverly Hills, CA: 20th Century Fox Home Entertainment, 2004.

Ahmed, Sarah. *The Cultural Politics of Emotion*. New York: Routledge, 2004.

Aisch, Gregor, Jon Huang, and Cecelia Kang. "Dissecting the #PizzaGate Conspiracy Theories." *New York Times*, December 10, 2016. https://www .nytimes.com/interactive/2016/12/10/business/media/pizzagate.html.

Alexander, Jeffrey C. "Toward a Theory of Cultural Trauma." In *Cultural Trauma and Collective Identity*, by Jeffrey C. Alexander, Ron Eyerman, Bernard Giesen, Neil J. Smelser, and Piotr Sztompka, 1–30. Berkeley: University of California Press, 2004.

Ali, Lorraine. "Anger Is an Energy for a New Wave of Women in Pop Culture." *Los Angeles Times*, July 15, 2016. https://www.latimes.com/entertainment/tv /la-ca-anger-angry-women-20160707-snap-story.html.

Allen, Leona. "Was Gayle King Wrong to Question Kobe Bryant's Legacy? It's Complicated." *Dallas Morning News*, February 14, 2020. https://www .dallasnews.com/opinion/commentary/2020/02/16/was-gayle-king-wrong -to-question-kobe-bryants-legacy-its-complicated/?utm_source=pushly//.

"American Humor: Hardly a Laughing Matter." *Time*, March 4, 1966, 46–47.

Anderson, Benedict. *Imagined Communities: Reflections on the Origin and Spread of Nationalism*. New ed. New York: Verso, 2006.

Andreeva, Nellie. "'The Opposition' to End as Comedy Central Orders New Jordan Klepper Weekly Series." *Deadline Hollywood*, June 15, 2018. https://deadline.com/2018/06/the-opposition-canceled-end-comedy -central-orders-new-jordan-klepper-weekly-series-1202411168/.

Animated Anon. *South Park Family Guy Muhammad*. Vimeo video. Posted January 11, 2015. https://vimeo.com116475218.

Arthurs, Jane. "Sex and the City and Consumer Culture: Remediating Postfeminist Drama." *Feminist Media Studies* 3, no. 1 (2003): 83–98.

Associated Press. "Cartoon on MTV Blamed for Fire." *New York Times*, October 10, 1993. https://www.nytimes.com/1993/10/10/us/cartoon-on-mtv -blamed-for-fire.html.

———. "Humor Muted on Late-Night Shows." *USA Today*, September 17, 2001. http://usatoday30.usatoday.com/life/enter/tv/2001-09-17-late-night -humor.htm#more.

———. "'JFK' Director Condemned: Warren Commission Attorney Calls Stone Film 'a Big Lie.'" *Washington Post*, December 16, 1991.

———. "Los Angeles Riot Toll Dropped to 51 after Review." *New York Times*, August 13, 1992. http://www.nytimes.com/1992/08/13/us/los-angeles-riot -toll-dropped-to-51-after-review.html.

"Attack on America—Cheers, Tears Fill Yankee Stadium—Thousands Gather to Honor Victims in 'Prayer for America.'" *Yakima Herald-Republic*, September 24, 2001, A9.

Attardo, Salvatore, Arthur Asa Berger, Peter Derks, Charles Gruner, Paul Lewis, Des MacHale, Lawrence E. Mintz et al. "Debate: Humor and Political Correctness." *Humor* 10, no. 4 (1997): 453–513.

Bakhtin, Mikhail. *The Dialogic Imagination: Four Essays*. Edited by Michael Holquist. Translated by Caryl Emerson and Michael Holquist. Austin: University of Texas Press, 1981.

———. *Rabelais and His World*. Translated by Hélène Iswolsky. First Midland Book ed. Bloomington: Indiana University Press, 1984.

Banner-Haley, Charles T. *The Fruits of Integration: Black Middle-Class Ideology and Culture, 1960–1990*. Jackson: University Press of Mississippi, 1994.

Bardan, Alice. "'The Tattler's Tattle': Fake News, Linguistic National Intimacy, and New Media in Romania." *Popular Communication* 10, no. 1–2 (February 2012): 145–157.

Barreca, Regina. *They Used to Call Me Snow White . . . But I Drifted: Women's Strategic Use of Humor*. Hanover, NH: University Press of New England, 2013.

Bassist, Elissa. "Why Daniel Tosh's 'Rape Joke' at the Laugh Factory Wasn't Funny." Daily Beast, July 11, 2012. https://www.thedailybeast.com/why -daniel-toshs-rape-joke-at-the-laugh-factory-wasnt-funny.

Baudrillard, Jean. "The Spirit of Terrorism." In *The Spirit of Terrorism*, translated by Chris Turner, 1–41. London: Verso, 2002.

Baym, Geoffrey, and Jeffrey P. Jones. "News Parody in Global Perspective: Politics, Power, and Resistance." *Popular Communication*, no. 1–2 (February 10, 2013): 2–13.

Behnam, Nicole. "Talent Agency Drops Ari Shaffir in Light of Kobe Bryant Remarks." *Jewish Journal*, January 28, 2020. https://jewishjournal.com /culture/hollywood-schmooze/309984/talent-agency-drops-ari-shaffir-in -light-of-kobe-bryant-remarks/.

Berg, David. "Berg: After 9/11, the President Said We Need Comedy." *Washington Times*, September 8, 2011. http://www.washingtontimes.com/news /2011/sep/8/defining-terrorism-down-263023106/?page=1.

Berger, Alisha. "Playing in the Neighborhood." *New York Times*, August 1, 1999.

Bergson, Henri. *Laughter: An Essay on the Meaning of the Comic*. Translated by Cloudesly Brereton and Fred Rothwell. Rockville, MD: Arc Manor, 2008.

Berlant, Lauren, and Sianne Ngai. "Comedy Has Issues." *Critical Inquiry* 43, no. 2 (Winter 2017): 233–249.

Bernstein, Arielle. "Mad Women: How Angry Sisterhood Is Taking Over the Small Screen." *Guardian*, March 7, 2018. https://www.theguardian.com/tv -and-radio/2018/mar/07/mad-women-angry-sisterhood-taking-over-tv.

Billig, Michael. *Banal Nationalism*. London: Sage, 1995.

Blanchard, John, Kelly Makin, Stephen Surjik, and Robert Boyd. *Kids in the Hall—The Complete Collection + Digital*. DVD. Minneapolis, MN: Mill Creek Entertainment, 2018.

Blanton, Thomas C. "The President's Daily Brief." National Security Archive, April 8, 2004. https://nsarchive2.gwu.edu//NSAEBB/NSAEBB116/index .htm.

Bodroghkozy, Aniko. "Black Weekend: A Reception History of Network Television News and the Assassination of John F. Kennedy." *Television and New Media* 14, no. 6 (September 4, 2012): 560–578.

———. *Groove Tube: Sixties Television and Youth Rebellion*. Durham, NC: Duke University Press, 2001.

Boorstin, Daniel J. *The Image: A Guide to Pseudo-Events in America*. 25th anniversary ed. New York: Vintage, 1987.

Braxton, Greg. "Has Black Comedy Been Beaten Blue?" *Los Angeles Times*, February 20, 1994.

Brooks, Peter. *The Melodramatic Imagination: Balzac, Henry James, Melodrama, and the Mode of Excess*. New Haven, CT: Yale University Press, 1976.

Brooks, Tim, and Earle Marsh. *The Complete Directory to Prime Time Network and Cable TV Shows*. 9th ed. New York: Ballantine Books, 2007.

Caldwell, John Thornton. *Televisuality: Style, Crisis, and Authority in American Television*. New Brunswick, NJ: Rutgers University Press, 1995.

"The Campaign Jokes." *Time*, September 18, 1964.

Campbell, James E. *Polarized: Making Sense of a Divided America*. Princeton, NJ: Princeton University Press, 2016.

Canby, Vincent. "Sahl (He's Not All Sunshine) Digressing at the Village Gate." *New York Times*, August 31, 1968.

Carter, Brandon. "Jimmy Kimmel Makes Emotional ObamaCare Plea while Revealing Newborn Son's Heart Defect." *In the Know* (blog). The Hill, May 2, 2017. https://thehill.com/blogs/in-the-know/in-the-know/331500-jimmy-kimmel-makes-emotional-plea-for-obamacare.

Carroll, Noël. "Horror and Humor." *Journal of Aesthetics and Art Criticism* 57, no. 2 (Spring 1999): 145–160.

Caruth, Cathy. "An Interview with Jean Laplanche." *Postmodern Culture* 11, no. 2 (2001). http://www.iath.virginia.edu/pmc/text-only/issue.101/11.2caruth.txt.

Champion, Jared. "'This Kindergarten Country of Ours': Daniel Tosh's Postmodern Social Politics." *Journal of Popular Culture* 51, no. 3 (2018): 595–614.

Coaston, Jane. "ABC Canceled Roseanne's Show over a Racist Tweet. Her Feed's Been Full of Racism and Conspiracy Theories for a Decade." Vox, May 29, 2018. https://www.vox.com/2018/5/29/17406014/roseanne-racism-abc-trump-twitter.

Cohen, Ted. *Jokes: Philosophical Thoughts on Joking Matters*. Chicago: University of Chicago Press, 1999.

Comedy Central. "This Can't Wait: 'Roseanne' Gets Canceled—The Opposition w/ Jordan Klepper—Uncensored." YouTube video. Posted May 29, 2018. https://www.youtube.com/watch?v=QY28g6IBWdE.

Couldry, Nick. *Media Rituals: A Critical Approach*. New York: Routledge, 2003.

Curtin, Michael. *Redeeming the Wasteland: Television Documentary and Cold War Politics*. New Brunswick, NJ: Rutgers University Press, 1995.

Daly, Christopher B. *Covering America: A Narrative History of a Nation's Journalism*. Amherst: University of Massachusetts Press, 2012.

Daniel, Dayan, and Elihu Katz. *Media Events: The Live Broadcasting of History*. Cambridge, MA: Harvard University Press, 1992.

Day, Amber. "And Now . . . the News?: Mimesis and the Real in *The Daily Show*." In *Satire TV: Politics and Comedy in the Post-Network Era*, edited by Jonathan Gray, Jeffrey P. Jones, and Ethan Thompson, 85–103. New York:

New York University Press, 2009.

———. *Satire and Dissent: Interventions in Contemporary Political Debate*. Bloomington: University of Indiana Press, 2011.

Derrida, Jacques. *Archive Fever: A Freudian Impression*. Translated by Eric Prenowitz. Chicago: University of Chicago Press, 1998.

"Detention Centers, Baguettes & the World Cup (with Eric Lampaert)." *The Jim Jefferies Show Podcast*, June 17, 2018. MP3 audio, 50:33. https://art19 .com/shows/the-jim-jefferies-show-podcast/episodes/28b76694-dcfc-4e4a -ace2-74447f2ec41d.

Diffrient, David Scott. *M*A*S*H**. Detroit, MI: Wayne State University Press, 2008.

DiGiacomo, Frank. "Front Page 6." *New York Observer*, October 8, 2001. http:// observer.com/2001/10/front-page-6/.

Doane, Mary Ann. "Information, Crisis, Catastrophe." In *Logics of Television: Essays in Cultural Criticism*, edited by Patricia Mellencamp, 222–239. Bloomington: Indiana University Press, 1990.

Dockterman, Eliana. "The Battle over Brett Kavanaugh Has Ended. But the Pain His Hearing Triggered Has Not." *Time*, October 11, 2018. https:// time.com/5413109/brett-kavanaugh-supreme-court-survivors-trigger -ptsd/.

Douglas, Mary. "Jokes." In *Rethinking Popular Culture: Contemporary Perspectives in Cultural Studies*, edited by Chandra Mukerji and Michael Schudson, 291–310. Berkeley: University of California Press, 1991.

Douglas, Susan. *Listening In: Radio and the American Imagination*. Minneapolis: University of Minnesota Press, 2004.

Durkheim, Emile. *The Elementary Forms of Religious Life*. Translated by Joseph Ward Swain. London: George Allen & Unwin, 1915.

D'Zurilla, Christie. "Gilbert Gottfried Fired by Aflac over Japan Tsunami Jokes [Poll]." *Los Angeles Times*, March 4, 2011. http://latimesblogs.latimes.com /gossip/2011/03/gilbert-gottfried-fired-aflac-tsunami-jokes.html.

Eco, Umberto. "The Frames of Comic 'Freedom.'" In *Carnival!*, edited by Thomas A. Sebeok, 1–9. Berlin: Mouton, 1984.

Fandos, Nicholas, and Michael D. Shear. "Before Kavanaugh Hearing, New Accusations and Doubts Emerge." *New York Times*, September 26, 2018.

Farrell, Paul. "Ari Shaffir Says Twitter Account Was 'Hacked' after Kobe Tweet." *Heavy*, January 26, 2020. https://heavy.com/sports/2020/01/ari -shaffir-kobe-bryant/.

Federal Communications Commission. *Public Service Responsibility of Broadcast Licensees*. Washington, DC: Government Printing Office, 1946.

Fenster, Mark. *Conspiracy Theories: Secrecy and Power in American Culture*. Revised and updated ed. Minneapolis: University of Minnesota Press, 2008.

Feuer, Jane. "The Concept of Live Television: Ontology as Ideology." In *Regarding Television: Critical Approaches—an Anthology*, edited by E. Ann Kaplan, 12–21. Frederick, MD: University Publications of America, 1983.

Fiske, John. *Media Matters: Race and Gender in U.S. Politics*. Minneapolis: University of Minnesota Press, 1996.

Fleming, Crystal M., and Lorraine E. Roses. "Black Cultural Capitalists: African-American Elites and the Organization of the Arts in Early Twentieth Century Boston." *Poetics* 35, no. 6 (2007): 368–387.

Flint, Joe. "Cable TV Shows Are Sped Up to Squeeze in More Ads." *Wall Street Journal*, February 18, 2015. https://www.wsj.com/articles/cable-tv -shows-are-sped-up-to-squeeze-in-more-ads-1424301320?mod=WSJ_hpp _MIDDLENexttoWhatsNewsThird.

Foucault, Michel. *The Archaeology of Knowledge and the Discourse on Language.* Translated by A. M. Sheridan Smith. New York: Pantheon Books, 2010.

———. *Discipline and Punish: The Birth of the Prison.* Translated by Alan Sheridan. 2nd Vintage Books ed. New York: Vintage, 1977.

———. *The History of Sexuality.* Vol. 1, *An Introduction.* Translated by Robert Hurley. Vintage Books ed. New York: Vintage, 1990.

Foucault, Michel, and Cahiers du Cinema. "Film and Popular Memory: An Interview with Michel Foucault." *Radical Philosophy* 11 (Summer 1975): 24–29.

Friends: The Complete Eighth Series. DVD. Burbank, CA: Warner Home Video, 2004.

Freud, Sigmund. *Beyond the Pleasure Principle.* Translated by James Strachey. New York: Liveright, 1950.

———. "Humour." In *Collected Papers: Authorized Translation Under the Supervision of Joan Riviere,* edited by James Strachey, translated by Joan Riviere. 1st American ed., 159–166. Vol. 5. New York: Basic Books, 1959.

———. *Jokes and Their Relation to the Unconscious.* Edited and translated by James Strachey. New York: Norton, 1963.

Gass, Nick. "Obama Decries Latest Mass Shooting: 'We've Become Numb to This.'" Politico, October 1, 2015. https://www.politico.com/story/2015/10 /obama-oregon-shootings-214352.

Gates, Racquel. "Bringing the Black: Eddie Murphy and African American Humor on *Saturday Night Live.*" In *Saturday Night Live and American TV,* edited by Nick Marx, Matt Sienkiewicz, and Ron Becker, 151–172. Bloomington: Indiana University Press, 2013.

Gellner, Ernest. *Nations and Nationalism.* 2nd ed. Malden, MA: Blackwell Publishing, 2013.

Genzlinger, Neil. "No Puppet to Political Correctness." *New York Times,* December 4, 2009.

Gilbert, Joanne R. *Performing Marginality: Humor, Gender, and Cultural Critique.* Detroit, MI: Wayne State University Press, 2004.

Gilbert, Sophie. "Is Television Ready for Angry Women?" *Atlantic,* June 2018. https://www.theatlantic.com/magazine/archive/2018/06/marti-noxon /559115/.

Gitlin, Todd. *Inside Prime Time.* Rev. ed. Berkeley: University of California Press, 2000.

Godfrey (@ComedianGodfrey). "Mocking the death of Kobe Bryant was the wrong move dude!!" Instagram photo, January 29, 2020. https://www .instagram.com/p/B769QLIHzgI/.

Golden Age Cartoons. "A Guide to Censored MGM Cartoons." February 5, 2007. https://web.archive.org/web/20070205112019/http://looney .goldenagecartoons.com/ltcuts/mgmcuts.html.

Gray, Herman. *Watching Race: Television and the Struggle for "Blackness."* Minneapolis: University of Minnesota Press, 1995.

Gray, Jonathan. *Watching with the Simpsons: Television, Parody, and Intertextuality*. New York: Routledge, 2006.

Green, Adam. "Normalizing Torture, One Rollicking Hour at a Time." *New York Times*, May 22, 2005.

Greenier, Richard. "On the Trail of America's Paranoid Class: Oliver Stone's JFK." *National Interest*, Spring 1992.

Grossberg, Josh. "Did Scientology Go Gunning for *South Park* Guys?" E! Online, October 24, 2011. http://www.eonline.com/news/271142/did-scientology-go-gunning-for-south-park-guys.

Gurney, David. "Everything Changes Forever (Temporarily): Late-Night Television Comedy after 9/11." In *A Decade of Dark Humor: How Comedy, Irony, and Satire Shaped Post-9/11 America*, edited by Ted Gournelos and Viveca Greene, 3–19. Jackson: University Press of Mississippi, 2011.

Habermas, Jürgen. *The Structural Transformation of the Public Sphere: An Inquiry into a Category of Bourgeois Society*. Edited by Thomas Burger and Fredrick Lawrence. Cambridge, MA: MIT Press, 1989.

Haggins, Bambi. *Laughing Mad: The Black Comic Persona in Post-Soul America*. New Brunswick, NJ: Rutgers University Press, 1997.

Hall, Jeffrey A. "Aligning Darkness with Conspiracy Theory: The Discursive Effects of African American Interest in Gary Webb's 'Dark Alliance.'" *Howard Journal of Communication* 17, no. 3 (2006): 205–222.

Hall, Rachel. *The Transparent Traveler: The Performance and Culture of Airport Security*. Durham, NC: Duke University Press, 2015.

Hall, Stuart. "The Problem of Ideology: Marxism without Guarantees." In *Stuart Hall: Critical Dialogues in Cultural Studies*, edited by David Morley and Kuan-Hsing Chen, 25–45. New York: Routledge, 1996.

———. "What Is This 'Black' in Black Popular Culture." In *Stuart Hall: Critical Dialogues in Cultural Studies*, edited by David Morley and Kuan-Hsing Chen, 465–475. New York: Routledge, 1996.

Hawley, Kevin. "Diversity, Localism, and the Public Interest: The Politics of Assessing Media Performance." *International Journal of Media and Cultural Politics* 1, no. 1 (2005): 103–106.

Henderson, Felicia D. "The Culture behind Closed Doors: Issues of Gender and Race in the Writers' Room." *Cinema Journal* 50, no. 2 (Winter 2011): 145–152.

Hendra, Tony. *Going Too Far: The Rise and Demise of Sick, Gross, Black, Sophomoric, Weirdo, Pinko, Anarchist, Underground, Anti-establishment Humor*. New York: Dolphin Doubleday, 1987.

Herbert, Steven. "Fox's 'In Living Color' Plans Lampoon of Koon Television: Police Officer's Attorney Protests Parody as 'Sad Public Treatment of My Client.'" *Los Angeles Times*, April 24, 1993.

Herper, Matthew. "Jimmy Kimmel Turns a Tearful Story about His Newborn into an Obamacare Defense." *Forbes*, May 2, 2017. https://www.forbes.com/sites/matthewherper/2017/05/02/jimmy-kimmel-tearfully-explains-how-surgeons-saved-his-newborn-and-why-that-means-obamacare-should-stay/#4649dfb35cb4.

Hicks, Jonathan. "A Big Bet for the Godfather of Rap." *New York Times*, June 14, 1992.

Hill, Carl. *The Soul of Wit: Joke Theory from Grimm to Freud*. Lincoln: University of Nebraska Press, 1993.

Hirschorn, Michael. "Irony, the End of: Why Graydon Carter Wasn't Entirely Wrong." *New York Magazine*, August 27, 2011. http://nymag.com/news /9-11/10th-anniversary/irony/.

Ho, Raymond K. K. "How Many Children Must We Bury?" *Chicago Tribune*, December 26, 1994. https://www.chicagotribune.com/news/ct-xpm-1994 -12-26-9412260033-story.html.

Hobsbawm, Eric J. *Nations and Nationalism since 1780: Programme, Myth, Reality*. 2nd ed. Cambridge: Cambridge University Press, 2017.

Holpuch, Amanda. "Daniel Tosh Apologises for Rape Joke as Fellow Comedians Defend Topic." *Guardian*, July 11, 2012. https://www.theguardian.com /culture/us-news-blog/2012/jul/11/daniel-tosh-apologises-rape-joke.

Hughes, Geoffrey. *Political Correctness: A History of Semantics and Culture*. Malden, MA: Wiley-Blackwell, 2010.

Huizinga, Johan. *Homo Ludens: A Study of the Play-Element in Culture*. New York: J. & J. Harper Editions, 1970.

Hutcheon, Linda. *Irony's Edge: The Theory and Politics of Irony*. London: Routledge, 1995.

———. *A Theory of Parody: The Teachings of Twentieth-Century Art Forms*. 1st Illinois paperback ed. Urbana: University of Illinois Press, 2000.

Ignatiev, Noel. *How the Irish Became White*. New York: Routledge, 1995.

"Inside Look: 'The Boyfriend.'" *Seinfeld*. Season 3. Culver City, CA: Columbia TriStar Home Entertainment, 2004. DVD.

Itzkoff, Dave. "Fox Postpones Animated Comedies with Hurricane Story Line." *ArtsBeat* (blog). *New York Times*, April 29, 2011. https://artsbeat .blogs.nytimes.com/2011/04/29/fox-postpones-animated-comedies-with -hurricane-story-line/?partner=rss&emc=rss.

———. "'South Park' Episode Is Altered after Muslim Group's Warning." *ArtsBeat* (blog). *New York Times*, April 22, 2010. http://artsbeat.blogs.nytimes .com/2010/04/22/south-park-episode-is-altered-after-muslim-groups -warning/?_r=0.

Jacobs-Huey, Lanita. "The Arab Is the New Nigger: African American Comics Confront the Irony and Tragedy of September 11." *Transforming Anthropology* 14, no. 1 (2006): 60–64.

Jameson, Fredric. *Postmodernism, or, the Cultural Logic of Late Capitalism*. Durham, NC: Duke University Press, 1991.

Jeffreys, Daniel. "JFK's Trouble with George." *Independent*, March 24, 1997. http://www.independent.co.uk/news/media/jfks-trouble-with-george -1274767.html.

Johnson, E. Patrick. *Appropriating Blackness: Performance and the Politics of Authenticity*. Durham, NC: Duke University Press, 2003.

Jones, Isabel. "Why Sarah Jessica Parker Called Dating John Kennedy Jr. 'The Kennedy Fiasco.'" *InStyle*, May 15, 2019. https://www.instyle.com/news/tbt -sarah-jessica-parker-john-f-kennedy-jr.

Joyrich, Lynne. *Re-viewing Reception: Television, Gender, and Postmodern Culture*. Bloomington: Indiana University Press, 1996.

Kakutani, Michiko. "Critic's Notebook: The Age of Irony Isn't Over after All;

Assertions of Cynicism's Demise Belie History." *New York Times*, October 9, 2001. http://www.nytimes.com/2001/10/09/arts/critic-s-notebook -age-irony-isn-t-over-after-all-assertions-cynicism-s-demise.html?ref= michikokakutani.

Kaplan, E. Ann. *Trauma Culture: The Politics of Terror and Loss in Media and Literature*. New Brunswick, NJ: Rutgers University Press, 2005.

Katz, Elihu, and Tamar Liebes. "'No More Peace!': How Disaster, Terror and War Have Upstaged Media Events." *International Journal of Communication* 1 (2007): 157–166.

Kazin, Michael. "The Nation; Conspiracy Theories: The Paranoid Streak in American History." *Los Angeles Times*, October 27, 1996.

Keneally, Meghan. "6 Men Trump Has Defended amid Accusations of Assault or Misconduct." ABC News, September 22, 2018. https://abcnews.go.com /US/men-trump-defended-amid-assault-accusations/story?id=53045851.

King, Scott. "Inside the Mind and Career of Ventriloquist Comedian Jeff Dunham." *Forbes*, October 31, 2018. https://www.forbes.com/sites/scottking /2018/10/31/inside-the-mind-and-career-of-ventriloquist-comedian-jeff -dunham/.

Klapp, Orrin E. *Heroes, Villains, and Fools: The Changing American Character*. Englewood Cliffs, NJ: Prentice-Hall, 1962.

Knight, Peter. *Conspiracy Culture: From the Kennedy Assassination to* The X-Files. London: Routledge, 2000.

Krefting, Rebecca. *All Joking Aside: American Humor and Its Discontents*. Baltimore, MD: Johns Hopkins University Press, 2014.

Kumar, Sangeet. "Transgressing Boundaries as the Hybrid Global: Parody and Postcoloniality on Indian Television." *Popular Communication* 10, no. 1–2 (February 2012): 80–93.

Lamb, David. "A Long Way from Camelot: Vaughn Meader's JFK Impersonation Made Him a Star. Then an Assassin's Bullet Took Everything Away." *Los Angeles Times*, April 20, 1997.

Lee, Malcolm D., dir. *Undercover Brother*. Universal City, CA: Universal Studios Home Entertainment, 2015. DVD.

Lee, Spike, dir. *When the Levees Broke: A Requiem in Four Acts*. New York: HBO Documentary Films, 2006. DVD.

Lehrer, Jonah. "The Forgetting Pill: How a New Drug Can Target Your Worst Memories—and Erase Them Forever." *Wired*, March 2012.

Leman, Patrick. "The Born Conspiracy: When an Unforgettable Event Rocks Our World, Why Do We So Often Mistrust the Official Explanation? Psychologist Patrick Leman Has a Theory." *New Scientist*, July 14, 2007. http:// www.lexisnexis.com.turing.library.northwestern.edu/hottopics/lnacademic /?verb=sr&csi=158275.

Leonard, John. "Private Lives: Stand Up, Comedy." *New York Times*, January 18, 1978.

Lerner, Kevin M. "Magazines as Sites of Satire, Parody, and Political Resistance." In *The Handbook of Magazine Studies*, edited by Miglena Sternadori, 345–357. Hoboken, NJ: John Wiley & Sons, 2020.

Lessing, Doris. *Time Bites: Views and Reviews*. London: Fourth Estate, 2004.

Levine, Lawrence W. *Black Culture and Black Consciousness: Afro-American Folk Thought from Slavery to Freedom*. Oxford: Oxford University Press, 1977.

Limon, John. *Stand Up Comedy in Theory, or, Abjection in America.* Durham, NC: Duke University Press, 2000.

Linn, Edward. "The Comic Who'll Never Be In." *Saturday Evening Post,* September 19, 1964, 28–29.

Loofbourow, Lili. "All Hail the Angry Women of 2016." *Week,* December 28, 2016. https://theweek.com/articles/669346/all-hail-angry-women-2016.

Loth, Renee. "Oliver Stone's 'JFK' Reopens Old Wounds: In a Society That Often Views Life through Pop Culture, Film May Force Reexamination." *Boston Globe,* December 22, 1991.

Lowry, Brian. "The Jeff Dunham Show." *Variety,* October 22, 2009.

Luscombe, Belinda. "The Puppet Master." *Time,* June 8, 2009. http://content.time.com/time/magazine/article/0,9171,1901490,00.html.

MacCarthy, Mark M. "Broadcast Self-Regulation: The NAB Codes, Family Viewing Hour, and Television Violence." *Yeshiva University Cardozo Arts & Entertainment Law Journal* 13 (1995): 667–696.

Macks, Jon. *Monologue: What Makes America Laugh before Bed.* New York: Penguin, 2015.

Marc, David. *Comic Visions: Television Comedy and American Culture.* Malden, MA: Wiley-Blackwell, 1998.

———. *Demographic Vistas: Television in American Culture.* Rev. ed. Philadelphia: University of Pennsylvania Press, 1996.

Marx, Karl, and Frederich Engels. *The German Ideology.* Amherst, NY: Prometheus, 1998.

McCarthy, Anna. *The Citizen Machine: Governing by Television in 1950s America.* New York: New York University Press, 2010.

McCracken, Elizabeth. "The Temporary Kennedy." *New York Times Magazine,* December 26, 2004. http://www.nytimes.com/2004/12/26/magazine/the-temporary-kennedy.html.

McLellan, Dennis. "Obituaries; Vaughn Meader, 68; Comedian Known for Impersonating JFK." *Los Angeles Times,* October 30, 2004.

McNaughton, Ian, and John Howard Davies, dirs. *The Complete Monty Python's Flying Circus.* New York: A&E Home Video, 2000. DVD.

Medhurst, Andy. *A National Joke: Popular Comedy and English Cultural Identities.* London: Routledge, 2011.

Mellencamp, Patricia. "TV Time and Catastrophe, or Beyond the Pleasure Principle of Television." In *Logics of Television: Essays in Cultural Criticism,* edited by Patricia Mellencamp, 240–266. Bloomington: Indiana University Press, 1990.

Miller, Joshua Rhett. "Comedian Defends 'Achmed the Dead Terrorist' Puppet Routine against South African Ban." Fox News, October 2, 2008. https://www.foxnews.com/story/comedian-defends-achmed-the-dead-terrorist-puppet-routine-against-south-african-ban.

Miller, Nancy K. "Reporting the Disaster." In *Trauma at Home: After 9/11,* edited by Judith Greenberg, 39–47. Lincoln: University of Nebraska Press, 2003.

Mills, Brett, and Erica Horton. *Creativity in the British Television Comedy Industry.* Abingdon, Oxfordshire: Routledge, 2017.

Minow, Newton N. "Television and Public Interest." Last updated May 2, 2019. http://www.americanrhetoric.com/speeches/newtonminow.htm.

Mintz, Lawrence E. "American Humor as Unifying and Divisive." *Humor* 12, no. 3 (1999): 237–252.

Mooallem, Jon. "Comedy for Dummies." *New York Times Magazine*, November 1, 2009.

Muldauer, Maureen. *Smothered: The Censorship Struggles of the Smothers Brothers Comedy Hour*. New Video Group, 2003. DVD.

Naficy, Hamid. "Mediating the Other: American Pop Culture Representations of Postrevolutionary Iran." In *The U.S. Media and the Middle East: Image and Perception*, edited by Yahya R. Kamalipour, 73–90. Westport, CT: Greenwood, 1995.

Newcomb, Horace, and Paul M. Hirsch. "Television as a Cultural Forum." In *Television: The Critical View*, edited by Horace Newcomb, 5th ed., 503–515. New York: Oxford University Press, 1994.

"N.Y. Comedy Club Receives Threats after Comedian's Jokes about Kobe Bryant." *Hollywood Reporter*, January 29, 2020. https://www.hollywoodreporter .com/news/new-york-comedy-club-receives-threats-comedians-kobe -bryant-jokes-1274600.

Nowatzki, Robert. "Paddy Jumps Jim Crow: Irish Americans and Blackface Minstrelsy." *Éire-Ireland* 41, no. 3/4 (Fall/Winter 2006): 162–184.

O'Neal, Sean. "An Uncensored Version of South Park's Controversial Muhammed Episode Has Surfaced." AV Club, January 31, 2014. http://www.avclub.com/article/the-uncensored-version-of-south-parks -controversia-107422.

Oakley, Bill, Josh Weinstein, and Jim Reardon. "Commentary, Episode 179." *The Simpsons Complete Ninth Season*. Beverly Hills, CA: 20th Century Fox Home Entertainment, 2006. DVD.

"Oswald Shooting a First in Television History." *Broadcasting*, December 2, 1963.

Paley Center for Media, dir. *Family Guy: Cast and Creators Live at the Paley Center*. 2006; Paley Center for Media, 2010. DVD.

———. "The Museum of Radio and Television Presents Two Five-Letter Words: Lenny Bruce." Press release. October 1, 2004. http://www .paleycenter.org/pressrelease-2004-lenny-bruce.

Palmer, Jerry. *The Logic of the Absurd: On Film and Television Comedy*. London: BFI, 1987.

Parker, Trey, dir. *South Park*. "200." Aired April 14, 2010, on Comedy Central.

———, dir. *South Park*. "Super Best Friends." Aired July 4, 2001, on Comedy Central.

———, dir. *Team America: World Police*. Hollywood, CA: Paramount, 2004. DVD.

PBS NewsHour. "Ford Says She's Coped with PTSD-Like Symptoms after Incident with Kavanaugh." YouTube video. Posted September 27, 2018. https://www.youtube.com/watch?v=N58umMFF7xg.

Penley, Constance. *NASA/Trek: Popular Science and Sex in America*. New York: Verso, 1997.

Peyser, Marc. "Worst Predictions #6: Graydon Carter Proclaims the End of Irony." *Newsweek*. Accessed February 2, 2020. http://2010.newsweek.com /top-10/worst-predictions/graydon-carter.html.

Pinchevski, Amit. "Screen Trauma: Visual Media and Post-Traumatic Stress Disorder." *Theory, Culture, and Society* 33, no. 4 (2016): 51–75.

Porter, Edwin S. *Uncle Josh at the Moving Picture Show*. Edison Manufacturing Co., 1902. 35 mm film. Library of Congress, MOV video, 1:57 at 16 fps. https://www.loc.gov/item/00694324.

Powell, Michael. "JFK Jr.: As Child and Man, America's Crown Prince." *Washington Post*, July 18, 1999.

Provenza, Paul, dir. *The Aristocrats*. New York: Thinkfilm, 2006. DVD.

Queenan, Joe. *Closing Time: A Memoir*. New York: Viking, 2009.

Radstone, Susannah. "Trauma and Screen Studies: Opening the Debate." *Screen* 42, no. 2 (Summer 2001): 188–193.

———. "Trauma Theory: Contexts, Politics, Ethics." *Paragraph* 30, no. 1 (March 2007): 9–29.

Randall, Eric. "The 'Death of Irony,' and Its Many Reincarnations." *Atlantic Wire*, September 9, 2011. http://www.theatlanticwire.com/national/2011 /09/death-irony-and-its-many-reincarnations/42298/#.

Reinhold, Robert. "Rebuilding Lags in Los Angeles a Year after Riots." *New York Times*, May 10, 1993. http://www.nytimes.com/1993/05/10/us /rebuilding-lags-in-los-angeles-a-year-after-riots.html.

Rogin, Michael. *Blackface, White Noise: Jewish Immigrants in the Hollywood Melting Pot*. Berkeley: University of California Press, 1996.

Roediger, David R. *The Wages of Whiteness: Race and the Making of the American Working Class*. Rev. ed. London: Verso, 2007.

Rosenblatt, Roger. "The Age of Irony Comes to an End." *Time*, September 24, 2001. http://content.time.com/time/magazine/article/0,9171,1000893,00 .html.

Rothe, Anne. *Popular Trauma Culture: Selling the Pain of Others in the Mass Media*. New Brunswick, NJ: Rutgers University Press, 2011.

Roush, Matt. "A Nation Rallies." *TV Guide*, December 22, 2001.

Rowe, Kathleen. *The Unruly Woman: Gender and the Genres of Laughter*. Austin: University of Texas Press, 1995.

Rubin, Rebecca. "'Broad City' Helps Bleep Trump's Name from the Internet." *Variety*, October 25, 2017. https://variety.com/2017/tv/news/broad-city -bleeps-trump-internet-1202599285/.

Sahl, Mort. *Heartland*. New York: Harcourt Brace Jovanovich, 1976.

Saper, Bernard. "Joking in the Context of Political Correctness." *Humor* 8, no. 1 (1995): 65–76.

Scepanski, Philip. "Sacred Catastrophe, Profane Laughter: *Family Guy*'s Comedy in the Ritual of National Trauma." In *The Comedy Studies Reader*, edited by Nick Marx and Matt Sienkiewicz, 33–44. Austin: University of Texas Press, 2018.

Scheck, Frank. "Critic's Notebook: Stephen Colbert Turns Election Night Comedy Special into a Wake." *Hollywood Reporter*, November 8, 2016. https://www.hollywoodreporter.com/news/critics-notebook-election-night -945640.

Schneider, Michael. "Michael Jackson Episode Removed from 'The Simpsons.'" *Variety*, March 7, 2019. https://variety.com/2019/tv/news/the-simpsons -michael-jackson-leaving-neverland-stark-raving-dad-1203158114/.

Schou, Nick. "The Truth in 'Dark Alliance.'" *Los Angeles Times*, August 18, 2006.

Sconce, Jeffrey. "What If? Charting Television's New Textual Boundaries." In *Television After TV: Essays on a Medium in Transition*, edited by Lynn Spigel and Jan Olsson, 93–112. Durham, NC: Duke University Press, 2004.

Scott, Allen J. *On Hollywood: The Place, The Industry*. Princeton, NJ: Princeton University Press, 2005.

Seelye, Katherine Q. "John F. Kennedy, Jr.: Heir to a Formidable Dynasty." *New York Times*, July 19, 1999.

"'Sex and the City' Trivia." *Entertainment Weekly*, May 16, 2008. http://www.ew.com/ew/article/0,,20201140,00.html.

Shaffir, Ari (@arishaffir). "This is NOT an Apology." Instagram photo, January 28, 2020. https://www.instagram.com/p/B73EHlTFrBy/.

Siemaszko, Corky. "InfoWars' Alex Jones Is a 'Performance Artist,' His Lawyer Says in Divorce Hearing." NBC News, April 17, 2017. https://www.nbcnews.com/news/us-news/not-fake-news-infowars-alex-jones-performance-artist-n747491.

Sienkiewicz, Matt. "Speaking Too Soon: SNL, 9/11, and the Remaking of American Irony." In *Saturday Night Live and American TV*, edited by Nick Marx, Matt Sienkiewicz, and Ron Becker, 93–111. Bloomington: Indiana University Press, 2013.

Sims, David. "How Stephen Colbert Tried to Process Trump's Victory." *Atlantic*, November 9, 2016. https://theatlantic.com/entertainment/archive/2016/11/stephen-colbert-donald-trump-election-special/507110/.

———. "Tragedy + Comedy = Catharsis." *Atlantic*, November 17, 2015. https://www.theatlantic.com/entertainment/archive/2015/11/john-oliver-stephen-colbert-paris-attacks/416352/.

Sinha-Roy, Piya. "CBS Pulls 'Mike & Molly' Finale with Tornado Storyline from Air." Reuters, May 20, 2013. https://www.reuters.com/article/entertainment-us-mikeandmolly-tornado/cbs-pulls-mike-molly-finale-with-tornado-storyline-from-air-idUSBRE94K01B20130521.

Sipchen, Bob. "Denny—Beaten but Unbowed." *Los Angeles Times*, December 24, 1992.

Sloterdijk, Peter. *Critique of Cynical Reason*. Translated by Michael Eldred. Minneapolis: University of Minnesota Press, 1987.

Smith, Jacob. *Spoken Word: Postwar American Phonograph Cultures*. Berkeley: University of California Press, 2010.

Smith-Shomade, Beretta. *Shaded Lives: African-American Women and Television*. New Brunswick, NJ: Rutgers University Press, 2002.

"Smothers Brothers Comedy Hour, The: Smothered Sketches (The Glaser Foundation First Amendment Collection) (TV)." Paley Center for Media. Accessed April 21, 2019. https://www.paleycenter.org/collection/item/?q=Smothers+Brothers+Comedy+Hour&p=1&item=T:22125.

Snierson, Dan. "'Simpsons' Exec Producer Al Jean: 'I Completely Understand' If Reruns with Nuclear Jokes Are Pulled." *Entertainment Weekly*, March 27, 2011. https://ew.com/article/2011/03/27/simpsons-al-jean-nuclear-japan/.

Sontag, Susan. *Against Interpretation and Other Essays*. New York: Delta, 1961.

Spigel, Lynn. "Entertainment Wars: Television Culture after 9/11." *American Quarterly* 56, no. 2 (June 2004): 235–270.

Stanley, Alessandra. "Abu Ghraib and Its Multiple Failures." *New York Times*, February 22, 2007.

Strause, Jackie. "'Broad City': How Trump Fueled the Show's Feminist Manifesto." *Hollywood Reporter*, October 25, 2017. https://www.hollywoodreporter.com/live-feed/broad-city-trump-orgasm-episode-abbi-jacobson-election-frustrations-season-5-1051916.

Sturken, Marita. *Tourists of History: Memory, Kitsch, and Consumerism from Oklahoma City to Ground Zero*. Durham, NC: Duke University Press, 2007.

Sullivan, Margaret. "Tiptoeing around Trump's Racism Is a Betrayal of Journalistic Truth-Telling: The Longtime Goal of Impartiality Should Never Translate into Euphemism—or Avoiding Reality." *Washington Post*, July 15, 2019.

Takacs, Stacy. *Terrorism TV: Popular Entertainment in Post-9/11 America*. Lawrence: University Press of Kansas, 2012.

Taylor, Paul. "The Demographic Trends Shaping American Politics in 2016 and Beyond." Pew Research Center, January 27, 2016. https://www.pewresearch.org/fact-tank/2016/01/27/the-demographic-trends-shaping-american-politics-in-2016-and-beyond/.

"Television." *New York Times*, February 12, 1992.

"Text: President Bush Addresses the Nation." *Washington Post*, September 20, 2001. https://www.washingtonpost.com/wp-srv/nation/specials/attacked/transcripts/bushaddress_092001.html.

Thakore, Bhoomi K., and Bilal Hussain. "'Indians on TV (and Netflix)': The Comedic Trajectory of Aziz Ansari." In *The Comedy Studies Reader*, edited by Nick Marx and Matt Sienkiewicz, 195–205. Austin: University of Texas Press, 2018.

"The Third Campaign." *Time*, August 15, 1960, 42–49.

Thompson, Ethan. "Tosh.0, Convergence Comedy, and the 'Post-PC' TV Trickster." In *Taboo Comedy: Television and Controversial Humour*, edited by Chiara Bucaria and Luca Barra, 155–171. London: Palgrave MacMillan, 2017.

———. "What, Me Subversive?: Television and Parody in Postwar America." PhD diss., University of Southern California, 2004.

"Time for Tears, A." *National Lampoon*, February 1977.

Torres, Sasha. "Televising Guantánamo: Transmission of Feeling during the Bush Years." In *Political Emotions: New Agendas in Communication*, edited by Janet Staiger, Ann Cvetkovich, and Ann Reynolds, 45–65. New York: Routledge, 2010.

Travers, Ben. "'Broad City': Ilana Glazer and Abbi Jacobson Break Down the Badass Feminist Statement of 'Witches.'" IndieWire, October 25, 2017. https://www.indiewire.com/2017/10/broad-city-season-4-ilana-glazer-abbi-jacobson-donald-trump-episode-1201888833/.

Trump, Donald J. (@realDonaldTrump). Twitter, July 14, 2019, 8:27 a.m. https://twitter.com/realdonaldtrump/status/1150381394234941448?lang=en.

Turnock, Robert. *Interpreting Diana: Television Audiences and the Death of a Princess*. London: BFI, 2000.

"TV's Top 100 Episodes of All Time." *TV Guide*, June 15, 2009.

Vågnes, Øyvind. *Zaprudered: The Kennedy Assassination in Film and Visual Culture*. Austin: University of Texas Press, 2011.

Vianello, Robert. "The Power Politics of 'Live' Television." *Journal of Film and Video* 37, no. 3 (Summer 1985): 26–40.

Wadler, Joyce. "The Sexiest Kennedy." *People*, September 12, 1988.

Walker, Nancy A. *A Very Serious Thing: Women's Humor and American Culture*. Minneapolis: University of Minnesota Press, 1988.

Wallace, David Foster. "E Unibus Pluram: Television and U.S. Fiction." *Review of Contemporary Fiction* 13, no. 2 (Summer 1993): 151–194.

Wantuck, Andrew. "Mort Sahl." The Comedy & Magic Club. Accessed July 11, 2014. http://comedyandmagicclub.com/page.cfm?id=1661.

Watkins, Mel. *On the Real Side: A History of African-American Comedy from Slavery to Chris Rock*. Chicago: Lawrence Hill Books, 1999.

Watson, Mary Ann. *The Expanding Vista: American Television in the Kennedy Years*. New York: Oxford University Press, 1990.

Webb, Gary. *Dark Alliance: The CIA, the Contras, and the Crack Cocaine Explosion*. New York: Seven Stories Press, 1998.

Wertheim, Arthur Frank. "The Rise and Fall of Milton Berle." In *American History/American Television*, edited by John E. O'Connor, 55–77. New York: Ungary, 1983.

West, Darrell M. *Divided Politics, Divided Nation: Hyperconflict in the Trump Era*. Washington, DC: Brookings Institute Press, 2019.

"Who Are the Trenchcoat Mafia?" BBC Online Network, April 21, 1999. http://news.bbc.co.uk/2/hi/americas/325054.stm.

Williams, Kevin. *Read All about It: A History of the British Newspaper*. New York: Routledge, 2010.

Williams, Raymond. *Television: Technology and Cultural Form*. New York: Shocken, 1974.

Wilstein, Matt. "Jimmy Kimmel Delivers Tear-Filled Plea for Obamacare after Infant Son Nearly Dies." Daily Beast, May 2, 2017. https://www.thedailybeast.com/jimmy-kimmel-delivers-tear-filled-plea-for-obamacare-after-infant-son-nearly-dies.

Wycliffe, Don. "Dangers of Questioning Government Actions." *Chicago Tribune*, January 6, 2005.

"Young Troubadours of Camelot, The." *National Lampoon*, February 1977.

Zelizer, Barbie. *Covering the Body: The Kennedy Assassination, the Media, and the Shaping of Collective Memory*. Chicago: University of Chicago Press, 1992.

Zinoman, Jason. "How to Get Away with Sociopathy." *New York Times*, May 1, 2019.

Zizek, Slavoj. "Welcome to the Desert of the Real!" In *Cultures of Fear: A Critical Reader*, edited by Uli Linke and Danielle Taana Smith, 70–77. New York: Pluto Press, 2009.

Zook, Kristal Brent. *Color by FOX: The FOX Network and the Revolution in Black Television*. New York: Oxford University Press, 1999.

INDEX

Note: Numbers in *italics* refer to images.

Access Hollywood, 170, 174
Achmed the Dead Terrorist, 139–143, *142*, 156
Adult Swim, 14
Affordable Care Act. *See* Obamacare
African American comedies: and class issue, 113–114, 123; and creation of black demographic, 23, 110; "crossover" appeal of, 110–111, 112, 121; and cynicism, 127, 129; and performance of group membership/authenticity, 23–24, 109–112, 115–116, 120; producers of, 111; and racial gatekeeping, 113–114; treatment of conspiracy theories in, 93; treatment of Rodney King beating and riots in, 109–112. *See also individual programs*
Ahmed, Ahmed, 153–155, 157–158
Ahmed, Sara, 9
Aladdin, 145–146, 149
Alexander, Jeffrey C., 7
Ali, Lorraine, 170–171
Allen, Leona, 186
American Dad, 56, 144, 150
Anderson, Benedict, 4–5, 7, 21, 49. *See also* imagined community
anger, 69, 74, 86, 114, 136, 170–171
anti-rites, 16–18, 20
anti-Semitism, 93, 105, 157
Arthurs, Jane, 59
Aurora, Colorado, shooting, 12, *12*
Axis of Evil Comedy Tour, The, 25, 133–134; and airing grievances, 154–155; and alignment of subnational identities, 156–158; and appeal to sense of common citizenship, 155–156; and Islamophobia, 153; and self-deprecating humor, 158–159

Baier, Bret, 162
Bakhtin, Mikhail, 17, 53, 70, 175, 211n20
Barr, Roseanne, 89, 144
Batista, Bobbie, 58
Baudrillard, Jean, 9–10
Beavis and Butt-Head, 56
Bee, Samantha. See *Full Frontal with Samantha Bee*
Belafonte, Harry, 47, 48
Berger, Vic, 175–176
Bergson, Henri, 16, 53–54, 71, 125
Between Two Ferns, 208n11
Billig, Michael, 9
bin Laden, Osama, 1–2, 21, 50, 83–84, 134, 156
Black-ish, 132, 161
Black Lives Matter movement, 87, 132
Bodroghkozy, Aniko, 29, 47
Boondocks, The, 23, 93, 94–98, *96*, *97*
Boorstin, Daniel J., 10
Brennan, Christine, 185
Broad City, 25, 170, 174–176
Brooks, Peter, 11
Brown, Roy "Chubby," 140
Bruce, Lenny: and emotional nonconformity, 69, 72; and Vaughn Meader joke, 28, 30, 69, 201n16; personal reputation of, 32; and Mort Sahl, 91; "sick" satirical style of, 30; TV appearances of, 32
Bryant, Kobe, 185–188
Bush, George W.: and Hurricane Katrina, 181; and Islamophobia, 148; and 9/11, 12, 16, 18, 81–82, 86; representation of, on South Park, 105–106; on terrorists, 156

cable television, 6, 184, 201n28
Caldwell, John, 113
camp, 23, 83–85